HOUSES AND HOUSE-LIFE
OF THE AMERICAN ABORIGINES

CLASSICS IN ANTHROPOLOGY
Paul Bohannan, Editor

HOUSES AND HOUSE-LIFE
OF THE AMERICAN
ABORIGINES

By Lewis H. Morgan
With an Introduction
by Paul Bohannan

THE UNIVERSITY OF CHICAGO PRESS / CHICAGO & LONDON

Originally published as Volume IV of *Contributions to North American Ethnology* (Washington: Government Printing Office, 1881)

The University of Chicago Press, Chicago 60637
The University of Chicago Press, Ltd., London W.C. 1

INTRODUCTION

Only a handful of nineteenth-century social thinkers has had so extensive an impact on the twentieth century as has Lewis H. Morgan. All remembered students of society have influenced their societies in at least two ways: one is direct and results from their contribution to social science or philosophy; the other is covert and changes the matrix in terms of which whole cultures view the world and society. The two influences might be seen as the scientific battlefront and the fifth column. With few scholars is it so vital to make clear the distinctions between the scientist and the fifth columnist as it is with Morgan.

Morgan's Position and His Influence

It is well known that Morgan lived the life of a practical lawyer and businessman in Rochester, New York, making extensive ethnological investigations on his own time and for the most part at his own expense.[1]

---

[1] The best biography of Morgan is Carl Resek, *Lewis Henry Morgan, American Scholar* (Chicago: University of Chicago Press, 1960), which also includes a good bibliography of the writings by and about Morgan. Bernhard J. Stern, *Lewis Henry Morgan: Social Evolutionist* (Chicago: University of Chicago Press, 1931) has some material in it that is nowhere else available but is dated in its prejudices. Leslie White's "Introduction" to the new edition of Morgan's *Ancient Society* (Cambridge, Mass.: Harvard University Press, 1965) is a balanced judgment of Morgan and his work, and cites other further papers by White on Morgan. White has also published some of Morgan's correspondence—most particularly "The Correspondence between Lewis Henry Morgan and Joseph Henry," *University of Rochester Bulletin* 12, 1957—and edited some of his journals, particularly *The Indian Journals, 1859–62* (Ann Arbor: University of Michigan Press, 1959) and "Extracts from the European Travel Journal of Lewis H. Morgan," *Rochester Historical Society Publications* XVI (1937). A definitive biography of Morgan has yet to be written, and a completely new and competently edited version of *Systems of Consanguinity and Affinity in the Human Family* is badly needed by anthropologists, though the magnitude of that task almost demands another Morgan.

He stayed outside the academic whirlpool (Morgan turned down an "offer" from Cornell), although he was closely associated with the museums of the state of New York and with the Bureau of American Ethnology in its early days under Powell.

Morgan thought of himself as a scientist—one of his most eloquent pleas is the one for a new and scientific ethnography that appears at the end of this book. His social science, although it contains errors of fact and interpretation, was "right," both in the sense that it created channels within which the subject could move and also in the further sense that its tenets changed the images of self-perception current in the Western world. A man can fittingly be held responsible for his scientific work; he cannot of course be held responsible for the version that trickles into common culture.

Morgan was one of the primary inspirations of Marx and Engels. Engels' book on the family *is* Morgan, with minor modifications. Marx took extensive notes for, but never wrote, a book on Morgan's theories (White, *op. cit.*, p. xxxiii). *Ancient Society* has never been out of print since its original publication in 1877; it has been kept in the public eye by socialist or communist presses. Yet, as White has pointed out, Morgan was a child of the bourgeois, not the communist, revolution. He never doubted that the American system, as he knew it, was the *summum bonum* of social organization, as the closing few pages of this book clearly indicate.

Marx could not have afforded to be ignorant of Morgan, and was hence "influenced" by him. Marx "needed" Morgan in order to link sociopolitical phenomena to his concepts of evolution by revolution in modes of production. Morgan's "stages" of human progress were suited to Marx's needs, as Bachofen's, for example, were not.

For Morgan himself, however, the stages at the basis of his theory had an utterly different purpose. Morgan's task was to organize some of the vast bulk of data about exotic societies that had come pouring in during the decades before he worked, and to add system and sense to further collection. Geology, paleontology, biology, and ethnology had all developed, and the quantity of data about foreign parts that was contained in works by travelers and missionaries was truly mountainous.

The new vistas of the tremendous sweep of time and the panorama of geographical and human variety could not be accommodated from the old viewpoints. In fact, old categories had to crumble—the nineteenth century was ripe for a new world view—and genetic explanation was in the air.

Morgan probably never knew that his work was an important element in the foundation for that new world view. In fact, it is doubtful that he was aware that the world view was changing. Leslie White has emphasized that Morgan clung to the world view of early-nineteenth-century Protestant Christianity, for all that he personally never capitulated to its demands for individual salvation.

The problem that Morgan erected his stages to solve was a very much smaller one: he was interested in the American Indians, where they had come from, how they had got where they were, and in the similarities of their social organization to that of classical antiquity. Morgan was first and foremost an ethnographer. He even fell into most of the traps set for ethnographers: he raised general theories on the basis of those more specialized and limited theories he needed to understand "his people," the Iroquois. He managed to a degree rare in his day to get beyond mere primary ethnocentrism—that arising from his mother culture—but he was thereafter soon entrapped again in Iroquois culture, the first he came to understand intellectually. Morgan gathered most of his own data from the field and from a gigantic correspondence (he was among the first to use the method of questionnaires aimed at "scientific experts" rather than only informants).

Morgan's influence, in short, extended beyond his problem and his contribution to social science; he became one of the creators of a new world view, which came to be called "cultural evolution" or "social Darwinism." Creators of new world views in one age seem invariably to become scapegoats in the succeeding age. Morgan was, then, rejected beyond his measure as he had been accepted beyond it.

Just as the writers of one age, who are taken up for their fifth-column effect as much as for their scientific contributions, become the scapegoats of the next age, so the scapegoats of one age are likely to become the bellwethers of the next. Lowie, Boas, Radcliffe-Brown, and many others in the early twentieth century either damned Morgan with faint praise, ignored him, or attacked him scurrilously. Leslie White, almost alone, began the revival that is today generally recognized in the profession.

Morgan, himself, remained little read in the profession for some decades. He will come as a considerable surprise to those who read him afresh, divorced from both the exaggerated charges made by his detractors and the exaggerated claims of latter-day bandwagoneers.

Morgan turns out to be, first of all, a social anthropologist, in that he begins with social relationships and their structures rather than with culture traits and their clustering.

Morgan, read in terms of modern anthropological categories, is as much a functionalist as an evolutionist. He held a fully mature theory of the needs of social groups and human beings and an idea (though he did not use the words) of culture as the device by which such needs are met. He fully realized the interconnectedness of all the institutions in any cultural field. Morgan the ethnographer called for detailed studies of specific societies (of the sort that he himself did of the Iroquois). His words could be easily attributable to the early Boas, middle Mead, or mature Evans-Pritchard.

Morgan's Oeuvre

Morgan's work in anthropology is a structured oeuvre—unlike that of Tylor or Boas, who were both men of less tidy minds. Therefore, evaluating any piece of the work demands locating it in the developing structure. The structure is in fact explicit—and is a major factor leading to misrepresentation of Morgan's full position. Morgan summarized and repeated his position at the beginning of every book. Too often his critics have given more weight to his summaries than to his original statements. Leslie White (*op. cit.*, p. xxxvii) has pointed out that by the time *Ancient Society* was written Morgan believed that the theories he had set forth in his *Systems of Consanguinity* were "established with a certainty approaching the absolute." White's statement can be generalized and put another way. As Morgan reduced the length of these summaries, he also threw to the winds the caution with which his ideas were originally put forward. Each précis, therefore, shows its author's strengths and weaknesses in a particular perspective. Read in context, it is the perspective that Morgan had of his past work as he leaped into his next work. But read out of context, such passages from *Houses and House-Life,* as the following, seem merely dogmatic:

> Throughout aboriginal America the gens took its name from some animal or inanimate object and never from a person. (p. 8.)

> . . . the beginning of civilization, as that term is properly understood. (p. 4.)

> There was no possible way of becoming connected on equal terms with a confederacy except through membership in a gens and a tribe and a common speech. (p. 25.)

Morgan's summaries are, however, also sources of strength, making it possible to see his entire development from ethnographer to comparative social anthropologist. After his basic ethnography of the Iroquois,[2] he proceeded to a comparative study of kinship systems in order to validate and set into perspective some of his discoveries.[3] That study led him to a method and to a subject matter—social organization—with which he could attempt to set all ethnographic information into a single matrix.[4] His last book, the present one, makes as its special point a correlation between architecture and social structure.

Any evaluation of Morgan's books must therefore be done in two stages: first, by making a critique of the minutiae that have been corrected or affirmed by the forward march of the discipline, and second, by determining the viability of the large-scale ideas that dominate the entire oeuvre.

Houses and House-Life

Morgan's last book is still fascinating and instructive today. Although it can no longer be wholly accepted, no book of similar scope has

---

[2] *League of the Ho-de-no-sau-nee, or Iroquois.* Rochester: Sage and Bros., 1851; New York: Dodd, Mead and Co., 1901. New Haven: Behavior Science Reprints, 1954.

[3] *Systems of Consanguinity and Affinity of the Human Family.* Washington: Smithsonian Institution, 1870. (Vol. XVII of "Contributions to Knowledge.")

[4] *Ancient Society, or Researches in the Lines of Human Progress from Savagery through Barbarism to Civilization.* New York: Henry Holt and Company, 1877; Chicago: Charles H. Kerr and Company, 1910, 1912.

replaced it. Indeed, its theoretical point is only today beginning to be taken up by the specialist subject of proxemics, which is Edward Hall's word for the study of the relationship between social structures and space, particularly buildings and their placement, transportation modes and their demands on human beings. Therefore, this book, like all anthropological classics, must be read with an informed view of what the problem and the frame of reference were.

Morgan's problem in this book is a basic one: what does domestic architecture show anthropologists—either ethnologists or archaeologists —about social organization, and how does social organization combine with a system of production technology and an ecological adjustment to influence domestic and public architecture?

Morgan's method of procedure can only be called "functional-evolutionary," a term that will be discussed below.

The first chapter and much of the next three are made up of Morgan's condensation of his position. The Iroquois data have now become the model against which Morgan judges all other ethnographic data. The arguments of *Systems of Consanguinity* and *Ancient Society* are set forth with the sanctity of established fact. *Houses and House-Life* was to have formed a fifth section of *Ancient Society*, but it was omitted because of the already inordinate length of that manuscript. Morgan printed some of it as articles, and then later reworked it and added introductory summaries.

A weak point in this book is Chapter X, which is almost a reprint of one of the published articles.[5] Morgan himself said that this should have been rewritten to bring it into line with Bandelier's new material. Chapter X is also marred by a sarcasm toward his sources, authorities, and adversaries which is rare in Morgan. Not only could he have improved it by rewriting with better material (if, indeed, the Bandelier material was better—a moot point), but he could have made it very much more effective by making it more even-tempered.

There are a few other emendations that should be made in this book —none of them seriously affect the main argument, but some of them

---

[5] "Montezuma's Dinner," *North American Review* CXXII (April, 1876), 265–308.

should nevertheless be noted before we proceed to the much more significant insights and analyses that the book also contains. Morgan misinterpreted the social structure of the Aztecs and the Maya: his theory about unilineal descent groups and the position such groups occupied in his evolutionary stages, combined with the poor quality of the data on social organization left by the Spanish chroniclers, led Morgan to see descent groups where in fact there were none.

Morgan was also wrong about the Mound Builders of the Ohio and Mississippi valleys. It is an astounding fact that only since about 1960—almost a hundred years after Morgan wrote—has there been any adequate excavation of these sites. Morgan suggested that these mounds were house sites. Present-day opinion is that they were mortuary mounds. There were structures on them, but it is unlikely that they were houses; there were no middens, and evidence of row after row of houses has been found on the regular ground surface, nearby but separated from the mounds. The largest of these mounds to be excavated to date is the Cahokia site near St. Louis, where there are about twenty large, truncated mounds, with traces of some 385 houses in the fields adjacent.[6] Therefore, those parts of pages 228–44 of this book that describe the mounds as house sites, and the ingenious "restoration" that Morgan made in Figures 47 and 48 of a "High Bank Pueblo," are brilliant—though, unfortunately, inaccurate—guesses; they nevertheless had greater verisimilitude than any other explanations current at the time, or for decades afterward.

Two terms in *Houses and House-Life* call for special comment: land tenure, and what Morgan called "communism in living."

"Communism in living" meant to Morgan something quite different from what it means today, or indeed from what it meant to nineteenth-century "communists." To express something like Morgan's idea today, we would rather uncomfortably use the word "communalism." What is implied is that some sort of cohesive local community, larger than the nuclear family, is the basic unit of consumption and possibly also of pro-

---

[6] Reports on excavations between 1960 and 1962 will be published in the forthcoming series of Cahokia Reports from the Illinois State Museum, Springfield.

duction. Robert Owen's communities come far closer than do collective farms or even *kibbutzim* to what Morgan was describing.

Moreover, Morgan looked back to a period of communism, not forward. To him, the distribution of labor in the nineteenth-century monogamous household and in the new industrial system had far outdated what he called "communism in living." Morgan's terminological difficulties reflect a lack that we still feel: we need, and so far as I am aware do not have, a good comparative study of domestic groups, domestic economy, sexual and other division of domestic labor, and what general aspects of society do in fact seem to be co-ordinated with various types of domestic unit (and, to utilize Fortes' insights,[7] with various event sequences that mark domestic units in different societies of the world).

The land-tenure problem is not so simple—even now. Just as domestic groups have been inadequately analyzed comparatively, either by Morgan or by his successors, so have larger-scale local groups and the settlement patterns to which they have given rise. A difficulty lies in the assumption that settlement patterns are to be studied primarily in terms of "property," "ownership," and, indeed, "land tenure." Here is another example of the kind of ethnocentrism that tries to turn the terminology of a specialized Western institution into a terminology suitable for cross-cultural comparison. As usual, much of the obscurity results from the shadow that the Western institution casts.

"Land tenure" and other aspects of human settlement patterns supply a way of looking at territoriality in human beings. Even those animals that do not exhibit aggression in their territorial arrangements (and human beings are among those that do) must place themselves in terrestrial space. That placement is one of the important reflections— indeed, causes—of just what social arrangements are in fact made. Euro-American society has, for the past several centuries, maintained its territorial juxtaposition by means of contract (including treaties), with legal machinery of enforcement. The term "land tenure" is a carry-over from feudal days. Yet history has seen a change in the legal background, from the organizing principle of infeudation to the organizing principle of con-

---

[7] Meyer Fortes, "Introduction" to J. Goody, *Developmental Cycles in Domestic Groups* ("Cambridge Papers in Social Anthropology," No. 1), 1958.

tract. In the West, a local community nowadays results from contractual sale and rental of land as living sites and as a factor of production. The terms for connecting man with his place in the sun are legal terms.

Morgan too saw territoriality in the limiting terms of his own culture and his own profession:

There is not the slightest probability that any Indian, whether Iroquois, Mexican, or Peruvian, owned a foot of land that he could call his own, with power to sell and convey the same in fee simple to whomsoever he pleased. (p. 98.)

Of course there is not. But Morgan's explanation in terms of communal ownership is not the only explanation—it is merely the one that made it necessary for him to do the least adjustment. A better way of looking at the situation is to ask what the organizational basis of communities may be, and how these communities extend themselves on the surface of the earth, and how they go about exploiting that surface for their daily needs. What Morgan did not realize is that land tenure as he knew it would have destroyed—ultimately did destroy—the very kinship basis of the extended family household. To view the extended family as a corporation aggregate that "owns" the "land" is—to use a literary metaphor— a mere substitution of nouns rather than accurate translation. Better, the extended family lives in a space that is determined by social relationships —relationships among its own members, and between it and other similar groups. That space is exploited and protected. The notion of legal "rights" in the form of a "fee" was alien precisely because when the community (whatever it may have been) left this piece of land, and no longer exploited it, the "rights" lapsed. Morgan copes with this situation in terms of a generalized idea of rights of use.

In short, Morgan failed (as we all do) whenever his model for explanation ill fitted his data. One should always ask: (1) What is the source of my model? Then one can proceed to ask: (2) Is it flexible and inclusive enough, so that I am not destroying another folk model by using my model, whatever its source?

Morgan's Lasting Contributions

In assessing the lasting contributions of Morgan, it is necessary to go to the complete oeuvre, for, as we have noted, the books form a whole.

Morgan's most enduring achievements result from his ability occasionally to rise above the model presented him by his natal culture or by his profession—just as his (and our) failures result from a contrasting inability to do so. Other commentators may not concur, but it seems to me that the three greatest of his theoretical contributions are: his theory of kinship terminology (for all that much of it has been superseded today); his theory of the gens (which has not been superseded, because it is correct and more or less complete); and his holistic theory of domestic groups.

"Gens" is the Latin word for an agnatic group. Morgan adopted it as a term for any group of agnatic kinsmen or of uterine kinsmen, but never a combination of the two. Most later anthropologists have used the term "unilineal descent group" for this phenomenon.[8]

The principle of the unilineal descent group is simple: it is based on the belief that there is some kind of qualitative biological difference (the kind varies, and is beside the immediate point) between descent from the father and descent from the mother. Some traits and some social affiliations can thereupon be associated with one or the other. Kinship in general leads to extremely "dense" relationships (to use Durkheim's word) posited on many qualities and many duties. But the descent group allows a people to emphasize out of proportion one or two qualities for some kinsmen without denying the other qualities. Thus, a society is using the ethic of kinship in a new dimension: not merely to endorse the family and whatever domestic and local groups may be based on it, but to legitimize a much larger group that is capable of more specialized tasks precisely because it is not called upon to do all tasks.

Thus, the unilineal descent group or the gens is freed from family responsibility at the same time that it can utilize the emotional motivation of family and kinship ethics. The result is an extremely simple, resilient, and pliable institution. It can be the unit, larger than family or band, that is charged with political or legal life in the growing community; it

---

[8] Neither term is felicitous. "Gens" is unsuccessful because it is actually lifted out of an ethnographic context, and, for people who understand that context, will inevitably trail clouds of association when used for comparative purposes. "Unilineal descent group" is difficult because it contains a genetic explanation that may not in fact be the historically accurate one—that is, there are agnatic and uterine groups to which descent is epiphenomenal.

can be the unit of economic production and distribution; it can form the basis of the ceremonial and ritual of society; it can provide education, social insurance, emotional security, and many other of men's requirements—but it specifically cannot direct the more intimate functions of the family and household: control and expression of sexuality, reproduction and socialization of children, domestic division of labor.

Morgan understood these matters. He also understood that the number of people who can in fact be organized into a unilineal descent group has practical limits—the limits beyond which the ethic of kinship is no longer adequate to the job of maintaining predictable social life. It is then that the other types of ethic—the ethic of contract, that of social responsibility, that of public law, or of the golden rule, or of the market place—must be brought in to inform and illuminate new forms of social organization. Morgan's only mistake was to assume that the unilineal descent group had been historically universal simply because it filled a need that arose as population grew and technology improved. Widespread it certainly was. It worked well. But so did some other institutions based on contract, propinquity, or overtly expressed common interest.

Morgan was, moreover, the first to make an efficient distinction between family and household. A family is a kinship group. A household is a local group. In almost all societies of the world, the local group known as the household or domestic group is based on some combination of kinsmen—some part of the extended family. But that fact does not make family and household the same thing—they have, once for all, different defining characteristics.

Morgan's Problems Today

Two of the problems to which Morgan gave keenest attention are still at the anthropological frontier: evolution and proxemics. Morgan wrote before cultural evolution or even social Darwinism became dogma. Although most of the evolutionary theorists who came after him built on his work directly, nevertheless it is anachronistic to speak of him as merely an evolutionist. It would be just as anachronistic to say that Morgan was a functionalist, but even the most cursory reading of his books today will reveal principles that since his time have come to be called functionalist. Morgan antedated the distinction, and today we would have to say that funtionalist theory is embedded in his evolutionism, that evolutionary theory is embedded even in his ethnography. The two are not distinguished in Morgan, and therefore he gives us many important clues to the way in which the two fit together.

Two interlinked assumptions underlie functionalist theory: (1) that human institutions, and therefore culture, fulfil the needs of human creatures, and *ipso facto* satisfy the requisites of social life; (2) that within a single society or social field human institutions are perceptually and materially interconnected, and therefore a change in one is likely to bring about a change in the other.

Morgan assumed both these ideas and added a third: institutions, in the course of satisfying human needs and social requisites, lead people to more efficient or highly prized means of satisfying needs; in the process of so doing, these institutions may create a new, derived set of demands that they themselves can no longer fulfil.[9]

Thus, in satisfying needs, institutions create new needs; in the search for fulment, social change occurs; once change occurs in one institution, concomitant change occurs in some others; once these changes have occurred, simplifying solutions may be found that make reversal impossible because it would be complicating rather than simplifying and hence more trouble for less reward.

In such a scheme, a functionalist approach is basic to evolutionary theory, and functionalism without an evolutionary theory stops short of full explanation—each type may answer limited questions and different questions, but the *rapprochement* is vital to still other questions.

Morgan made all these points with great clarity. The first principle of functionalism cannot be better stated than in the sentence: "Every institution of mankind which attained permanence will be found linked with a perpetual want." (*Ancient Society*, p. 98.) The second point of functionalism—the interconnectedness of institutions and culture traits

---

[9] Marx also perceived these ideas, and went on to advocate the use of the resulting dysfunction to create revolution—hence evolution.

—is illustrated by Morgan's assumption of a relationship between family structure and kinship terminology, or that between family interaction and domestic architecture. The third point—that of functional evolution —is well illustrated in such statements as:

> The city brought with it new demands in the art of government by creating a changed condition of society. (*Ancient Society*, p. 264.)

> After an immensely protracted duration . . . the gentile organization finally surrendered its existence . . . to the demands of civilization. It had held exclusive possession of society through these several ethnical periods, and until it had won by experience all the elements of civilization, which it then proved unable to manage. (*Ancient Society*, p. 350.)

Within the present book, functional-evolutionary statements like the following occur:

> As a key to the interpretation of this architecture, two principles, the practice of hospitality and the practice of communism in living, have been employed. (p. 310.)

> It was the weakness of the family, its inability to face alone the struggle of life, which led to the construction of joint-tenement houses throughout North and South America by the Indian tribes; and it was the gentile organization which led them to fill these houses, on the principle of kin, with related families. (p. 268.)

The examples could be multiplied.

Indeed, one of Morgan's greatest evolutionary errors comes from too rigid a reading of functional requirements. Band organization is a limiting factor—bands can organize people only until population density and technology reach a certain level of complexity. After that, it is not adequate. The band must separate into two bands, or a new and simplifying social mechanism is needed. Such a point is not in question. Morgan, however, assumed that the unilineal descent group was the next step in all instances. We have already noted that many other types of organization can fulfil the same needs and therefore succeed the band in an evolutionary sense. Morgan had the right vision, but he narrowed it too soon.

Today we can see that it is the local groups—not the families—that can be placed on an evolutionary ladder.[10] Seeing that point might have allowed Morgan to avoid what was probably his most telling misstep: dependence on a theory of survivals in general and of kinship terminologies as survivals in particular. Today, most anthropologists accept the

---

[10] Elman R. Service, *Primitive Social Organization*. New York: Random House, 1964.

idea that local groups fit onto an evolutionary scale, and that some types of local groups are based on kinship principles but others are not. It is very doubtful, however, that known extant types of family structure form an evolutionary progression, although it is easier to move from each to some than to some others.[11] Morgan, to achieve his evolutionary stages, had to make a division between the family based on monogamous marriage and all the other types of known family forms, and then to postulate and arrange in moral sequence the earlier stages. Such stage building made an unwarranted assumption: that some forms of family organization are more complex than others. It would seem today that monogamous family forms can move to some polygamous form (what Morgan called the "syndyasmian family") as well as from it to monogamy. Morgan's earlier stages are either errors in reporting, reconstructions from inadequate facts, or not present today in human society. Today, however, we are returning to the idea that early forms of social organization among the early forms of man that were to become *homo sapiens* resembled that of the baboon troop.[12] In terms of group morphology then, Morgan's intuition was close; his reconstruction of process, via kinship terminology, is no longer adequate.

Another aspect of Morgan's evolutionary theory also provides some difficulty: stage building is simple only in theory. Today we know that to mark the end of a stage or "condition of civilization," as Morgan called it, it is necessary that new modes of communication, energy use, or social organization occur which not merely transcend earlier forms but render those earlier forms unusable. Resulting changes are thus irreversible in that they combine efficiency and simplicity to the point that a backward step would be not merely uncomfortable but more difficult of comprehension and achievement than a forward step. Fire making, family organization, domestication of animals, and planting of food crops—all these (and many others) are so simple and so efficient that, even though precise techniques may be lost, the idea is in the minds of men and will be

---

[11] G. P. Murdock, *Social Structure.* New York: Macmillan, 1949.

[12] S. L. Washburn and Irven DeVore, "Social Behavior of Baboons and Early Man," *in* S. L. Washburn (ed.), *Social Life of Early Man.* Chicago: Aldine Press, 1961.

carried through because the earlier alternative is more difficult. Thus, the great simplifying ideas—cooking, planting, money—are the "mutations" that lead to the "gene loss" of earlier forms.

Today, the evolutionary principles of Morgan lead, almost automatically as it were, into one of the standard practices of twentieth-century sociology—scaling. One of the fundamental scales is the Guttman. It works simply: if a collection of items "scale," items A, B, and C are always present if item D is present, but A, B, and C may be conjoined without D; moreover, where C is present, A and B are to be found, but A and B may be found without C, and so on. In tabular form, a perfect Guttman scale appears:

Items	A	B	C	D
	+	+	+	+
	+	+	+	−
	+	+	−	−
	+	−	−	−
	−	−	−	−

Several recent studies have brought the Guttman scale into play in determining questions of social complexity, and ultimately of evolution.[13]

The only major difficulty that needs to be mentioned here is one that Morgan would have grasped and pointed out immediately: functional equivalents may supplant one another and give the illusion of disjunction in the scaling order. One can avoid this difficulty in two ways: one is to do what Goodenough did and create a "quasi-scale"; the other is to enlarge the category of one of the units in the scale, and so have scales within scales. That is, if item B is replaced by item M, then item B must be called by a larger category name, the former item B relabeled B_1 and M renamed B_2. If $B_1 B_2$ do not scale, but rather are interchangeable (as I have claimed that all extant family forms seem to be), then the new

---

[13] Linton C. Freeman and Robert F. Winch, "Societal Complexity: An Empirical Test of a Typology of Societies," *American Journal of Sociology* LXII (March, 1957), 461–66. Richard D. Schwartz and James C. Miller, "Legal Evolution and Societal Complexity," *American Journal of Sociology* LXX (September, 1964), 159–69. Robert L. Carniero, "Scale Analysis as an Instrument for the Study of Cultural Evolution," *Southwestern Journal of Anthropology* XVIII (1962), 149–69. Ward L. Goodenough, "Some Applications of Guttman Scale Analysis to Ethnography and Culture Theory," *Southwestern Journal of Anthropology* XIX (Autumn, 1963), 235–50.

label for B still fits; if B_1 B_2 do scale, we have a subordinate type of scale or "quasi-scale" that illuminates the first.

Morgan's inadequacies for the mid-twentieth century can be seen if we accept the idea of two scales in evolutionary situations. Morgan set the boundaries of his stages by technological inventions. Some of these technological inventions do not scale: writing, for example, may or may not antedate pottery; the bow and arrow may or may not antedate metallurgy. In every instance, we must go to the data in any specific area, because no evolutionary scaling is possible. Such scaling can, on the other hand, be made in terms of energy use, as White[14] has done, or in terms of local organization.[15] Morgan used cultural inventions for his indicators of stages, then looked for functional and organizational correlates. Had he been more aware of functional equivalents, he would have made more nearly correct stages.

We can now restate Morgan's evolutionary position in terms of current problems. Families can perform all the necessary functions for the maintenance of the individual and society. They can, however, do it only within a comparatively small compass. Therefore, when they are successful, the compass of the society enlarges; society must break into what Durkheim would have called units in mechanical solidarity, which must remain independent of one another (which means, in this context, without effective social relationships between the independent units) or a new social institution must be added to assume responsibility where the capability of the family ceases. One of the widespread forms to assume this new task was the unilineal descent group—a culturally obvious group because it utilizes kinship solidarity as its means for demanding loyalty. Other types of groups, however, founded on propinquity or contract or the principle of the common weal, will also work.

Morgan's primary work on evolution came earlier in his career than did his work on proxemics. His publishing history, however, emphasizes the point disproportionately, because the material that became *Houses and House-Life* was removed from *Ancient Society* and so failed to show

---

[14] Leslie White, *The Science of Culture*. New York: Farrar, Strauss, 1949.

[15] Elman R. Service, *op. cit.*

how unitary the ideas were for Morgan. Morgan's evolutionary schemes are in terms of families and family types, associated with kinship terminology and with political structure. His work on proxemics concerns the way that local groups and families intercorrelate with settlement patterns and architecture. It is associated with his struggles to interrelate culture traits and social structure. Anthropology has been slow to realize the importance of Morgan's lead in this field which he, in a very real sense, founded but did not name. Some of the most interesting new work in this field is being done by Edward Hall.[16]

The contributions of Lewis H. Morgan show more contemporary vitality today than they have for several decades. Indeed, today students (who, from before 1930 almost until 1960 could get along without him) will find it necessary to turn back to Morgan, not merely to learn the history of their subject, but more importantly to avoid what Gunnar Myrdal once called, speaking of Lord Keynes, "unnecessary Anglo-Saxon originality."

PAUL BOHANNAN

---

[16] Edward T. Hall, "The Language of Space," *Journal of the American Institute of Architects*, February, 1961; "A System for the Notation of Proxemic Behavior," *American Anthropologist* 65 (1963), 1003–26; "Quality in Architecture: An Anthropological View," *Journal of the American Institute of Architects*, July, 1963.

PREFACE.

The following work substantially formed the Fifth Part of the original manuscript of "Ancient Society," under the title "Growth of the Idea of House Architecture." As the manuscript exceeded the limits of a single volume, this portion (Part V) was removed; and having then no intention to publish it separately, the greater part of it found its way into print in detached articles. A summary was given to Johnson's New Universal Cyclopedia in the article on the "Architecture of the American Aborigines." The chapter on the "Houses of the Aztecs" formed the basis of the article entitled "Montezuma's Dinner," published in the North American Review, in April, 1876. Another chapter, that on the "Houses of the Mound Builders," was published in the same Review in July, 1876. Finally, the present year, at the request of the executive committee of the "Archæological Institute of America," at Cambridge, I prepared from the same materials an article entitled "A Study of the Houses and House Life of the Indian Tribes," with a scheme for the exploration of the ruins in New Mexico, Arizona, the San Juan region, Yucatan, and Central America.

With some additions and reductions the facts are now presented in their original form; and as they will now have a wider distribution than the articles named have had, they will be new to most of my readers. The facts and suggestions made will also have the advantage of being presented in their proper connection. Thus additional strength is given to the argument as a whole. All the forms of this architecture sprang from a common mind, and exhibit, as a consequence, different stages of development of the same conceptions, operating upon similar necessities. They also represent these several conditions of Indian life with reasonable completeness. Their

houses will be seen to form one system of works, from the Long House of
the Iroquois to the Joint Tenement houses of adobe and of stone in New
Mexico, Yucatan, Chiapas, and Guatemala, with such diversities as the different degrees of advancement of these several tribes would naturally produce. Studied as one system, springing from a common experience, and
similar wants, and under institutions of the same general character, they
are seen to indicate a plan of life at once novel, original, and distinctive.

The principal fact, which all these structures alike show, from the
smallest to the greatest, is that the family through these stages of progress
was too weak an organization to face alone the struggle of life, and sought
a shelter for itself in large households composed of several families. The
house for a single family was exceptional throughout aboriginal America,
while the house large enough to accommodate several families was the rule.
Moreover, they were occupied as joint tenement houses. There was also a
tendency to form these households on the principle of gentile kin, the
mothers with their children being of the same gens or clan.

If we enter upon the great problem of Indian life with a determination
to make it intelligible, their house life and domestic institutions must furnish the key to its explanation. These pages are designed as a commencement of that work. It is a fruitful, and, at present, but partially explored
field. We have been singularly inattentive to the plan of domestic life
revealed by the houses of the aboriginal period. Time and the influences
of civilization have told heavily upon their mode of life until it has become
so far modified, and in many cases entirely overthrown, that it must be
taken up as a new investigation upon the general facts which remain. At
the epoch of European discovery it was in full vitality in North and South
America; but the opportunities of studying its principles and its results
were neglected. As a scheme of life under established institutions, it was
a remarkable display of the condition of mankind in two well marked
ethnical periods; namely, the Older Period and the Middle Period of
barbarism; the first being represented by the Iroquois and the second by
the Aztecs, or ancient Mexicans. In no part of the earth were these two
conditions of human progress so well represented as by the American
Indian tribes. A knowledge of the culture and of the state of the arts of

life in these periods is indispensable to a definite conception of the stages of human progress. From the laws which govern this progress, from the uniformity of their operation, and from the necessary limitations of the principle of intelligence, we may conclude that our own remote ancestors passed through a similar experience and possessed very similar institutions. In studying the condition of the Indian tribes in these periods we may recover some portion of the lost history of our own race. This consideration lends incentive to the investigation.

The first chapter is a condensation of four in "Ancient Society," namely, those on the gens, phratry, tribe, and confederacy of tribes. As they formed a necessary part of that work, they become equally necessary to this. A knowledge of these organizations is indispensable to an understanding of the house life of the aborigines. These organizations form the basis of American ethnology. Although the discussion falls short of a complete explanation of their character and of their prevalence, it will give the reader a general idea of the organization of society among them.

We are too apt to look upon the condition of savage and of barbarous tribes as standing on the same plane with respect to advancement. They should be carefully distinguished as dissimilar conditions of progress. Moreover, savagery shows stages of culture and of progress, and the same is true of barbarism. It will greatly facilitate the study of the facts relating to these two conditions, through which mankind have passed in their progress to civilization, to discriminate between ethnical periods, or stages of culture both in savagery and in barbarism. The progress of mankind from their primitive condition to civilization has been marked and eventful. Each great stage of progress is connected, more or less directly, with some important invention or discovery which materially influenced human progress, and inaugurated an improved condition. For these reasons the period of savagery has been divided into three subperiods, and that of barbarism also into three; the latter of which are chiefly important in their relation to the condition of the Indian tribes. The Older Period of barbarism, which commences with the introduction of the art of pottery, and the Middle Period, which commences with the use of adobe brick in the construction of houses, and with the cultivation of maize and plants by irrigation, mark two very different and very dissimilar conditions of life. The larger portion of the Indian tribes fall within one or the other of these periods. A small portion were in the Older Period of savagery, and none had reached the Later Period of barbarism, which immediately precedes civilization. In treating of the condition of the several tribes they will be assigned to the particular period to which they severally belong under this classification.

I regret to add that I have not been able, from failing health, to give to this manuscript the continuous thought which a work of any kind should receive from its author. But I could not resist the invitation of my friend Major J. W. Powell, the Director of the Bureau of Ethnology, to put these chapters together as well as I might be able, that they might be published by that Bureau. As it will undoubtedly be my last work, I part with it under some solicitude for the reason named; but submit it cheerfully to the indulgence of my readers.

I am greatly indebted to my friend Mr. J. C. Pilling, of the same Bureau, for his friendly labor and care in correcting the proof sheets, and for supervising the illustrations. Such favors are very imperfectly repaid by an author's thanks.

The late William W. Ely, M. D., LL.D., was, for a period of more than twenty-five years, my cherished friend and literary adviser, and to him I am indebted for many valuable suggestions, and for constant encouragement in my labors. The dedication of this volume to his memory is but a partial expression of my admiration of his beautiful character, and of my appreciation of his friendship.

LEWIS H. MORGAN.

ROCHESTER, N. Y., *June*, 1881.

CONTENTS

ILLUSTRATIONS

HOUSES AND HOUSE-LIFE OF THE AMERICAN ABORIGINES.

BY LEWIS H. MORGAN.

CHAPTER I.

SOCIAL AND GOVERNMENTAL ORGANIZATION.

In a previous work* I have considered the organization of the American aborigines in gentes, phratries, and tribes, with the functions of each in their social system. From the importance of this organization to a right understanding of their social and governmental life, a recapitulation of the principal features of each member of the organic series is necessary in this connection.

The gentile organization opens to us one of the oldest and most widely-prevalent institutions of mankind. It furnished the nearly universal plan of government of ancient society, Asiatic, European, African, American, and Australian. It was the instrumentality by means of which society was organized and held together. Commencing in savagery, and continuing through the three subperiods of barbarism, it remained until the establishment of political society, which did not occur until after civilization had commenced. The Grecian gens, phratry, and tribe, the Roman gens, *curia*, and tribe find their analogues in the gens, phratry, and tribe of the American aborigines. In like manner the Irish *sept*, the Scottish *clan*, the *phrara* of the Albanians, and the Sanskrit *ganas*, without extending the comparison further, are the same as the American Indian gens, which has usually been

---

* "Ancient Society; or, Researches in the Lines of Human Progress from Savagery through Barbarism to Civilization." Henry Holt & Co. 1877.

called a clan. As far as our knowledge extends, this organization runs through the entire ancient world upon all the continents, and it was brought down to the historical period by such tribes as attained to civilization. Nor is this all. Gentile society wherever found is the same in structural organization and in principles of action ; but changing from lower to higher forms with the progressive advancement of the people. These changes give the history of development of the same original conceptions.

THE GENS.

Gens, γένος, and *ganas* in Latin, Greek, and Sanskrit have alike the primary signification of *kin*. They contain the same element as *gigno*, γίγνομας, and *ganamai*, in the same languages, signifying *to beget;* thus implying in each an immediate common descent of the members of a gens. A gens, therefore, is a body of consanguinei descended from the same common ancestor, distinguished by a gentile name, and bound together by affinities of blood. It includes a moiety only of such descendants. Where descent is in the female line, as it was universally in the archaic period, the gens is composed of a supposed female ancestor and her children, together with the children of her female descendants, through females, in perpetuity; and where descent is in the male line—into which it was changed after the appearance of property in masses—of a supposed male ancestor and his children, together with the children of his male descendants, through males, in perpetuity. The family name among ourselves is a survival of the gentile name, with descent in the male line, and passing in the same manner. The modern family, as expressed by its name, is an unorganized gens, with the bond of kin broken, and its members as widely dispersed as the family name is found.

Among the nations named, the gens indicated a social organization of a remarkable character, which had prevailed from an antiquity so remote that its origin was lost in the obscurity of far distant ages. It was also the unit of organization of a social and governmental system, the fundamental basis of ancient society. This organization was not confined to the Latin,

Grecian, and Sanskrit speaking tribes, with whom it became such a conspicuous institution. It has been found in other branches of the Aryan family
of nations, in the Semitic, Uralian, and Turanian families, among the tribes
of Africa and Australia, and of the American aborigines.

The gens has passed through successive stages of development in its
transition from its archaic to its final form with the progress of mankind.
These changes were limited in the main to two : firstly, changing descent
from the female line, which was the archaic rule, as among the Iroquois,
to the male line, which was the final rule, as among the Grecian and Roman
gentes; and, secondly, changing the inheritance of the property of a
deceased member of the gens from his gentiles, who took it in the archaic
period, first to his agnatic kindred, and finally to his children. These
changes, slight as they may seem, indicate very great changes of condition
as well as a large degree of progressive development.

The gentile organization, originating in the period of savagery, enduring through the three subperiods of barbarism, finally gave way, among
the more advanced tribes, when they attained civilization—the requirements
of which it was unable to meet. Among the Greeks and Romans political
society supervened upon gentile society, but not until civilization had commenced. The township (and its equivalent, the city ward), with its fixed
property, and the inhabitants it contained, organized as a body politic,
became the unit and the basis of a new and radically different system of
government. After political society was instituted this ancient and time-
honored organization, with the phratry and tribe developed from it, gradually yielded up their existence. It was under gentile institutions that
barbarism was won by some of the tribes of mankind while in savagery,
and that civilization was won by the descendants of some of the same tribes
while in barbarism. Gentile institutions carried a portion of mankind from
savagery to civilization.

This organization may be successfully studied both in its living and in
its historical forms in a large number of tribes and races. In such an investigation it is preferable to commence with the gens in its archaic form.
I shall commence, therefore, with the gens as it now exists among the
American aborigines, where it is found in its archaic form, and among whom

its theoretical constitution and practical workings can be investigated more successfully than in the historical gentes of the Greeks and Romans. In fact, to understand fully the gentes of the latter nations a knowledge of the functions and of the rights, privileges, and obligations of the members of the American Indian gens is imperatively necessary.

In American ethnography *tribe* and *clan* have been used in the place of gens as equivalent terms from not perceiving the universality of the latter. In previous works, and following my predecessors, I have so used them. A comparison of the Indian clan with the gens of the Greeks and Romans reveals at once their identity in structure and functions. It also extends to the phratry and tribe. If the identity of these several organizations can be shown, of which there can be no doubt, there is a manifest propriety in returning to the Latin and Grecian terminologies, which are full and precise as well as historical.

The plan of government of the American aborigines commenced with the gens and ended with the confederacy, the latter being the highest point to which their governmental institutions attained. It gave for the organic series: first, the gens, a body of consanguinei having a common gentile name; second, the phratry, an assemblage of related gentes united in a higher association for certain common objects; third, the tribe, an assemblage of gentes, usually organized in phratries, all the members of which spoke the same dialect; and fourth, a confederacy of tribes, the members of which respectively spoke dialects of the same stock language. It resulted in a gentile society (*societas*) as distinguished from a political society or state (*civitas*). The difference between the two is wide and fundamental. There was neither a political society, nor a citizen, nor a state, nor any civilization in America when it was discovered. One entire ethnical period intervened between the highest American Indian tribes and the beginning of civilization, as that term is properly understood.

The gens, though a very ancient social organization founded upon kin, does not include all the descendants of a common ancestor. It was for the reason that when the gens came in marriage between single pairs was unknown, and descent through males could not be traced with certainty. Kindred were linked together chiefly through the bond of their maternity.

In the ancient gens descent was limited to the female line. It embraced all such persons as traced their descent from a supposed common female ancestor, through females, the evidence of the fact being the possession of a common gentile name. It would include this ancestor and her children, the children of her daughters, and the children of her female descendants, through females, in perpetuity, while the children of her sons and the children of her male descendants, through males, would belong to other gentes, namely, those of their respective mothers. Such was the gens in its archaic form, when the paternity of children was not certainly ascertainable, and when their maternity afforded the only certain criterion of descents.

This state of descents which can be traced back to the Middle Status of savagery, as among the Australians, remained among the American aborigines through the Upper Status of savagery, and into and through the Lower Status of barbarism, with occasional exceptions. In the Middle Status of barbarism the Indian tribes began to change descent from the female line to the male, as the syndyasmian family of the period began to assume monogamian characteristics. In the Upper Status of barbarism descent had become changed to the male line among the Grecian tribes, with the exception of the Lycians, and among the Italian tribes, with the exception of the Etruscans. Between the two extremes, represented by the two rules of descent, three entire ethnical periods intervene, covering many thousands of years.

As intermarriage in the gens was prohibited, it withdrew its members from the evils of consanguine marriages, and thus tended to increase the vigor of the stock. The gens came into being upon three principal conceptions, namely, the bond of kin, a pure lineage through descent in the female line, and non-intermarriage in the gens. When the idea of a gens was developed, it would naturally have taken the form of gentes in pairs, because the children of the males were excluded, and because it was equally necessary to organize both classes of descendants. With two gentes started into being simultaneously the whole result would have been attained, since the males and females of one gens would marry the females and males of the other, and the children, following the gentes of their respective mothers, would be divided between them.   Resting on the bond of kin as its cohesive principle, the gens afforded to each individual member that personal protection which no other existing power could give.

After enumerating the rights, privileges, and obligations of its members, it will be necessary to follow the gens in its organic relations to a phratry tribe and confederacy, in order to find the uses to which it was applied, the privileges which it conferred, and the principles which it fostered.   The gentes of the Iroquois will be taken as the standard exemplification of this institution in the Ganowánian family.   They had carried their scheme of government from the gens to the confederacy, making it complete in each of its parts, and an excellent illustration of the capabilities of the gentile organization in its archaic form.

When discovered the Iroquois were in the Lower Status of barbarism, and well advanced in the arts of life pertaining to this condition.   They manufactured nets, twine, and rope from filaments of bark; wove belts and burden straps, with warp and woof from the same materials; they manufactured earthen vessels and pipes from clay mixed with silicious materials and hardened by fire, some of which were ornamented with rude medallions; they cultivated maize, beans, squashes, and tobacco in garden beds, and made unleavened bread from pounded maize, which they boiled in earthen vessels;* they tanned skins into leather, with which they manufactured kilts, leggins, and moccasins; they used the bow and arrow and war-club as their principal weapons; used flint-stone and bone implements, wore skin garments, and were expert hunters and fishermen.   They constructed long joint tenement houses, large enough to accommodate five, ten, and twenty families, and each household practiced communism in living, but they were unacquainted with the use of stone or adobe-brick in house architecture, and with the use of the native metals.   In mental capacity and in general advancement they were the representative branch of the Indian family north of New Mexico.   General F. A. Walker has sketched their military career in two paragraphs: "The career of the Iroquois was simply terrific. They were the scourge of God upon the aborigines of the continent."†

---

* These loaves or cakes were about six inches in diameter and an inch thick.
† North American Review, April No., 1873, p. 370, Note.

From lapse of time the Iroquois tribes have come to differ slightly in the number and in the names of their respective gentes, the largest number being eight, as follows:

	Senecas.	Cayugas.	Onondagas.	Oneidas.	Mohawks.	Tuscaroras.
1	Wolf.	Wolf.	Wolf.	Wolf.	Wolf.	Gray Wolf.
2	Bear.	Bear.	Bear.	Bear.	Bear.	Bear.
3	Turtle.	Turtle.	Turtle.	Turtle.	Turtle.	Great Turtle.
4	Beaver.	Beaver.	Beaver.			Beaver.
5	Deer.	Deer.	Deer.			Yellow Wolf.
6	Snipe.	Snipe.	Snipe.			Snipe.
7	Heron.	Eel.	Eel.			Eel.
8	Hawk.	Hawk.	Ball.			Little Turtle.

These changes show that certain gentes in some of the tribes have become extinct through the vicissitudes of time, and that others have been formed by the segmentation of over-full gentes.

With a knowledge of the rights, privileges, and obligations of the members of a gens, its capabilities as the unit of a social and governmental system will be more fully understood, as well as the manner in which it entered into the higher organizations of the phratry, tribe, and confederacy.

The gens is individualized by the following rights, privileges, and obligations conferred and imposed upon its members, and which made up the *jus gentilicium*:

    I. *The right of electing its sachem and chiefs.*

    II. *The right of deposing its sachem and chiefs.*

    III. *The obligation not to marry in the gens.*

    IV. *Mutual rights of inheritance of the property of deceased members.*

    V. *Reciprocal obligations of help, defense, and redress of injuries*

    VI. *The right of bestowing names upon its members.*

    VII. *The right of adopting strangers into the gens.*

    VIII. *Common religious rites.*

    IX. *A common burial place.*

    X. *A council of the gens.*

These functions and attributes gave vitality as well as individuality to the organization, and protected the personal rights of its members.

Such were the rights, privileges, and obligations of the members of an Iroquois gens; and such were those of the members of the gentes of the Indian tribes generally, as far as the investigation has been carried.

For a detailed exposition of these characteristics the reader is referred to *Ancient Society*, pp. 72–85.

All the members of an Iroquois gens were personally free, and they were bound to defend each other's freedom; they were equal in privileges and in personal rights, the sachem and chiefs claiming no superiority; and they were a brotherhood bound together by the ties of kin. Liberty, equality, and fraternity, though never formulated, were cardinal principles of the gens. These facts are material, because the gens was the unit of a social and governmental system, the foundation upon which Indian society was organized. A structure composed of such units would of necessity bear the impress of their character, for as the unit so the compound. It serves to explain that sense of independence and personal dignity universally an attribute of Indian character.

Thus substantial and important in the social system was the gens as it anciently existed among the American aborigines, and as it still exists in full vitality in many Indian tribes. It was the basis of the phratry, of the tribe, and of the confederacy of tribes.

At the epoch of European discovery the American Indian tribes generally were organized in gentes, with descent in the female line. In some tribes, as among the Dakotas, the gentes had fallen out; in others, as among the Ojibwas, the Omahas, and the Mayas of Yucatan, descent had been changed from the female to the male line Throughout aboriginal America the gens took its name from some animal or inanimate object and never from a person. In this early condition of society the individuality of persons was lost in the gens. It is at least presumable that the gentes of the Grecian and Latin tribes were so named at some anterior period; but when they first came under historical notice they were named after persons. In some of the tribes, as the Moki Village Indians of Arizona, the members of the gens claimed their descent from the animal whose name they bore—their remote ancestors having been transformed by the Great Spirit from the animal into the human form. The Crane gens of

the Ojibwas have a similar legend.   In some tribes the members of a gens
will not eat the animal whose name they bear, in which they are doubtless
influenced by this consideration.

With respect to the number of persons in a gens, it varied with the
number of the gentes, and with the prosperity or decadence of the tribe.
Three thousand Senecas divided equally among eight gentes would give an
average of three hundred and seventy-five persons to a gens.   Fifteen
thousand Ojibwas divided equally among twenty-three gentes would give
six hundred and fifty persons to a gens.   The Cherokees would average
more than a thousand to a gens   In the present condition of the principal
Indian tribes the number of persons in each gens would range from one
hundred to a thousand.

One of the oldest and most widely prevalent institutions of mankind,
the gentes have been closely identified with human progress upon which
they have exercised a powerful influence.   They have been found in tribes
in the Status of savagery, in the Lower, in the Middle, and in the Upper
Status of barbarism on different continents, and in full vitality in the Grecian and Latin tribes after civilization had commenced.   Every family of
mankind, except the Polynesian, seems to have come under the gentile
organization, and to have been indebted to it for preservation and for the
means of progress.   It finds its only parallel in length of duration in systems of consanguinity, which, springing up at a still earlier period, have
remained to the present time, although the marriage usages in which they
originated have long since disappeared.

From its early institution, and from its maintenance through such
immense stretches of time, the peculiar adaptation of the gentile organization to mankind, while in a savage and in a barbarous state, must be
regarded as abundantly demonstrated.

THE PHRATRY.

The phratry ($\varphi\rho\alpha\tau\rho\iota\alpha$) is a brotherhood, as the term imports, and a
natural growth from the organization into gentes.   It is an organic union
or association of two or more gentes of the same tribe for certain common

objects. These gentes were usually such as had been formed by the segmentation of an original gens.

The phratry existed in a large number of the tribes of the American aborigines, where it is seen to arise by natural growth, and to stand as the second member of the organic series, as among the Grecian and Latin tribes. It did not possess original governmental functions, as the gens tribe and confederacy possessed them; but it was endowed with certain useful powers in the social system, from the necessity for some organization larger than a gens and smaller than a tribe, and especially when the tribe was large. The same institution in essential features and in character, it presents the organization in its archaic form and with its archaic functions. A knowledge of the Indian phratry is necessary to an intelligent understanding of the Grecian and the Roman.

The eight gentes of the Seneca-Iroquois tribe were reintegrated in two phratries, as follows:

First Phratry.

Gentes.—1. Bear. 2. Wolf. 3. Beaver. 4. Turtle.

Second Phratry.

Gentes.—5. Deer. 6. Snipe. 7. Heron. 8. Hawk.

Each phratry (De-ă-non-dă'-a-yoh) is a brotherhood, as this term also imports. The gentes in the same phratry are brother gentes to each other, and cousin gentes to those of the other phratry. They are equal in grade, character, and privileges. It is a common practice of the Senecas to call the gentes of their own phratry brother gentes, and those of the other phratry their cousin gentes, when they mention them in their relation to the phratries. Originally marriage was not allowed between the members of the same phratry; but the members of either could marry into any gens of the other. This prohibition tends to show that the gentes of each phratry were subdivisions of an original gens, and therefore the prohibition against marrying into a person's own gens had followed to its subdivisions. This restriction, however, was long since removed, except with respect to the gens of the individual. A tradition of the Senecas affirms that the Bear and the Deer were the original gentes, of which the others were subdivisions. It is thus seen that the phratry had a natural foundation in the kinship of the gentes of which it was composed. After their subdivision from increase of numbers there was a natural tendency to their reunion in a higher organization for objects common to them all. The same gentes are not constant in a phratry indefinitely, as appears from the composition of the phratries in the remaining Iroquois tribes. Transfers of particular gentes from one phratry to the other must have occurred when the equilibrium in their respective numbers was disturbed. It is important to know the simple manner in which this organization springs up, and the facility with which it is managed as a part of the social system of ancient society. With the increase of numbers in a gens, followed by local separation of its members, segmentation occurred, and the seceding portion adopted a new gentile name. But a tradition of their former unity would remain and become the basis of their reorganization in a phratry.

From the differences in the composition of the phratries in the several tribes it seems probable that the phratries are modified in their gentes at intervals of time to meet changes of condition. Some gentes prosper and increase in numbers, while others, through calamities, decline, and others become extinct; so that transfers of gentes from one phratry to another were found necessary to preserve some degree of equality in the number of phrators in each. The phratric organization has existed among the Iroquois from time immemorial. It is probably older than the confederacy which was established more than four centuries ago. The amount of difference in their composition, as to the gentes they contain, represents the vicissitudes through which each tribe has passed in the interval. In any view of the matter it is small, tending to illustrate the permanence of the phratry as well as the gens.

The Iroquois tribes had a total of thirty-eight gentes, and in four of the tribes a total of eight phratries.

The phratry among the Iroquois was partly for social and partly for religious objects. Its functions and uses can be best shown by practical illustrations. We begin with the lowest, with games, which were of common occurrence at tribal and confederate councils. In the ball game, for example, among the Senecas, they play by phratries, one against the other; and they bet against each other upon the result of the game. Each phratry puts forward its best players, usually from six to ten on a side, and the members of each phratry assemble together, but upon opposite sides of the field in which the game is played.   Before it commences, articles of personal property are hazarded upon the result by members of the opposite phratries.   These are deposited with keepers to abide the event.   The game is played with spirit and enthusiasm, and is an exciting spectacle. The members of each phratry, from their opposite stations, watch the game with eagerness, and cheer their respective players at every successful turn of the game.*

Again, when a murder had been committed it was usual for the gens of the murdered person to meet in council, and, after ascertaining the facts, to take measures for avenging the deed.   The gens of the criminal also held a council, and endeavored to effect an adjustment or condonation of the crime with the gens of the murdered person; but it often happened that the gens of the criminal called upon the other gentes of their phratry, when the slayer and the slain belonged to opposite phratries, to unite with them to obtain a condonation of the crime.   In such a case the phratry held a council, and then addressed itself to the other phratry, to which it sent a delegation with a belt of white wampum asking for a council of the phratry and for an adjustment of the crime.   They offered reparation to the family and gens of the murdered person in expressions of regret and in presents of value.   Negotiations were continued between the two councils until an affirmative or a negative conclusion was reached.   The influence of a phratry composed of several gentes would be greater than that of a single gens; and by calling into action the opposite phratry the probability of a condonation would be increased, especially if there were extenuating circumstances.   We may thus see how naturally the Grecian phratry, prior to civilization, assumed the principal though not exclusive management of cases of murder, and also of the purification of the murderer if he escaped punishment, and after the institution of political society with what propriety the phratry assumed the duty of prosecuting the murderer in the courts of justice.

At the funerals of persons of recognized importance in the tribe the

---

* League of the Iroquois, p. 294.

phratric organization manifested itself in a conspicuous manner. The phrators of the decedent in a body were the mourners, and the members of the opposite phraty conducted the ceremonies. At the funeral of Handsome Lake (Gä-ne-o-di'-yo), one of the eight Seneca sachems (which occurred some years ago), there was an assemblage of sachems and chiefs to the number of twenty-seven, and a large concourse of members of both phratries. The customary address to the dead body, and the other addresses before the removal of the body, were made by members of the opposite phratry. After the addresses were concluded the body was borne to the grave by persons selected from the last named phratry, followed, first, by the sachems and chiefs, then by the family and gens of the decedent, next by his remaining phrators, and last by the members of the opposite phratry. After the body had been deposited in the grave the sachems and chiefs formed in a circle around it for the purpose of filling it with earth. Each in turn, commencing with the senior in years, cast in three shovelfuls, a typical number in their religious system, of which the first had relation to the Great Spirit, the second to the Sun, and the third to Mother Earth. When the grave was filled the senior sachem, by a figure of speech, deposited "the horns" of the departed sachem, emblematic of his office, upon the top of the grave over his head, there to remain until his successor was installed. In that subsequent ceremony "the horns" were said to be taken from the grave of the deceased ruler and placed upon the head of his successor. The social and religious functions of the phratry, and its naturalness in the organic system of ancient society, are rendered apparent by this single usage.

The phratry was also directly concerned in the election of sachems and chiefs of the several gentes, upon which they had a negative as well as a confirmative vote. After the gens of a deceased sachem had elected his successor, or had elected a chief of the second grade, it was necessary, as elsewhere stated, that their choice should be accepted and confirmed by each phratry. It was expected that the gentes of the same phratry would confirm the choice almost as a matter of course, but the opposite phratry also must acquiesce, and from this source opposition sometimes appeared. A council of each phratry was held and pronounced upon the question of acceptance or rejection.   If the nomination made was accepted by both it became complete, but if either refused it was thereby set aside and a new election was made by the gens.   When the choice made by the gens had been accepted by the phratries it was still necessary, as before stated, that the new sachem, or the new chief, should be invested by the council of the confederacy, which alone had power to invest with office.

The phratry was without governmental functions in the strict sense of the phrase, these being confined to the gens tribe and confederacy; but it entered into their social affairs with large administrative powers, and would have concerned itself more and more with their religious affairs as the condition of the people advanced.   Unlike the Grecian phratry and the Roman *curia*, it had no official head.   There was no chief of the phratry as such, and no religious functionaries belonging to it as distinguished from the gens and tribe.   The phratric institution among the Iroquois was in its rudimentary archaic form; but it grew into life by natural and inevitable development, and remained permanent because it met necessary wants.   Every institution of mankind which attained permanence will be found linked with a perpetual want.   With the gens tribe and confederacy in existence the presence of the phratry was substantially assured.   It required time, however, and further experience to manifest all the uses to which it might be made subservient.

Among the Village Indians of Mexico and Central America the phratry must have existed, reasoning upon general principles, and have been a more fully developed and influential organization than among the Iroquois.   Unfortunately mere glimpses at such an institution are all that can be found in the teeming narratives of the Spanish writers within the first century after the Spanish conquest.   The four "lineages" of the Tlascalans who occupied the four quarters of the pueblo of Tlascala were, in all probability, so many phratries.   They were sufficiently numerous for four tribes, but as they occupied the same pueblo and spoke the same dialect the phratric organization was apparently a necessity.   Each lineage or phratry, so to call it, had a distinct military organization, a peculiar costume and banner, and its head war-chief (*Teuctli*), who was its general military commander.   They went forth to battle by phratries.   The organization of a military force by phratries and by tribes was not unknown to the Homeric Greeks. Thus, Nestor advises Agamemnon to "separate the troops by phratries and by tribes, so that phratry may support phratry and tribe tribe."* Under gentile institutions of the most advanced type the principle of kin became to a considerable extent the basis of the army organization. The Aztecs, in like manner, occupied the pueblo of Mexico in four distinct divisions, the people of each of which were more nearly related to each other than to the people of the other divisions. They were separate lineages, like the Tlascalan, and it seems highly probable were four phratries, separately organized as such. They were distinguished from each other by costumes and standards, and went out to war as separate divisions. Their geographical areas were called the four quarters of Mexico.

With respect to the prevalence of this organization among the Indian tribes in the Lower Status of barbarism, the subject has been but slightly investigated. It is probable that it was general in the principal tribes from the natural manner in which it springs up as a necessary member of the organic series, and from the uses, other than governmental, to which it was adapted.

In some of the tribes the phratries stand out prominently upon the face of their organization. Thus the Chocta gentes are united in two phratries, which must be mentioned first in order to show the relation of the gentes to each other. The first phratry is called "Divided People," and contains four gentes. The second is called "Beloved People," and also contains four gentes. This separation of the people into two divisions by gentes created two phratries. Some knowledge of the functions of these phratries is of course desirable; but without it, the fact of their existence is established by the divisions themselves. The evolution of a confederacy from a pair of gentes—for less than two are never found in any tribe—may be deduced theoretically from the known facts of Indian experience. Thus the gens increases in the number of its members and divides into two; these again subdivide, and in time reunite in two or more phratries. These phratries form a tribe, and its members speak the same dialect. In course of time this tribe falls into several by the process of segmentation, which in turn

---

* *Iliad*, ii, 362.

reunite in a confederacy. Such a confederacy is a growth, through the tribe and phratry, from a pair of gentes.

The Chickasas are organized in two phratries, of which one contains four and the other eight gentes, as follows:

I. *Panther Phratry.*

Gentes.—1. Wild Cat.   2. Bird.   3. Fish.   4. Deer.

II. *Spanish Phratry.*

Gentes.—5. Raccoon.   6. Spanish.   7. Royal.   8. Hush-ko'-ni.   9. Squirrel.   10. Alligator.   11. Wolf.   12. Blackbird.

A very complete illustration of the manner in which phratries are formed by natural growth through the subdivision of gentes is presented by the organization of the Mohegan tribe. It had three original gentes, the Wolf, the Turtle, and the Turkey.

Each of these subdivided, and the subdivisions became independent gentes; but they retained the names of the original gentes as their respective phratric names. In other words, the subdivisions of each gens reorganized in a phratry. It proves conclusively the natural process by which in course of time a gens breaks up into several, and these remain united in a phratric organization, which is expressed by assuming a phratric name. They are as follows:

I. *Wolf Phratry.*

Gentes.—1. Wolf.   2. Bear.   3. Dog.   4. Opossum.

II. *Turtle Phratry.*

Gentes.—5. Little Turtle.   6. Mud Turtle.   7. Great Turtle.   8. Yellow Eel.

III. *Turkey Phratry.*

Gentes.—9. Turkey.   10. Crane.   11. Chicken.

It is thus seen that the original Wolf gens divided into four gentes, the Turtle into four, and the Turkey into three. Each new gens took a new name, the original retaining its own, which became by seniority that of the phratry. It is rare among the American Indian tribes to find such plain evidence of the segmentation of gentes in their external organization, followed by the formation into phratries of their respective subdivisions.

It shows also that the phratry is founded upon the kinship of the gentes. As a rule, the name of the original gens out of which others had formed is not known ; but in each of these cases it remains as the name of the phratry.   Since the latter, like the Grecian, was a social and religious rather than a governmental organization, it is externally less conspicuous than a gens or tribe, which were essential to the government of society.   The name of but one of the twelve Athenian phratries has come down to us in history.   Those of the Iroquois had no name but that of a brotherhood.

The phratry also appears among the Thlinkits of the Northwest coast upon the surface of their organization into gentes.   They have two phratries, as follows :

I. *Wolf Phratry.*

Gentes.—1. Bear.   2. Eagle.   3. Dolphin.   4. Shark.   5. Alca.

II. *Raven Phratry.*

Gentes.—6. Frog.   7. Goose.   8. Sea-lion.   9. Owl.   10. Salmon.

Intermarriage in the phratry is prohibited, which shows of itself that the gentes of each phratry were derived from an original gens.   The members of any gens in the Wolf phratry could marry into any gens of the opposite phratry, and *vice versa.*

From the foregoing facts the existence of the phratry is established in several linguistic stocks of the American aborigines.   Its presence in the tribes named raises a presumption of its general prevalence in the Ganowánian family.   Among the Village Indians, where the numbers in a gens and tribe were greater, it would necessarily have been more important, and consequently more fully developed.   As an institution it was still in its archaic form, but it possessed the essential elements of the Grecian and the Roman.

THE TRIBE.

It is difficult to describe an Indian tribe by the affirmative elements of its composition.   Nevertheless it is clearly marked, and is the ultimate organization of the great body of the American aborigines.   The large number of independent tribes into which they had fallen by the natural process of segmentation is the striking characteristic of their condition.   Each tribe was individualized by a name, by a separate dialect, by a supreme government, and by the possession of a territory which it occupied and defended as its own.   The tribes were as numerous as the dialects, for separation did not become complete until dialectical variation had commenced.   Indian tribes, therefore, are natural growths through the separation of the same people in the area of their occupation, followed by divergence of speech, segmentation, and independence.

The exclusive possession of a dialect and of a territory has led to the application of the term *nation* to many Indian tribes, notwithstanding the fewness of the people in each.   *Tribe* and *nation*, however, are not strict equivalents.   A nation does not arise, under gentile institutions, until the tribes united under the same government have coalesced into one people, as the four Athenian tribes coalesced in Attica, three Dorian tribes at Sparta, and three Latin and Sabine tribes at Rome.   Federation requires independent tribes in separate territorial areas; but coalescence unites them by a higher process in the same area, although the tendency to local separation by gentes and by tribes would continue   The confederacy is the nearest analogue of the nation, but not strictly equivalent.   Where the gentile organization exists, the organic series gives all the terms which are needed for a correct description.

An Indian tribe is composed of several gentes, developed from two or more, all the members of which are intermingled by marriage, and all of whom speak the same dialect.   To a stranger the tribe is visible, and not the gens.   The instances are extremely rare, among the American aborigines, in which the tribe embraced peoples speaking different dialects. When such cases are found it has resulted from the union of a weaker with a stronger tribe speaking a closely related dialect, as the union of the Missouris with the Otoes after the overthrow of the former.   The fact that the great body of the aborigines were found in independent tribes illustrates the slow and difficult growth of the idea of government under gentile institutions.   A small portion only had attained to the ultimate stage known among them, that of a confederacy of tribes speaking dialects of the same stock language. A coalescence of tribes into a nation had not occurred in any case in any part of America.

A constant tendency to disintegration, which has proved such a hinderance to progress among savage and barbarous tribes, existed in the elements of the gentile organization. It was aggravated by a further tendency to divergence of speech, which was inseparable from their social state and the large areas of their occupation. An oral language, although remarkably persistent in its vocables, and still more persistent in its grammatical forms, is incapable of permanence. Separation of the people in area was followed in time by variation in speech; and this, in turn, led to separation in interests and ultimate independence. It was not the work of a brief period, but of centuries of time, aggregating finally into thousands of years; and the multiplication of the languages and dialects of the different families of North and South America probably required for their formation the time measured by three ethnical periods.

New tribes, as well as new gentes, were constantly forming by natural growth, and the process was sensibly accelerated by the great expanse of the American continent. The method was simple. In the first place there would occur a gradual outflow of people from some overstocked geographical center, which possessed superior advantages in the means of subsistence. Continued from year to year, a considerable population would thus be developed at a distance from the original seat of the tribe. In course of time the emigrants would become distinct in interests, strangers in feeling, and, last of all, divergent in speech. Separation and independence would follow, although their territories were contiguous. A new tribe was thus created. This is a concise statement of the manner in which the tribes of the American aborigines were formed, but the statement must be taken as general. Repeating itself from age to age in newly acquired as well as in old areas, it must be regarded as a natural as well as inevitable result of the gentile organization, united with the necessities of their condition. When increased numbers pressed upon the means of subsistence, the surplus removed to a new seat, where they established themselves with facility, because the government was perfect in every gens, and in any number of gentes united in a band. Among the Village Indians the same thing repeated itself in a slightly different manner. When a village became overcrowded with numbers, a colony went up or down on the same stream and commenced a new village.   Repeated at intervals of time, several such villages would appear, each independent of the other and a self-governing body, but united in a league or confederacy for mutual protection. Dialectic variation would finally spring up, and thus complete their growth into tribes

The manner in which tribes are evolved from each other can be shown directly by examples. The fact of separation can be derived in part from tradition, in part from the possession by each of a number of the same gentes, and deduced in part from the relations of their dialects. Tribes formed by the subdivisions of an original tribe would possess a number of gentes in common, and speak dialects of the same language. After several centuries of separation they would still have a number of the same gentes. Thus the Hurons, now Wyandots, have six gentes of the same name with six of the gentes of the Seneca-Iroquois, after at least four hundred years of separation. The Potawattamies have eight gentes of the same name with eight among the Ojibwas, while the former have six, and the latter fourteen, which are different, showing that new gentes have been formed in each tribe by segmentation since their separation. A still older offshoot from the Ojibwas, or from the common parent tribe of both, the Miamis, have but three gentes in common with the former, namely, the Wolf, the Loon, and the Eagle.   The minute social history of the tribes of the Ganowánian family is locked up in the life and growth of the gentes. If investigation is ever turned strongly in this direction, the gentes themselves would become reliable guides, in respect to the order of separation from each other of the tribes of the same stock.

This process of subdivision has been operating among the American aborigines for thousands of years, until several hundred tribes have been developed from about seventy stocks as existing in as many families of language.

Their experience, probably, was but a repetition of that of the tribes of Asia, Europe, and Africa when they were in corresponding conditions.

From the preceding observations it is apparent that an American Indian tribe is a very simple as well as humble organization. It required but a few hundred, and, at most, a few thousand people to form a tribe and place it in a respectable position in the Ganowánian family.

It remains to present the functions and attributes of an Indian tribe, which are contained in the following propositions:

I. *The possession of a territory and a name.*

II. *The exclusive possession of a dialect.*

III. *The right to invest sachems and chiefs elected by the gentes.*

IV. *The right to depose these sachems and chiefs.*

V. *The possession of a religious faith and worship.*

VI. *A supreme government consisting of a council of chiefs.*

VII. *A head-chief of the tribe in some instances.*

For a discussion of these characteristics of a tribe, reference is made to Ancient Society, pp. 113–118.

The growth of the idea of government commenced with the organization into gentes in savagery. It reveals three great stages of progressive development between its commencement and the institution of political society after civilization had been attained. The first stage was the government of a tribe by a council of chiefs elected by the gentes. It may be called a government of *one power;* namely, *the council.* It prevailed generally among tribes in the Lower Status of barbarism. The second stage was a government co-ordinated between a council of chiefs and a general military commander, one representing the civil and the other the military functions. This second form began to manifest itself in the Lower Status of barbarism after confederacies were formed, and it became definite in the Middle Status. The office of general, or principal military commander, was the germ of that of a chief executive magistrate, the king, the emperor, and the president. It may be called a government of *two powers,* namely, *the council of chiefs* and *the general.* The third stage was the government of a people or nation by a council of chiefs, an assembly of the people, and a general military commander. It appeared among the tribes who had attained to the Upper Status of barbarism; such, for example, as the Homeric Greeks and the Italian tribes of the period of Romulus. A large increase in the number of people united in a nation, their establishment in walled cities, and the creation of wealth in lands and in flocks and herds, brought in the assembly of the people as an instrument of government. The council of chiefs, which still remained, found it necessary, no doubt, through popular constraint, to submit the most important public measures to an assembly of the people for acceptance or rejection; whence the popular assembly. This assembly did not originate measures. It was its function to adopt or reject, and its action was final. From its first appearance it became a permanent power in the government. The council no longer passed important public measures, but became a preconsidering council, with power to originate and mature public acts to which the assembly alone could give validity. It may be called a government of *three powers*, namely, *the preconsidering council*, the *assembly of the people*, and *the general*. This remained until the institution of political society, when, for example, among the Athenians, the council of chiefs became the senate, and the assembly of the people the ecclesia or popular assembly. The same organizations have come down to modern times in the two houses of Parliament, of Congress, and of legislatures. In like manner the office of general military commander, as before stated, was the germ of the office of the modern chief executive magistrate.

Recurring to the tribe, it was limited in the numbers of the people, feeble in strength, and poor in resources; but yet a completely organized society. It illustrates the condition of mankind in the Lower Status of barbarism. In the Middle Status there was a sensible increase of numbers in a tribe, and an improved condition; but with a continuance of gentile society without essential change. Political society was still impossible from want of advancement. The gentes organized into tribes remained as before, but confederacies must have been more frequent. In some areas, as in the Valley of Mexico, large numbers were developed under a common government, with improvements in the arts of life; but no evidence exists of the overthrow among them of gentile society and the substitution of political. It is impossible to found a political society or a state upon gentes.

A state must rest upon territory and not upon persons; upon the township as the unit of a political system, and not upon the gens, which is the unit of a social system. It required time and a vast experience, beyond that of the American Indian tribes, as a preparation for such a fundamental change of systems. It also required men of the mental stature of the Greeks and Romans, and with the experience derived from a long chain of ancestors, to devise and gradually introduce that new plan of government under which civilized nations are living at the present time.

THE CONFEDERACY OF TRIBES.

A tendency to confederate for mutual defense would very naturally exist among kindred and contiguous tribes. When the advantages of a union had been appreciated by actual experience, the organization, at first a league, would gradually cement into a federal unity. The state of perpetual warfare in which they lived would quicken this natural tendency into action among such tribes as were sufficiently advanced in intelligence and in the arts of life to perceive its benefits. It would be simply a growth from a lower into a higher organization by an extension of the principle which united the gentes in a tribe.

As might have been expected, several confederacies existed in different parts of North America when discovered, some of which were quite remarkable in plan and structure. Among the number may be mentioned the Iroquois Confederacy of five independent tribes, the Creek Confederacy of six, the Ottawa Confederacy of three, the Dakota League of the "Seven Council Fires," the Moki Confederacy in New Mexico of Seven Pueblos, and the Aztec Confederacy of three tribes in the Valley of Mexico. It is probable that the Village Indians in other parts of Mexico, in Central and in South America, were quite generally organized in confederacies consisting of two or more kindred tribes. Progress necessarily took this direction from the nature of their institutions and from the law governing their development. Nevertheless the formation of a confederacy out of such materials, and with such unstable geographical relations, was a difficult undertaking. It was easiest of achievement by the Village Indians from the nearness to each other of their pueblos and from the smallness of their areas; but it was accomplished in occasional instances by tribes in the Lower Status of barbarism, and notably by the Iroquois. Wherever a confederacy was formed it would of itself evince the superior intelligence of the people.

The two highest examples of Indian confederacies in North America were those of the Iroquois and of the Aztecs. From their acknowledged superiority as military powers, and from their geographical positions, these confederacies in both cases produced remarkable results. Our knowledge of the structure and principles of the former is definite and complete, while of the latter it is far from satisfactory. The Aztec Confederacy has been handled in such a manner historically as to leave it doubtful whether it was simply a league of three kindred tribes, offensive and defensive, or a systematic confederacy like that of the Iroquois. That which is true of the latter was probably in a general sense true of the former, so that a knowledge of one will tend to elucidate the other.

The conditions under which confederacies spring into being and the principles on which they are formed are remarkably simple. They grow naturally with time out of pre-existing elements. Where one tribe had divided into several, and these subdivisions occupied independent but contiguous territories, the confederacy reintegrated them in a higher organization on the basis of the common gentes they possessed and of the affiliated dialects they spoke. The sentiment of kin embodied in the gens, the common lineage of the gentes, and their dialects, still mutually intelligible, yielded the material elements for a confederation. The confederacy, therefore, had the gentes for its basis and center, and stock language for its circumference. No one has been found that reached beyond the bounds of the dialects of a common language. If this natural barrier had been crossed it would have forced heterogeneous elements into the organization. Cases have occurred where the remains of a tribe, not cognate in speech, as the Natchez,* have been admitted into an existing confederacy; but this exception would not invalidate the general proposition. It was impossible for an Indian power to arise upon the American continent through a con-

---

* They were admitted into the Creek Confederacy after their overthrow by the French.

federacy of tribes organized in gentes, and advance to a general supremacy, unless their numbers were developed from their own stock. The multitude of stock languages is a standing explanation of the failure. There was no possible way of becoming connected on equal terms with a confederacy excepting through membership in a gens and tribe and a common speech.

The Iroquois have furnished an excellent illustration of the manner in which a confederacy is formed by natural growth assisted by skillful legislation. Originally emigrants from beyond the Mississippi, and possibly a branch of the Dakota stock, they first made their way to the valley of the St. Lawrence and settled themselves near Montreal. Forced to leave this region by the hostility of surrounding tribes, they sought the central region of New York. Coasting the eastern shore of Lake Ontario in canoes, for their numbers were small, they made their first settlement at the mouth of the Oswego River, where, according to their traditions, they remained for a long period of time. They were then in at least three distinct tribes, the Mohawks, the Onondagas, and the Senecas. One tribe subsequently established themselves at the head of the Canandaigua Lake and became the Senecas. Another tribe occupied the Onondaga Valley and became the Onondagas. The third passed eastward and settled first at Oneida, near the site of Utica, from which place the main portion removed to the Mohawk Valley and became the Mohawks. Those who remained became the Oneidas. A portion of the Onondagas or Senecas settled along the eastern shore of the Cayuga Lake and became the Cayugas New York, before its occupation by the Iroquois, seems to have been a part of the area of the Algonkin tribes. According to Iroquois traditions, they displaced its anterior inhabitants as they gradually extended their settlements eastward to the Hudson and westward to the Genesee. Their traditions further declare that a long period of time elapsed after their settlement in New York before the confederacy was formed, during which they made common cause against their enemies, and thus experienced the advantages of the federal principle both for aggression and defense. They resided in villages, which were usually surrounded with stockades, and subsisted upon fish and game and the products of a limited horticulture. In numbers they did not at any time exceed 20,000 souls, if they ever reached that number. Precarious subsistence and incessant warfare repressed numbers in all the aboriginal tribes, including the Village Indians as well. The Iroquois were enshrouded in the great forests which then overspread New York, against which they had no power to contend. They were first discovered A. D. 1608. About 1675 they attained their culminating point, when their dominion reached over an area remarkably large, covering the greater parts of New York, Pennsylvania, and Ohio,* and portions of Canada north of Lake Ontario. At the time of their discovery they were the highest representatives of the red race north of New Mexico in intelligence and advancement, though perhaps inferior to some of the Gulf tribes in the arts of life. In the extent and quality of their mental endowments they must be ranked among the highest Indians in America. There are over six thousand Iroquois in New York, besides scattered bands in other parts of the United States, and a still larger number in Canada; thus illustrating the efficiency as well as persistency of the arts of barbarous life in sustaining existence It is, moreover, now ascertained that they are slowly increasing.

When the confederacy was formed, about A. D. 1400–1450,† the conditions previously named were present. The Iroquois were in five independent tribes, occupied territories contiguous to each other, and spoke dialects of the same language which were mutually intelligible. Beside these facts, certain gentes were common in the several tribes, as has been shown. In their relations to each other, as separated parts of the same gens, these common gentes afforded a natural and enduring basis for a confederacy. With these elements existing, the formation of a confederacy became a question of intelligence and skill. Other tribes in large numbers were standing in precisely the same relations in different parts of the continent without confederating. The fact that the Iroquois tribes accomplished the work affords evidence of their superior capacity. Moreover, as the

---

* About 1651-'55 they expelled their kindred tribes, the Eries, from the region between the Genesee River and Lake Erie, and shortly afterwards the Neutral Nations from the Niagara River, and thus came into possession of the remainder of New York, with the exception of the Lower Hudson and Long Island.

† The Iroquois claimed that it had existed from one hundred and fifty to two hundred years when they first saw Europeans. The generations of sachems in the history by David Cusick (a Tuscarora) would make it more ancient. Schoolcraft's History, Condition and Prospects of the Indian Tribes, 5, p. 631.

confederacy was the ultimate stage of organization among the American aborigines, its existence would be expected in the most intelligent tribes only.

It is affirmed by the Iroquois that the confederacy was formed by a council of wise men and chiefs of the five tribes which met for that purpose on the north shore of Onondaga Lake, near the site of Syracuse; and that before its session was concluded the organization was perfected and set in immediate operation. At their periodical councils for raising up sachems they still explain its origin as the result of one protracted effort of legislation. It was probably a consequence of a previous alliance for mutual defense, the advantages of which they had perceived and which they sought to render permanent.

The origin of the plan is ascribed to a mythical, or, at least, traditionary person, *Hä-yo-went'-hä*, the Hiawatha of Longfellow's celebrated poem, who was present at this council and the central person in its management. In his communications with the council he used a wise man of the Onondagas, *Da-gä-no-we'-dä*, as an interpreter and speaker to expound the structure and principles of the proposed confederacy. The same tradition further declares that when the work was accomplished *Hä-yo-went'-hä* miraculously disappeared in a white canoe, which arose with him in the air and bore him out of their sight. Other prodigies, according to this tradition, attended and signalized the formation of the confederacy, which is still celebrated among them as a masterpiece of Indian wisdom. Such in truth it was; and it will remain in history as a monument of their genius in developing gentile institutions. It will also be remembered as an illustration of what tribes of mankind have been able to accomplish in the art of government while in the Lower Status of barbarism, and under the disadvantages this condition implies.

Which of the two persons was the founder of the confederacy it is difficult to determine. The silent *Hä-yo-went'-hä* was, not unlikely, a real person of Iroquois lineage;* but tradition has enveloped his character so completely in the supernatural that he loses his place among them as one of their number. If Hiawatha were a real person, *Da-gä-no-we'-dä* must hold

---

* My friend Horatio Hale, the eminent philologist, came, as he informed me, to this conclusion.

a subordinate place; but if a mythical person invoked for the occasion, then to the latter belongs the credit of planning the confederacy.

The Iroquois affirm that the confederacy, as formed by this council, with its powers, functions, and mode of administration, has come down to them through many generations to the present time with scarcely a change in its internal organization. When the Tuscaroras were subsequently admitted, their sachems were allowed by courtesy to sit as equals in the general council, but the original number of sachems was not increased, and in strictness those of the Tuscaroras formed no part of the ruling body.

The general features of the Iroquois Confederacy may be summarized in the following propositions:

I. *The Confederacy was a union of Five Tribes, composed of common gentes, under one government on the basis of equality; each Tribe remaining independent in all matters pertaining to local self-government.*

II. *It created a General Council of Sachems, who were limited in number, equal in rank and authority, and invested with supreme powers over all matters pertaining to the Confederacy.*

III. *Fifty Sachemships were created and named in perpetuity in certain gentes of the several Tribes; with power in these gentes to fill vacancies, as often as they occurred, by election from among their respective members, and with the further power to depose from office for cause; but the right to invest these Sachems with office was reserved to the General Council.*

IV. *The Sachems of the Confederacy were also Sachems in their respective Tribes, and with the Chiefs of these Tribes formed the Council of each, which was supreme over all matters pertaining to the Tribe exclusively.*

V. *Unanimity in the Council of the Confederacy was made essential to every public act.*

VI. *In the General Council the Sachems voted by Tribes, which gave to each Tribe a negative upon the others.*

VII. *The Council of each Tribe had power to convene the General Council; but the latter had no power to convene itself.*

VIII. *The General Council was open to the orators of the people for the discussion of public questions; but the Council alone decided.*

IX. *The Confederacy had no chief Executive Magistrate or official head.*

X. *Experiencing the necessity for a General Military Commander, they created the office in a dual form, that one might neutralize the other. The two principal War-chiefs created were made equal in powers.*

These several propositions will be considered and illustrated, but without following the precise form or order in which they are stated.

At the institution of the confederacy fifty permanent sachemships were created and named, and made perpetual in the gentes to which they were assigned. With the exception of two, which were filled but once, they have been held by as many different persons in succession as generations have passed away between that time and the present. The name of each sachemship is also the personal name of each sachem while he holds the office, each one in succession taking the name of his predecessor. These sachems, when in session, formed the council of the confederacy in which the legislative, executive, and judicial powers were vested, although such a discrimination of functions had not come to be made. To secure order in the succession, the several gentes in which these offices were made hereditary were empowered to elect successors from among their respective members when vacancies occurred, as elsewhere explained. As a further measure of protection to their own body, each sachem, after his election and its confirmation, was invested with his office by a council of the confederacy. When thus installed his name was "taken away" and that of the sachemship was bestowed upon him. By this name he was afterwards known among them. They were all upon equality in rank, authority, and privileges.

These sachemships were distributed unequally among the five tribes; but without giving to either a preponderance of power; and unequally among the gentes of the last three tribes. The Mohawks had nine sachems, the Oneidas nine, the Onondagas fourteen, the Cayugas ten, and the Senecas eight. This was the number at first, and it has remained the number to the present time. A table of these sachemships, founded at the institution of the Confederacy, with the names which have been borne by their sachems in succession, from its formation to the present time, is subjoined, with their names in the Seneca dialect, and their arrangement in classes to facilitate the attainment of unanimity in council. In foot-notes will be found the signification of these names, and the gentes to which they belonged.

Table of sachemships of the Iroquois.[1]

MOHAWKS.

I. 1. Da-gä-e'-o-gă.[1] 2. Hä-yo-went'-ha.[2] 3. Da-gä-no-we'-dä.[3]

II. 4. So-ä-e-wä'-ah.[4] 5. Da-yo'-ho-go.[5] 6. O-ä-ä'-go-wä.[6]

III. 7. Da-an-no-gä'e-neh.[7] 8. Sä-da'-gä-e-wä-deh.[8] 9. Häs-dä-weh'-se-ont-hä.[9]

ONEIDAS.

I. 1. Ho-däs'-hä-teh.[10] 2. Ga-no-gweh'-yo-do.[11] 3. Da-yo-hä'-gwen-da.[11]

II. 4. So-no-sase'.[13] 5. To-no-ä-gă'-o.[14] 6. Hä-de-ä-dun-nent'-hä.[15]

III. 7. Da-wä-dä'-o-dä-yo.[16] 8. Gä-ne-ä-dus'-ha-yeh.[17] 9. Ho-wus'-hä-da-o.[18]

ONONDAGAS.

I. 1. To-do-dä'-ho.[19] 2. To-nes'-sa-ah. 3. Da-ät'-ga-dose.[20]

II. 4. Gä-neä-dä'-je-wake.[21] 5. Ah-wä'-ga-yat.[22] 6. Da-ä-yat'-gwä-e.

III. 7. Ho-no-we-nă-to.[23]

IV. 8. Gä-wă-nă'-san-do.[24]. 9. Hä-e'-ho.[25] 10. Ho-yo-ne-ä'-ne.[26] 11. Sa-dä'-kwä-seh.[27]

V. 12. Sä-go-ga-hä'.[28] 13. Ho-sa-hä'-do[29] 14. Skä-no'-wun-de.[30]

---

[1] These names signify as follows: 1. "Neutral," or "The Shield." 2. "Man who Combs." 3. "Inexhaustible." 4. "Small Speech." 5. "At the Forks." 6. "At the Great River." 7. "Dragging his Horns." 8. "Even-Tempered," 9. "Hanging up Rattles." The sachems in class one belonged to the Turtle gens, in class two to the Wolf gens, and in class three to the Bear gens.
10. "A Man bearing a Burden." 11. "A Man covered with Cat-tail Down." 12. "Opening through the Woods." 13. "A Long String." 14. "A Man with a Headache." 15. "Swallowing Himself." 16. "Place of the Echo." 17. "War-club on the Ground." 18. "A Man Steaming Himself." The sachems in the first class belong to the Wolf gens, in the second to the Turtle gens, and in the third to the Bear gens.
19. "Tangled," Bear gens. 20. "On the Watch," Bear gens. This sachem and the one before him were hereditary councillors of the To-do-dä'-ho, who held the most illustrious sachemship. 21. "Bitter Body," Snipe gens. 22. Turtle gens. 23. This sachem was hereditary keeper of the wampum; Wolf gens.
24. Deer gens. 25. Deer gens. 26. Turtle gens. 27. Bear gens. 28. "Having a Glimpse," Deer gens. 29. "Large Mouth," Turtle gens. 30. "Over the Creek," Turtle gens.

CAYUGAS.

I. 1. Da-gä'-ă-yo.[31] 2. Da-je-no'-dä-weh-o.[32] 3. Gä-dä'-gwà-sa.[33]
4. So-yo-wasé.[34] 5. Hä-de-äs'yo-no.[35]

II. 6. Da-yo-o-yo'go.[36] 7. Jote-ho-weh'-ko.[37] 8. De-ä-wate'-ho.[38]

III. 9. To-dä-e-ho'.[39] 10. 10. Des-gä'-heh.[40]

SENECAS.

I. 1. Ga-ne-o-di'-yo.[40] 2. Sä-dä-gä'-o-yase.[41]

II. 3. Gä-no-gi'-e.[42] 4. Sä-geh'-jo-wä.[43]

III. 5. Sä-de-a-no'-wus.[44] 6. Nis-hä-ne-a'-nent.[45]

IV. 7. Gä-no-go-e-dä'-we.[46] 8. Do-ne-ho-gä'-weh.[47]

Two of these sachemships have been filled but once since their creation. *Hä-yo-went'-hä* and *Da-gä-no-we'-da* consented to take the office among the Mohawk sachems, and to leave their names in the list upon condition that after their demise the two should remain thereafter vacant. They were installed upon these terms, and the stipulation has been observed to the present day. At all councils for the investiture of sachems their names are still called with the others as a tribute of respect to their memory. The general council, therefore, consisted of but forty-eight members.

Each sachem had an assistant sachem, who was elected by the gens of his principal from among its members, and who was installed with the same forms and ceremonies. He was styled an "aid." It was his duty to stand behind his superior on all occasions of ceremony, to act as his messenger, and in general to be subject to his directions. It gave to the aid the office of chief, and rendered probable his election as the successor of his principal after the decease of the latter. In their figurative language these aids of the sachems were styled "Braces in the Long House," which symbolized the confederacy.

---

31. "Man Frightened," Deer gens. 32. Heron gens. 33. Bear gens. 34. Bear gens. 35. Turtle gens. 36. Not ascertained. 37. "Very Cold," Turtle gens. 38. Heron gens. 39. Snipe gens. 40. Snipe gens. 41. "Handsome Lake," Turtle gens. 42. "Level Heavens," Snipe gens. 43. Turtle gens. 44. "Great Forehead," Hawk gens. 45. "Assistant," Bear gens. 46. "Falling Day," Snipe gens. 47. "Hair Burned Off," Snipe gens. 48. "Open Door," Wolf gens."

The names bestowed upon the original sachems became the names of their respective successors in perpetuity.   For example, upon the demise of *Gä-ne-o-di'-yo*, one of the eight Seneca sachems, his successor would be elected by the Turtle gens in which this sachemship was hereditary, and when raised up by the general council he would receive this name, in place of his own, as a part of the ceremony.   On several different occasions I have attended their councils for raising up sachems both at the Onondaga and Seneca reservations, and witnessed the ceremonies herein referred to. Although but a shadow of the old confederacy now remains, it is fully organized with its complement of sachems and aids, with the exception of the Mohawk tribe, which removed to Canada about 1775.   Whenever vacancies occur their places are filled, and a general council is convened to install the new sachems and their aids.   The present Iroquois are also perfectly familiar with the structure and principles of the ancient confederacy.

For all purposes of tribal government the five tribes were independent of each other.   Their territories were separated by fixed boundary lines, and their tribal interests were distinct.   The eight Seneca sachems, in conjunction with the other Seneca chiefs, formed the council of the tribe by which its affairs were administered, leaving to each of the other tribes the same control over their separate interests.   As an organization the tribe was neither weakened nor impaired by the confederate compact.   Each was in vigorous life within its appropriate sphere, presenting some analogy to our own States within an embracing Republic.   It is worthy of remembrance that the Iroquois commended to our forefathers a union of the colonies similar to their own as early as 1755.   They saw in the common interests and common speech of the several colonies the elements for a confederation, which was as far as their vision was able to penetrate.

The tribes occupied positions of entire equality in the confederacy in rights, privileges, and obligations.   Such special immunities as were granted to one or another indicate no intention to establish an unequal compact or to concede unequal privileges.   There were organic provisions apparently investing particular tribes with superior power; as, for example, the Onondagas were allowed fourteen sachems and the Senecas but eight; and a larger body of sachems would naturally exercise a stronger influence in council than a smaller. But in this case it gave no additional power, because the sachems of each tribe had an equal voice in forming a decision, and a negative upon the others. When in council they agreed by tribes, and unanimity in opinion was essential to every public act. The Onondagas were made "Keepers of the Wampum," and "Keepers of the Council Brand," the Mohawks "Receivers of Tribute" from subjugated tribes, and the Senecas "Keepers of the Door" of the Long House. These and some other similar provisions were made for the common advantage.

The cohesive principle of the confederacy did not spring exclusively from the benefits of an alliance for mutual protection, but had a deeper foundation in the bond of kin. The confederacy rested upon the tribes ostensibly, but primarily upon common gentes. All the members of the same gens, whether Mohawks, Oneidas, Onondagas, Cayugas, or Senecas, were brothers and sisters to each other in virtue of their descent from the same common ancestor, and they recognized each other as such with the fullest cordiality. When they met, the first inquiry was the name of each other's gens, and next the immediate pedigree of their respective sachems; after which they were usually able to find, under their peculiar system of consanguinity*, the relationship in which they stood to each other. Three of the gentes—namely, the Wolf, Bear, and Turtle—were common to the five tribes; these and three others were common to three tribes. In effect, the Wolf gens, through the division of an original tribe into five, was now in five divisions, one of which was in each tribe. It was the same with the Bear and the Turtle gentes. The Deer, Snipe, and Hawk gentes were common to the Senecas, Cayugas, and Onondagas. Between the separated parts of each gens, although its members spoke different dialects of the same language, there existed a fraternal connection which linked the nations together with indissoluble bonds. When the Mohawk of the Wolf gens recognized an Oneida, Onondaga, Cayuga, or Seneca of the same gens as a brother, and when the members of the other divided gentes did the same,

---

* The children of brothers are themselves brothers and sisters to each other; the children of the latter were also brothers and sisters, and so downwards indefinitely. The children and descendants of sisters are the same. The children of a brother and sister are cousins; the children of the latter are cousins, and so downwards indefinitely. A knowledge of the relationships to each other of the members of the same gens is never lost.

the relationship was not ideal, but a fact founded upon consanguinity, and upon faith in an assured lineage older than their dialects and coeval with their unity as one people.   In the estimation of an Iroquois every member of his gens, in whatever tribe, was as certainly a kinsman as an own brother. This cross-relationship between persons of the same gens in the different tribes is still preserved and recognized among them in all its original force. It explains the tenacity with which the fragments of the old confederacy still cling together.   If either of the five tribes had seceded from the confederacy it would have severed the bond of kin, although this would have been felt but slightly.   But had they fallen into collision it would have turned the gens of the Wolf against their gentile kindred, Bear against Bear; in a word, brother against brother.   The history of the Iroquois demonstrates the reality as well as persistency of the bond kin, and the fidelity with which it was respected.   During the long period through which the confederacy endured they never fell into anarchy nor ruptured the organization.

The "Long House" (*Ho-de'-no-sote*) was made the symbol of the confederacy,[1] and they styled themselves the "People of the Long House" (*Ho-de'-no-sau-nee*).   This was the name, and the only name, with which they distinguished themselves.   The confederacy produced a gentile society more complex than that of a single tribe, but it was still distinctively a gentile society.   It was, however, a stage of progress in the direction of a nation, for nationality is reached under gentile institutions.   Coalescence is the last stage in this process   The four Athenian tribes coalesced in Attica into a nation by the intermingling of the tribes in the same area, and by the gradual disappearance of geographical lines between them.   The tribal names and organizations remained in full vitality as before, but without the basis of an independent territory.   When political society was instituted on the basis of the deme or township, and all the residents of the deme became a body politic, irrespective of their gens or tribe, the coalescence became complete.

The coalescence of the Latin and Sabine gentes into the Roman people

---

[1] The Long House was not peculiar to the Iroquois, but used by many other tribes, as the Powhattan Indians of Virginia, the Nyacks of Long Island, and other tribes.

and nation was a result of the same processes. In all alike the gens, phratry, and tribe were the first three stages of organization. The confederacy followed as the fourth. But it does not appear, either among the Grecian or Latin tribes in the Later Period of barbarism, that it became more than a loose league for offensive and defensive purposes. Of the nature and details of organization of the Grecian and Latin confederacies our knowledge is limited and imperfect, because the facts are buried in the obscurity of the traditionary period. The process of coalescence arises later than the confederacy in gentile society; but it was a necessary as well as a vital stage of progress by means of which the nation, the state, and political society were at last attained. Among the Iroquois tribes it had not manifested itself.

The valley of Onondaga, as the seat of the central tribe, and the place where the Council Brand was supposed to be perpetually burning, was the usual though not the exclusive place for holding the councils of the confederacy. In ancient times it was summoned to convene in the autumn of each year, but public exigencies often rendered its meetings more frequent. Each tribe had power to summon the council, and to appoint the time and place of meeting at the council-house of either tribe, when circumstances rendered a change from the usual place at Onondaga desirable. But the council had no power to convene itself.

Originally the principal object of the council was to raise up sachems to fill vacancies in the ranks of the ruling body occasioned by death or deposition; but it transacted all other business which concerned the common welfare. In course of time, as they multiplied in numbers and their intercourse with foreign tribes became more extended, the council fell into three distinct kinds, which may be distinguished as Civil, Mourning, and Religious. The first declared war and made peace, sent and received embassies, entered into treaties with foreign tribes, regulated the affairs of subjugated tribes, and took all needful measures to promote the general welfare. The second raised up sachems and invested them with office. It received the name of Mourning Council because the first of its ceremonies was the lament for the deceased ruler whose vacant place was to be filled. The third was held for the observance of a general religious festival. It was made an occasion for the confederated tribes to unite under the auspices of a general council in the observance of common religious rites; but as the Mourning Council was attended with many of the same ceremonies it came in time to answer for both. It is now the only council they hold, as the civil powers of the confederacy terminated with the supremacy over them of the state.

When the sachems met in council at the time and place appointed, and the usual reception ceremony had been performed, they arranged themselves in two divisions and seated themselves upon opposite sides of the council-fire. Upon one side were the Mohawk, Onondaga, and Seneca sachems. The tribes they represented were, when in council, brother tribes to each other and father tribes to the other two. In like manner their sachems were brothers to each other and fathers to those opposite. They constituted a phratry of tribes and of sachems, by an extension of the principle which united gentes in a phratry. On the opposite side of the fire were the Oneida and Cayuga and at a later day the Tuscarora sachems. The tribes they represented were brother tribes to each other and son tribes to the opposite three. Their sachems also were brothers to each other, and sons of those in the opposite division. They formed a second tribal phratry. As the Oneidas were a subdivision of the Mohawks, and the Cayugas a subdivision of the Onondagas or Senecas, they were in reality junior tribes; whence their relation of seniors and juniors, and the application of the phratric principle. When the tribes are named in council the Mohawks, by precedence, are mentioned first. Their tribal epithet was "The Shield" (*Da-gä-e-o'-dä*). The Onondagas came next, under the epithet of "Name-Bearer" (*Ho-de-san-no'-ge-tä*), because they had been appointed to select and name the fifty original sachems. Next in the order of precedence were the Senecas, under the epithet of "Door-Keeper" (*Ho-nan-ne-ho'-ont*) They were made perpetual keepers of the western door of the Long House. The Oneidas, under the epithet of "Great Tree" (*Ne-ar'-de-on-dar'-go-war*), and the Cayugas, under that of "Great Pipe" (*So-nus'-ho-gwar-to-war*), were named fourth and fifth. The Tuscaroras, who came late into the confederacy, were named last, and had no distinguishing epithet. Forms, such as these, were more important in ancient society than we would be apt to suppose.

Unanimity among the sachems was required upon all public questions, and essential to the validity of every public act. It was a fundamental law of the confederacy. They adopted a method for ascertaining the opinions of the members of the council which dispensed with the necessity of casting votes. Moreover, they were entirely unacquainted with the principle of majorities and minorities in the action of councils. They voted in council by tribes, and the sachems of each tribe were required to be of one mind to form a decision. Recognizing unanimity as a necessary principle, the founders of the confederacy divided the sachems of each tribe into classes as a means for its attainment. This will be seen by consulting the table (*supra*, p. 30). No sachem was allowed to express an opinion in council in the nature of a vote until he had first agreed with the sachem or sachems of his class upon the opinion to be expressed, and had been appointed to act as speaker for the class. Thus the eight Seneca sachems being in four classes, could have but four opinions, and the ten Cayuga sachems, being in the same number of classes, could have but four. In this manner the sachems in each class were first brought to unanimity among themselves. A cross-consultation was then held between the four sachems appointed to speak for the four classes; and when they had agreed they designated one of their number to express their resulting opinion, which was the answer of their tribe. When the sachems of the several tribes had, by this ingenious method, become of one mind separately, it remained to compare their several opinions, and if they agreed the decision of the council was made. If they failed of agreement the measure was defeated and the council was at an end. The five persons appointed to express the decision of the five tribes may possibly explain the appointment and the functions of the six electors, so called, in the Aztec confederacy.

By this method of gaining assent the equality and independence of the several tribes were recognized and preserved. If any sachem was obdurate or unreasonable, influences were brought to bear upon him, through the preponderating sentiment, which he could not well resist, so that it seldom happened that inconvenience or detriment resulted from their adherence to the rule. Whenever all efforts to procure unanimity had failed, the whole matter was laid aside because further action had become impossible.

Under a confederacy of tribes the office of general (*Hos-gä-ä-geh'-da-go-wä*), "Great War Soldier," makes its first appearance. Cases would now arise when the several tribes in their confederate capacity would be engaged in war, and the necessity for a general commander to direct the movements of the united bands would be felt. The introduction of this office as a permanent feature in the government was a great event in the history of human progress. It was the beginning of a differentiation of the military from the civil power, which, when completed, changed essentially the external manifestation of the government; but even in later stages of progress, when the military spirit predominated, the essential character of the government was not changed. Gentilism arrested usurpation. With the rise of the office of general, the government was gradually changed from a government of one power into a government of two powers. The functions of government became, in course of time, co-ordinated between the two. This new office was the germ of that of a chief executive magis- trate, for out of the general came the king, the emperor, and the president, as elsewhere suggested. The office sprang from the military necessities of society, and had a logical development.

When the Iroquois confederacy was formed, or soon after that event two permanent war-chiefships were created and named, and both were assigned to the Seneca tribe. One of them (*Ta-wan'-ne-ars*, signifying needle-breaker) was made hereditary in the Wolf, and the other (*So-no'-so-wä*, signifying great oyster shell) in the Turtle gens. The reason assigned for giving them both to the Senecas was the greater danger of attack at the west end of their territories. They were elected in the same manner as the sachems, were raised up by a general council, and were equal in rank and power. Another account states that they were created later. They discovered immediately after the confederacy was formed that the structure of the Long House was incomplete, because there were no officers to execute the military commands of the confederacy. A council was con- vened to remedy the omission, which established the two perpetual war-chiefs named. As general commanders they had charge of the military affairs of the confederacy, and the command of its joint forces when united in a general expedition. Governor Blacksnake, recently deceased, held the office first named, thus showing that the succession has been regularly maintained. The creation of two principal war-chiefs instead of one, and with equal powers, argues a subtle and calculating policy to prevent the domination of a single man even in their military affairs. They did without experience precisely as the Romans did in creating two consuls instead of one, after they had abolished the office of *rex*. Two consuls would balance the military power between them, and prevent either from becoming supreme. Among the Iroquois this office never became influential.

In Indian ethnography the subjects of primary importance are the gens, phratry, tribe, and confederacy. They exhibit the organization of society. Next to these are the tenure and functions of the office of sachem and chief, the functions of the council of chiefs, and the tenure and functions of the office of principal war-chief. When these are ascertained the structure and principles of their governmental system will be known. A knowledge of their usages and customs, of their arts and inventions, and of their plan of life will then fill out the picture. In the work of American investigators too little attention has been given to the former. They still afford a rich field in which much information may be gathered. Our knowledge, which is now general, should be made minute and comparative. The Indian tribes in the Lower and in the Middle Status of barbarism represent two of the great stages of progress from savagery to civilization. Our own remote forefathers passed through the same conditions, one after the other, and possessed, there can scarcely be a doubt, the same, or very similar institutions, with many of the same usages and customs. However little we may be interested in the American Indians personally, their experience touches us more nearly, as an exemplification of the experience of our own ancestors. Our primary institutions root themselves in a prior gentile society in which the gens, phratry, and tribe were the organic series, and in which the council of chiefs was the instrument of government. The phenomena of their ancient society must have presented many points in common with that of the Iroquois and other Indian tribes. This view of the matter lends an additional interest to the study of comparative institutions of mankind.

The Iroquois confederacy is an excellent exemplification of a gentile society under this form of organization. It seems to realize all the capabilities of gentile institutions in the Lower Status of barbarism, leaving an opportunity for further development, but no subsequent plan of government until the institutions of political society, founded upon territory and upon property, with the establishment of which the gentile organization would be overthrown. The intermediate stages were transitional, remaining military democracies to the end, except where tyrannies founded upon usurpation were temporarily established in their places. The confederacy of the Iroquois was essentially democratic, because it was composed of gentes each of which was organized upon the common principles of democracy, not of the highest but of the primitive type; and because the tribes reserved the right of local self-government. They conquered other tribes and held them in subjection, as for example the Delawares; but the latter remained under the government of their own chiefs, and added nothing to the strength of the confederacy. It was impossible in this state of society to unite tribes under one government who spoke different languages, or to hold conquered tribes under tribute with any benefit but the tribute.

This exposition of the Iroquois confederacy is far from exhaustive of the facts, but it has been carried far enough to answer my present object. The Iroquois were a vigorous and intelligent people, with a brain approaching in volume the Aryan average. Eloquent in oratory, vindictive in war, and indomitable in perseverance, they have gained a place in history. If their military achievements are dreary with the atrocities of savage warfare, they have illustrated some of the highest virtues of mankind in ther relations with each other. The confederacy which they organized must be regarded as a remarkable production of wisdom and sagacity. One of its avowed objects was peace—to remove the cause of strife by uniting their tribes under one government, and then extending it by incorporating other tribes of the same name and lineage. They urged the Eries and the Neutral Nation to become members of the confederacy, and for their refusal expelled them from their borders. Such an insight into the highest objects of government is creditable to their intelligence. Their numbers were small, but they counted in their ranks a large number of able men.   This proves the high grade of the stock.*

---

* For the prevalence of the organization into gentes or clans among the Indian tribes, see Ancient Society, ch. vi.   Since the publication of that work the same organization has been found by Mr. Bandelier by personal exploration among the Pueblo tribes in New Mexico, who speak the Quéris language, among whom his work thus far has been confined.   Descent is in the female line.   The same idefatigable student has found very satisfactory evidence of the same organization among the ancient Mexicans. (See article on "The Social Organization and Mode of Government of the Ancient Mexicans," Peabody Museum, Twelfth Annual Report, p. 576.)   He has also found additional evidence of the same organization among the Sedentary Tribes in Central America.   It seems highly probable that this organization was anciently universal among the tribes in the Ganowánian family.

CHAPTER II.

THE LAW OF HOSPITALITY AND ITS GENERAL PRACTICE.

When America was discovered in its several parts the Indian tribes were found in dissimilar conditions. The least advanced tribes were without the art of pottery, and without horticulture, and were, therefore, in savagery. But in the arts of life they were advanced as far as is implied by its Upper Status, which found them in possession of the bow and arrow. Such were the tribes in the Valley of the Columbia, in the Hudson Bay Territory, in parts of Canada, California, and Mexico, and some of the coast tribes of South America. The use of pottery, and the cultivation of maize and plants, were unknown among them. They depended for subsistence upon fish, bread, roots, and game. The second class were intermediate between them and the Village Indians. They subsisted upon fish and game and the products of a limited horticulture, and were in the Lower Status of barbarism. Such were the Iroquois, the New England and Virginia Indians, the Creeks, Cherokees, and Choctaws, the Shawnees, Miamis, Mandans, Minnitarees, and other tribes of the United States east of the Missouri River, together with certain tribes of Mexico and South America in the same condition of advancement. Many of them lived in villages, some of which were stockaded, but village life was not as distinctive and common among them as it was among the most advanced tribes. The third class were the Village Indians proper, who depended almost exclusively upon horticulture for subsistence, cultivating maize and plants by irrigation. They constructed joint tenement houses of adobe bricks and of stone, usually more than one story high. Such were the tribes of New Mexico, Mexico, Central America, and upon the plateau of the Andes. These tribes were in the Middle Status of barbarism.

The weapons, arts, usages, and customs, inventions, architecture, institutions, and form of government of all alike bear the impress of a common mind, and reveal, in their wide range, the successive stages of development of the same original conceptions. Our first mistake consisted in overrating the degree of advancement of the Village Indians, in comparison with that of the other tribes; our second in underrating that of the latter; from which resulted a third, that of separating one from the other, and regarding them as different races. The evidence of their unity of origin has now accumulated to such a degree as to leave no reasonable doubt upon the question. The first two classes of tribes always held the preponderating power, at least in North America, and furnished the migrating bands which replenished the ranks of the Village Indians, as well as the continent, with inhabitants. It remained for the Village Indians to invent the process of smelting iron ore to attain to the Upper Status of barbarism, and, beyond that, to invent a phonetic alphabet to reach the first stage of civilization. One entire ethnical period intervened between the highest class of Indians and the beginning of civilization.*

It seems singular that the Village Indians, who first became possessed of maize, the great American cereal, and of the art of cultivation, did not rise to supremacy over the continent. With their increased numbers and more stable subsistence they might have been expected to extend their

---

*PROPOSED ETHNIC OR CULTURE PERIODS.

PERIOD OF SAVAGERY.		PERIOD OF BARBARISM.	
Subperiods.	Conditions.	Subperiods.	Conditions.
Older Period	Lower Status.	Older Period	Lower Status.
Middle Period	Middle Status.	Middle Period	Middle Status.
Later Period	Upper Status.	Later Period	Upper Status.

PERIOD OF CIVILIZATION.

RECAPITULATION.

OLDER PERIOD OF SAVAGERY.—*From the infancy of the human race to the knowledge of fire and the acquisition of a fish subsistence.*

MIDDLE PERIOD.—*From the acquisition of a fish subsistence to the invention of the bow and arrow.*

LATER PERIOD.—*From the invention of the bow and arrow to the invention of the art of pottery.*

OLDER PERIOD OF BARBARISM.—*From a knowledge of pottery to the domestication of animals in the eastern hemisphere, and in the western to the cultivation of maize and plants by irrigation.*

MIDDLE PERIOD.—*From the domestication of animals, &c., to the invention of the process of smelting iron ore.*

LATER PERIOD.—*From the knowledge of iron to the invention of a phonetic alphabet, or to the use of hieroglyphs upon stone as an equivalent.*

CIVILIZATION.—*From the invention of a phonetic alphabet and the use of letters in literary composition to the present time.*

power and spread their migrating bands over the most valuable areas to the gradual displacement of the ruder tribes.   But in this respect they signally failed.   The means of sustaining life among the latter were remarkably persistent.   The higher culture of the Village Indians, such as it was, did not enable them to advance, either in their weapons or in the art of war, beyond the more barbarous tribes, except as a superior house architecture tended to render their villages and their habitations impregnable to Indian assault.   Moreover, in the art of government they had not been able to rise above gentile institutions and establish political society.   This fact demonstrates the impossibility of privileged classes and of potentates, under their institutions, with power to enforce the labor of the people for the erection of palaces for their use, and explains the absence of such structures.

Horticulture and other domestic arts spread from the Village Indians to the tribes in the Lower Status of barbarism, and thus advanced them materially in their onward progress toward the higher condition of the Village Indians.   Numerous tribes were thus raised out of savagery into barbarism by appropriating the arts of life of tribes above them.   This process has been a constant phenomenon in the history of the human race. It is well illustrated in America, where the Red Race, one in origin and possessed of homogeneous institutions, were in three different ethnical conditions or stages of culture.

There are certain usages and customs of the Indian tribes generally which tend to explain their plan of life—their large households, their houses, and their house architecture.   They deserve a careful consideration and even further investigation beyond the bounds of our present knowledge. The influence of American civilization has very generally broken up their old plan of life, and introduced a new one more analogous to our own. It has been much the same in Spanish America.   The old usages and customs, in the particulars about to be stated, have now so far disappeared in their pure forms that their recovery is not free from difficulty.   Those to be considered are the following:

I. *The law of hospitality.*

II. *Communism in living.*

III. *The ownership of lands in common.*

IV. *The practice of having but one prepared meal each day—a dinner.*

V. *Their separation at meals, the men eating first and by themselves, and the women and children afterards.*

The discussion will be confined to the period of European discovery and to later periods while these practices remained. The object will be to show that these usages and customs existed among them when America was discovered in its several parts, and that they remained in practice for some time after these several periods.

THE LAW OF HOSPITALITY.

Among the Iroquois hospitality was an established usage. If a man entered an Indian house in any of their villages, whether a villager, a tribesman, or a stranger, it was the duty of the women therein to set food before him. An omission to do this would have been a discourtesy amounting to an affront. If hungry, he ate; if not hungry, courtesy required that he should taste the food and thank the giver. This would be repeated at every house he entered, and at whatever hour in the day. As a custom it was upheld by a rigorous public sentiment. The same hospitality was extended to strangers from their own and from other tribes. Upon the advent of the European race among them it was also extended to them. This characteristic of barbarous society, wherein food was the principal concern of life, is a remarkable fact. The law of hospitality, as administered by the American aborigines, tended to the final equalization of subsistence. Hunger and destitution could not exist at one end of an Indian village or in one section of an encampment while plenty prevailed elsewhere in the same village or encampment. It reveals a plan of life among them at the period of European discovery which has not been sufficiently considered.

A singular illustration of the powerful influence of the custom upon the Indian mind came to my notice some years ago at the Seneca Reservation in New York. A Seneca chief, well to do in the world, with farm lands and domestic animals which afforded him a comfortable subsistence, had lost his wife by death, and his daughter, educated in the usages of civilized life, took the position of housekeeper. The old man, referring to the ancient custom, requested his daughter to keep the usual food constantly prepared ready to offer to any person who entered their house, saying that he did not wish to see this custom of their forefathers laid aside. Their changed condition, and particularly the adoption of the regular meals of civilized society, for the time of which the visitor might reasonably be expected to wait, did not in his mind outweigh the sanctity of the custom.[1]

In July, 1743, John Bartram made a journey from Philadelphia to Onondaga to attend, with Conrad Weisar, a council of the Onondaga, Mohawk, Oneida, and Cayuga chiefs. At Shamokin he quartered with a trader who had an Indian wife, and at a village of the Delawares. "As soon as we alighted," he remarks, "they showed us where to lay our luggage, and then brought us a bowl of boiled squashes, cold. This I then thought poor entertainment, but before I came back I had learned not to despise good Indian food. This hospitality is agreeable to the honest simplicity of ancient times, and is so persistently adhered to that not only what is already dressed is immediately set before a traveler, but the most pressing business is postponed to prepare the best they can get for him, keeping it as a maxim that he must always be hungry. Of this we found the good effects in the flesh and bread they got ready for us."[2] We have here a perfect illustration among the Delawares of the Iroquois rule to set food before a person when he first entered the house. Although they had in this case nothing better than boiled squash to offer, it was done immediately, after which they commenced preparing a more substantial repast. Delaware and Iroquois usages were the same.

The council at Onondaga lasted two days, at the close of which they had each day a dinner in common. "This council [first day] was followed by a feast. After four o'clock we all dined together upon four great kettles of Indian-corn soup, which we emptied, and then every chief retired to his home. * * * The conference [second day] held till three, after which we dined. The repast consisted of three great kettles of Indian-corn soup, or thin hominy, with dried eels and other fish boiled in it, and one kettle

---

[1] William Parker was the chief named, a noble specimen of a Seneca Iroquois.
[2] Bartram's Observations, &c., London edition, 1751, p. 16.

full of young squashes and their flowers boiled in water, and a little meal mixed. This dish was but weak food. Last of all was served a great bowl-full of Indian dumplings made of new soft corn cut or scraped off the ear, with the addition of some boiled beans, lapped well in Indian-corn leaves. This is good hearty provision."[1]

"Again," he remarks, "we prepared for setting forward, and many of the chiefs came once more to make their farewells. Some of them brought us provisions for our journey. We shook hands again and set out at nine."[2]

One of the earliest notices of the hospitality of the Indian tribes of the United States was by the expedition of Philip Amidas and Arthur Barlow, under the auspices of Sir Walter Raleigh, which visited the Algonkin tribes of North Carolina in the summer of 1584. They landed at the Island of Wocoken, off Albemarle Sound, when "there came down from all parts great store of people," whose chief was Granganimeo. "He was very just of his promises, for oft we trusted him, and would come within his day to keep his word. He sent us commonly every day a brace of ducks, conies, hares, and fish, sometimes melons, walnuts, cucumbers, pease, and divers roots. * * * After this acquaintance, myself, with seven more, went thirty miles into the river Occam, that runneth toward the city Skicoack, and the evening following we came to an isle called Roanoak, from the harbor where we entered seven leagues: At the north end were nine houses, builded with cedar, fortified round with sharp trees [palisaded] and the entrance like a turnpike [turnspit]. When we came towards it, the wife of Granganimeo came running out to meet us (her husband was absent), commanding her people to draw our boat ashore for beating on the billows. Others she appointed to carry us on their backs aland, others to bring our oars into the house for stealing. When we came into the other room (for there were five in the house) she caused us to sit down by a great fire; and after took off our clothes and washed them, of some our stockins, and some our feet in warm water; and she herself took much pains to see all things well ordered and to provide us victuals. After we had thus dried ourselves she brought us into an inner room, where she sat on the board standing along the house, somewhat like frumenty, sodden venison, and roasted fish; in

---

[1] Bartram's Journal, p. 59. [2] Ib., p. 63.

like manner melons raw, boiled roots, and fruits of divers kinds. Their
drink is commonly water boiled with ginger, sometimes with sassafras, and
wholesome herbs.   *   *   *   A more kind, loving people cannot be   Beyond this isle is the main land, and the great river Occam, on which stand-
eth a town called Pomeiok."[1]

This is about the first, if not the first, English picture we have of
Indian life and of English and Indian intercourse in America. It is highly
creditable to both parties; to the Indians for their unaffected kindness and
hospitality, and to the English for their appreciation of both, and for the
absence of any act of injustice. At the same time it was simply an application by the natives of their rules of hospitality among themselves to their
foreign visitors, and not a new thing in their experience.

In the narrative of the expedition of Hernando de Soto to Florida in
1539, by a gentleman of Elvas, there are references to the customs of the
Indian tribes of South Carolina, the Cherokees, Choctas, and Chickasas,
and of some of the tribes west of the Mississippi, whom the expedition
visited one after another. They are brief and incomplete, but sufficiently
indicate the point we are attempting to illustrate. It was a hostile rather
than a friendly visitation, and the naturally free hospitality of the natives
was frequently checked and turned into enemity, but many instances of
friendly intercourse are mentioned in this narrative. " The fourth of April
the governor passed by a town called *Altamaca*, and the tenth of the month
he came to *Ocute*. The cacique sent him two thousand Indians with a
present, to wit, many conies and partridges, bread of maize, two hens and
many dogs."[2] Again: " Two leagues before he came to Chiaha, there met
him fifteen Indians loaded with maize which the cacique had sent; and
they told him on his behalf that he waited his coming with twenty barns
full of it."[3] " At Coça the chief commanded his Indians to void their houses,
wherein the governor and his men were lodged. There was in the barns
and in the fields great store of maize and French beans. The country was
greatly inhabited with many great towns and many sown fields which

---

[1] Smith's History of Virginia, &c. Reprint from London edition of 1627. Richmond edition,
1819, i, 83, 84. Amidas and Barlow's account is also in Hakluyt's Coll. of Voyages, iii, 301–7.

[2] Historical Collections of Louisiana, part ii. A Narrative of the Expedition of Hernando de
Soto into Florida, by a Gentleman of Elvas, p. 139.

[3] Ib. p. 147.

reached from one to the other."[1] After crossing the Mississippi, of which De Soto was the first discoverer, he "rested in *Pacaha* forty days, in all which time the two caciques served him with great store of fish, mantles, and skins, and strove who should do him greatest service."[2]

The justly celebrated Moravian missionary, John Heckewelder, obtained, through a long experience, an intimate acquaintance with the manners and customs of the Indian tribes. He was engaged in direct missionary labor, among the Delawares and Munsees chiefly, for fifteen years (1771–1786) on the Muskingum and Cuyahoga in Ohio, where, besides the Delawares and Munsees, he came in contact with Tuscaroras and other tribes of Iroquois lineage. He was conversant with the usages and customs of the Indian tribes of Pennsylvania and New York. His general knowledge justifies the title of his work, "History, Manners, and Customs of the Indian Nations, who once inhabited Pennsylvania and the neighboring States," and gives the highest credibility to his statements.

In discussing the general character of the Indians, he remarks as follows: "They think that he [the Great Spirit] made the earth and all that it contains for the common good of mankind; when he stocked the country that he gave them with plenty of game, it was not for the benefit of a few, but of all. Everything was given in common to the sons of men. Whatever liveth on the land, whatsoever groweth out of the earth, and all that is in the rivers and waters flowing through the same, was given jointly to all, and every one is entitled to his share. From this principle hospitality flows as from its source. With them it is not a virtue, but a strict duty; hence they are never in search of excuses to avoid giving, but freely supply their neighbors' wants from the stock prepared for their own use. They give and are hospitable to all without exception, and will always share with each other and often with the stranger to the last morsel. They rather would lie down themselves on an empty stomach than have it laid to their charge that they had neglected their duty by not satisfying the wants of the stranger, the sick, or the needy. The stranger has a claim to their hospitality, partly on account of his being at a distance from his family and friends, and partly because he has honored them with his visit and ought to

---

[1] Ib. p. 152.　　　　　　　[2] Ib. p. 175.

leave them with a good impression on his mind; the sick and the poor because they have a right to be helped out of the common stock, for if the meat they have been served with was taken from the woods it was common to all before the hunter took it; if corn or vegetables, it had grown out of the common ground, yet not by the power of man, but by that of the Great Spirit."[1]

This is a clear and definite statement of the principle of hospitality as it was observed by the Indian tribes at the epoch of their discovery, with the Indians' reasons on which the obligations rested. We recognize in this law of hospitality a conspicuous virtue of mankind in barbarism.

Lewis and Clarke refer to the usages of the tribes of the Missouri, which were precisely the same as those of the Iroquois. "It is the custom of all the nations on the Missouri," they remark, "to offer every white man food and refreshments when he first enters their tents."[2] This was simply applying their rules of hospitality among themselves to their white visitors.

About 1837–'38 George Catlin wintered at the Mandan Village, on the Upper Missouri. He was an accurate and intelligent observer, and his work on the "Manners and Customs of the North American Indians" is a valuable contribution to American ethnography. The principal Mandan village, which then contained fifty houses and fifteen hundred people, was surrounded with a palisade. It was well situated for game, but they did not depend exclusively upon this source of subsistence. They cultivated maize, squashes, pumpkins, and tobacco in garden beds, and gathered wild berries and a species of turnip on the praries. "Buffalo meat, however," says Mr. Catlin, "is the great staple and staff of life in this country, and seldom, if ever, fails to afford them an abundant means of subsistence. * * * During the summer and fall months they use the meat fresh, and cook it in a great variety of ways—by roasting, broiling, boiling, stewing, smoking, &c., and, by boiling the ribs and joints with the marrow in them, make a delicious soup, which is universally used and in vast quantities. The Mandans, I find, have no regular or stated times for their meals, but generally eat about twice in the twenty-four hours. The pot is always

---

[1] Heckewelder, Indian Nations, Philadelphia ed., 1876, p. 101.
[2] Travels, etc., London edition, 1814, p. 649.

boiling over the fire, and any one who is hungry, either from the household or from any other part of the village, has a right to order it taken off and to fall too, eating as he pleases. Such is an unvarying custom among the North American Indians, and I very much doubt whether the civilized world have in their institutions any system which can properly be called more humane and charitable. Every man, woman, or child in Indian communities is allowed to enter any one's lodge, and even that of the chief of the nation, and eat when they are hungry, provided misfortune or necessity has drawn them to it. Even so can the poorest and most worthless drone of the nation, if he is too lazy to hunt or to supply himself; he can walk into any lodge, and every one will share with him as long as there is anything to eat. He, however, who thus begs when he is able to hunt, pays dear for his meat, for he is stigmatized with the disgraceful epithet of poltroon and beggar."[1] Mr. Catlin puts the case rather strongly when he turns the free hospitality of the household into a right of the guest to entertainment independently of their consent. It serves to show that the provisions of the household, which, as he elsewhere states, consisted of from twenty to forty persons, were used in common, and that each household shared their provisions in the exercise of hospitality with any inhabitant of the village who came to the house hungry, and with strangers from other tribes as well. Moreover, he speaks of this hospitality as universal amongst the Indian tribes. It is an important statement, because few men in the early period of intercourse with the western tribes have traveled so extensively among them.

The tribes of the Columbia Valley lived upon fish, bread-roots, and game. Food was abundant at certain seasons, but there were times of scarcity even in this favored area. Whatever provisions they had were shared freely with each other, with guests, and with strangers. Lewis and Clarke, in 1804–1806, visited in their celebrated expedition the tribes of the Missouri and of the Valley of the Columbia. They experienced the same generous hospitality whenever the Indians possessed any food to offer, and their account is the first we have at all special of these numerous tribes. Frequent references are made to their hospitality. The Nez Percés "set

---

[1] Manners and Customs of the North American Indians, Hazard's edition, 1857, i, 200.

before them a small piece of buffalo meat, some dried salmon, berries, and several kinds of roots. Among these last is one which is round and much like an onion in appearance, and sweet to the taste. It is called *quamash*, and is eaten either in its natural state or boiled into a kind of soup or made into a cake, which is then called *pasheco*. After the long abstinence, this was a sumptuous treat; and we returned the kindness of the people by a few small presents, and then went on in company with one of the chiefs to a second village, in the same plain, at a distance of two miles. Here the party was treated with great kindness, and passed the night."[1] Of another tribe they remark, "As we approached the village most of the women, though apprised of our being expected, fled with their children into the neighboring woods. The men, however, received us without any apprehension, and gave us a plentiful supply of provisions. The plains were now crowded with Indians, who came to see the persons of the whites and the strange things they brought with them; but as our guide was perfectly a stranger to their language we could converse by signs only."[2]

The Indians of the Columbia, unlike the tribes previously named, boiled their food in wooden vessels, or in ground cavities lined with skins, by means of heated stones. They were ignorant of pottery. "On entering one of their houses he [Captain Clarke] found it crowded with men, women, and children, who immediately provided a mat for him to sit on, and one of the party undertook to prepare something to eat. He began by bringing in a piece of pine wood that had drifted down the river, which he split into small pieces with a wedge made of the elk's horn by means of a mallet of stone curiously carved. The pieces were then laid on the fire, and several round stones placed upon them. One of the squaws now brought a bucket of water, in which was a large salmon about half dried, and as the stones became heated they were put into the bucket till the salmon was sufficiently boiled for use It was then taken out, put on a platter of rushes neatly made, and laid before Captain Clarke, and another was boiled for each of his men."[3]

One or two additional cases, of which a large number are mentioned by these authors, will sufficiently illustrate the practice of hospitality of

---

[1] Travels, etc., p. 330. [2] Travels, etc., p. 334. [3] Travels, etc., 353.

these tribes and its universality. They went to a village of seven houses of the Chilluckittequaw tribe and to the house of the chief. "He received us kindly," they remark, "and set before us pounded fish, filberts, nuts, the berries of the sacacommis, and white bread made of roots. * * * The village is a part of the same nation with the village we passed above, the language of the two being the same, and their houses of similar form and materials, and calculated to contain about thirty souls. The inhabitants were unusually hospitable and good humored."[1] While among the Shoshonees, and before arriving at the Columbia, they "reached an Indian lodge of brush inhabited by seven families of the Shoshonees. They behaved with great civility, and gave the whole party as much boiled salmon as they could eat, and added a present of several dried salmon and a considerable quantity of chokechinies;"[2] and Captain Lewis remarks of the same people, that "an Indian invited him into his bower, and gave him a small morsel of boiled antelope, and a piece of fresh salmon roasted. This was the first salmon he had seen, and perfectly satisfied him that he was now on the waters of the Pacific."[3] Thus far among the tribes we find a literal repetition of the rule of hospitality as practiced by the Iroquois. Mr. Dall, speaking of the Aleüts, says, "hospitality was one of their prominent traits,"[4] and Powers, of the Pomo Indians of California remarks, that they would always divide the last morsel of dried salmon with genuine savage thriftlessness," and of the Mi-oal'-a-wa-gun, that, "like all California Indians, they are very hospitable."[5]

Father Marquette and Lieutenant Joliet, who first discovered the Upper Mississippi in 1673, had friendly intercourse with some of the tribes on its eastern bank, and were hospitably entertained by them. "The council being over, we were invited to a feast, which consisted of four dishes. The first was a dish of sagamite—that is, some Indian meal boiled in water and seasoned with grease—the master of ceremonies holding a spoonful of it, which he put thrice into my mouth and then did the like to M. Joliet. The

---

[1] Travels, etc., p. 375–376.
[2] Ib. p. 288.
[3] Ib. p. 268.
[4] On the Remains of Later Prehistoric Man, Alaska Ter., Smithsonian Cont., No. 318, p. 3. Travels, etc., Phila. ed., 1796, p. 171.
[5] Powell's Contributions to North American Ethnology, Power's Tribes of California, vol. iii, p. 153.

second dish consisted of three fish, whereof he took a piece, and having taken out the bones and blown upon it to cool it, he put it into my mouth. The third dish was a large dog, which they had killed on purpose, but understanding that we did not eat this animal they sent it away. The fourth was a piece of buffalo meat, of which they put the fattest pieces into our mouths."[1]

Lower down the river, below the mouth of the Ohio, they fell in with another tribe, of whom they speak as follows: " We therefore disembarked and went to their village. They entertained us with buffalo and bear's meat and white plums, which were excellent. We observed they had guns, knives, axes, shovels, glass beads, and bottles in which they put their powder. They wear their hair long as the Iroquois, and their women are dressed as the Hurons."[2]

In 1766 Jonathan Carver visited the Dakota tribes of the Mississippi, the Sauks and Foxes, and Winnebagos of Wisconsin, and the Ojibwas of Upper Michigan. He speaks generally of the hospitality of these tribes as follows: "No people are more hospitable, kind, and free than the Indians. They will readily share with any of their own tribe the last part of their provisions, and even with those of a different nation, if they chance to come in when they are eating. Though they do not keep one common stock, yet that community of goods which is so prevalent among them, and their generous disposition, render it nearly of the same effect."[3] The " community of goods, which is so prevalent among them," is explained by their large households formed of related families, who shared their provisions in common. The " seven families of Shoshonees" in one house, and also the houses " crowded with men, women, and children," mentioned by Lewis and Clarke, are fair samples of Indian households in the early period.

We turn again to the southern tribes of the United States, the Cherokes, Choctas, Chickasas, and Confederated Creek tribes. James Adair, whose work was published in 1775, remarks generally upon their usages in the following language: "They are so hospitable, kind-hearted, and

---

[1] Historical collections of Louisiana, part ii. An Account of the Discovery of some New Countries and Nations of North America in 1673, by Pere Marquette and Sieur Joliet, p. 287.

[2] Ib., p. 293.   [3] Carver's Travels, etc., Phila. ed. 1796, p. 171.

free, that they would share with those of their own tribe the last part of their own provisions, even to a single ear of corn; and to others, if they called when they were eating; for they have no stated meal time. An open generous temper is a standing virtue among them; to be narrow-hearted, especially to those in want, or to any of their own family, is accounted a great crime, and to reflect scandal on the rest of the tribe. Such wretched misers they brand with bad characters. * * * The Cherokee Indians have a pointed proverbial expression to the same effect—*sinnawàh nà wóra*, the great hawk is at home. However, it is a very rare thing to find any of them of a narrow temper; and though they do not keep one promiscuous common stock, yet it is to the very same effect; for every one has his own family or tribe; and when one of them is speaking, either of the individuals or habitations of any of his tribe, he says, 'he is of my house,' or 'it is my house.' * * * When the Indians are travel-ing in their own country, they inquire for a house of their own tribe [gens]; and if there be any, they go to it, and are kindly received, though they never saw the persons before—they eat, drink, and regale themselves with as much freedom as at their own table, which is the solid ground covered with a bear-skin. * * * Every town has a state-house or synedrion, as the Jewish sanhedrim, where, almost every night, the head men convene about public business; or the town's people to feast, sing, dance, and rejoice in the divine presence, as will fully be described hereafter. And if a stranger calls there, he is treated with the greatest civility and hearty kind-ness—he is sure to find plenty of their simple home fare, and a large cane-bed covered with the softened skins of bears or buffaloes to sleep on. But, when his lineage is known to the people (by a stated custom, they are slow in greeting one another), his relations, if he has any there, address him in a familiar way, invite him home, and treat him as a kinsman."[1] All these tribes were organized in gentes or clans, and the gentes of each tribe were usually reintegrated in two or more phratries. It is the gens to which Mr. Adair refers when he speaks of the "family," "relations," and "lineage." We find among them the same rule of hospitality, substantially, as prevailed among the Iroquois.

---

[1] History of the American Indians, London ed., 1775, p. 17.

It is a reasonable conclusion, therefore, that among all the tribes, north of New Mexico, the law of hospitality, as practiced by the Iroquois, was universally recognized; and that in all Indian villages and encampments without distinction the hungry were fed through the open hospitality of those who possessed a surplus. Notwithstanding this generous custom, it is well known that the Northern Indians were often fearfully pressed for the means of subsistence during a portion of each year. A bad season for their limited productions, and the absence of accumulated stores, not unfrequently engendered famine over large districts. From the severity of the struggle for subsistence, it is not surprising that immense areas were entirely uninhabited, that other large areas were thinly peopled, and that dense population nowhere existed.

Among the Village Indians of New Mexico the same hospitality is now extended to Americans visiting their pueblos, and which presumptively is simply a reflection of their usage among themselves and toward other tribes. In 1852 Dr. Tenbroeck, assistant surgeon United States Army, accompanied his command to the Moki pueblos. In his journal he remarks: "Between eleven and twelve to-day we arrived at the first towns of Moki. All the inhabitants turned out, crowding the streets and house-tops to have a view of the white men. All the old men pressed forward to shake hands with us, and we were most hospitably received and conducted to the governor's house, where we were at once feasted upon guavas and a leg of mutton broiled upon the coals. After the feast we smoked with them, and they then said that we should move our camp in, and that they would give us a room and plenty of wood for the men, and sell us corn for the animals."[1] In 1858 Lieut. Joseph C. Ives was at the Moki Pueblo of *Mooshahneh* [Mi-shong-i-ni-vi]. "The town is nearly square," he remarks, "and surrounded by a stone wall fifteen feet high, the top of which forms a landing extending around the whole. Flights of stone steps lead from the first to a second landing, upon which the doors of the houses open. Mounting the stairway opposite to the ladder, the chief crossed to the nearest door and ushered us into a low apartment, from which two or three others opened towards the interior of the dwelling. Our host courteously asked us to be seated upon

---

[1] Schoolcraft's History, Condition, and Prospects of the Indian Tribes, iv, 81.

some skins spread along the floor against the wall, and presently his wife brought in a vase of water and a tray filled with a singular substance that looked more like sheets of thin blue wrapping paper rolled up into bundles than anything else that I have ever seen. I learned afterwards that it was made of corn meal, ground very fine, made into a gruel, and poured over a heated stone to be baked. When dry it has a surface slightly polished like paper. The sheets are folded and rolled together, and form the staple article of food with the Moki Indians. As the dish was intended for our entertainment, and looked clean, we all partook of it. It had a delicate fresh-bread flavor, and was not at all unpalatable, particularly when eaten with salt."[1]

Lieutenant-Colonel (now General) Emory visited the Pima villages on the Gila River in 1846. " I rode leisurely in the rear through the thatched huts of the Pimos. Each abode consisted of a dome-shaped wicker-work about six feet high, and from twenty to fifty feet in diameter, thatched with straw or cornstalks. In front is usually a large arbor, on top of which is piled the cotton in the pod for drying. In the houses were stowed watermelons, pumpkins, beans, corn, and wheat, the three last articles generally in large baskets. Sometimes the corn was in baskets, covered with earth, and placed on the tops of the domes. A few chickens and dogs were seen, but no other domestic animals, except horses, mules, and oxen. * * * Several acquaintances, formed in our camp yesterday, were recognized, and they received me cordially, made signs to dismount, and when I did so offered watermelons and pinole. Pinole is the heart of Indian corn, baked, ground up, and mixed with sugar. When dissolved in water it affords a delicious beverage; it quenches thirst, and is very nutritious. * * * The population of the Pimos and Maricopas together is estimated variously at from three to ten thousand. The first is evidently too low. This peaceful and industrious race are in possession of a beautiful and fertile basin. Living remote from the civilized world, they are seldom visited by whites, and then only by those in distress, to whom they generously furnish horses and food."[2] In this case and in those stated by Lieutenant Ives and Dr.

---

[1] Report upon Colorado River of the West, Lieut. Ives, p. 121.
[2] Military Reconnaissance in New Mexico, pp. 85, 86.

Tenbroeck we find a repetition of the Iroquois rule to set food before the guest when he first enters the house.

With respect to the Village Indians of Mexico, Central and South America, our information is, in the main, limited to the hospitality extended to the Spaniards; but it is sufficient to show that it was a part of their plan of life, and, as it must be supposed, a repetition of their usages in respect to each other. In every part of America that they visited, the Spaniards, although often in numbers as a military force, were assigned quarters in Indian houses, emptied of their inhabitants for that purpose, and freely supplied with provisions. Thus at Zempoala " the lord came out, attended by ancient men, two persons of note supporting him by the arms, because it was the custom among them to come out in that manner when one great man received another. This meeting was with much courtesy and abundance of compliments, and people were already appointed to find the Spaniards quarters and furnish provisions."[1] When near Tlascala the Tlascallans "sent three hundred turkeys, two hundred baskets of cakes of *teutli*, which they call tamales, being about two hundred arrobas; that is, fifty hundred weight of bread, which was an extraordinary supply for the Spaniards, considering the distress they were in;"[2] and when at Tlascala, Cortes and his men " were generously treated, and supplied with all necessaries."[3] They "entered Cholula and went to a house where they lodged altogether, and their Indians with them, although upon their guard, being for the present plentifully supplied with provisions."[4] Although the Spaniards numbered about four hundred, and their allied Indians about a thousand, they found accommodations in a single joint tenement house of the aboriginal American model. Attention is called to this fact, because we shall find the Village Indians, as a rule, living in large houses, each containing many apartments, and accommodating five hundred or more persons. The household of several families of the northern Indians reappears in the southern tribes in a much greater household of a hundred or more families in a single joint tenement house, but not unlikely broken up into several household groups. The pueblo consisted sometimes of one, sometimes of two or three, and sometimes of a greater number of such houses. The plan of life within these

---

[1] Herrera's History of America, ii,.212.   [2] Ib., ii, 261.   [3] Ib., ii, 279.   [4] Ib., ii, 311.

houses is not well understood ; but it can still be seen in New Mexico, and it is to be hoped it will attract investigation.

Speaking of the Maya Indians of Yucatan, Herrera remarks that " they are still generous and free-hearted, so that they will make everybody eat that comes into their houses, which is everywhere practiced in travelling."[1] This is a fair statement of the Iroquois law of hospitality found among the Mayas, practiced among themselves and towards strangers from other tribes. When Grijalva, about 1517, discovered the Tabasco River, he held friendly intercourse with some of the tribes of Yucatan. " They immediately sent thirty Indians loaded with roasted fish, hens, several sorts of fruit, and bread made of Indian wheat.[2] When Cortes, in 1525, made his celebrated expedition to Honduras, he passed near the pueblo of Palenque and near that of Copan without being aware of either, and visited the shore of Lake Peten. " Being well received in the city of Apoxpalan, Cortes and all the Spaniards, with their horses, were quartered in one house, the Mexicans being dispersed into others, and all of them plentifully supplied with provisions during their stay."[3] They numbered one hundred and fifty Spanish horse and several hundred Aztecs. It was at this place, according to Herrera,[4] that Quatemozin, who accompanied Cortes as a prisoner, was barbarously executed by his command. Cortes next visited an island in Lake Peten, where he was sumptuously entertained by *Canec*, the chief of the tribe, where they " sat down to dinner in stately manner, and *Canec* ordered fowls, fish, cakes, honey, and fruit."[5]

In South America the same account of the hospitality of the Indian tribes is given by the early explorers. About the year 1500 Christopher Guerra made a voyage to the coast of Venezuela : " They came to an anchor before a town called Curiana, where the Indians entreated them to go ashore, but the Spaniards being no more than thirty-three in all durst not venture. * * * At length, being convinced of their sincerity, the Spaniards went ashore, and being courteously entertained, staid there twenty days. They plentifully supplied them for food with venison, rabbits, geese, ducks, parrots, fish, bread made of maize or Indian wheat, and other things,

---

[1] Herrera's History of America, iv, 171.
[2] Ib., ii, 126.
[3] Ib., iii, 359.
[4] Ib., iii, 361.
[5] Ib., iii, 362.

and brought them all the game they would ask for. * * * They perceived that they kept markets or fairs, and that they made use of jars,
pitchers, pots, dishes, and porringers, besides other vessels of several
shapes.",[1] Pizarro found the same custom among the Peruvians and other
tribes of the coast. At the time of his first visit to the coast of Peru he
found a female chief by whom he was entertained. "The lady came out
to meet them with a great retinue, in good order, holding green boughs and
ears of Indian wheat, having made an arbor where were seats for the
Spaniards, and for the Indians at some distance. They gave them to eat
fish and flesh dressed in several ways, much fruit, and such bread and
liquor as the country afforded."[2] When on the coast of Tumbez, and
before landing, "ten or twelve floats were immediately sent out with a
plenty of provisions, fruits, pots of water, and of chica, which is their liquor,
as also a lamb."[3] After entering Peru, on his second visit to the coast,
"Atahuallpa's messengers came and presented the governor with ten of
their sheep from the Inca, and some other things of small value, telling him
very courteously that Atahuallpa had commanded them to inquire what day
he intended to be at Caxamalca, that he might have provisions on the way."[4]
* * * The next day more messengers came from Atahuallpa with provisions, which he received with thanks."[5] The native historian, Garcilasso de la
Viga, remarks: "Nor were the Incas, among their other charities, forgetful
of the conveniences for travellers, but in all the great roads built houses or
inns for them, which they called corpahuaci, where they were provided
with victuals and other necessaries for their journies out of the royal
stores; and in case any traveller fell sick on the way, he was there attended
and care taken of him in a better manner perhaps than at his own home."[6]

These illustrations, which might be multiplied, are sufficient to show
the universality of the practice of hospitality among the Indian tribes of
America at the epoch of European discovery. Among all these forms, as
stated by different observers, the substance of the Iroquois law of hospitality is plainly found, namely: If a man entered an Indian house, whether
a villager, a tribesman, or a stranger, and at whatever hour of the day, it

---

[1] Herrera's Hist. America, iv, 248.   [2] Ib., i, 229.   [3] Ib., iv, 3.   [4] Ib., iii, 399.   [5] Ib., iv, 244.
[6] Royal Commentaries of Peru, Lond. ed., 1688; Rycaut Trans., p. 145.

was the duty of the women of the house to set food before him. An omission to do this would have been a discourtesy amounting to an affront. If hungry, he ate, if not hungry, courtesy required that he should taste the food and thank the giver. It is seen to have been a usage running through three ethnic conditions of the Indian race, becoming stronger as the means of subsistence increased in variety and amount, and attaining its highest development among the Village Indians in the Middle Status of barbarism. It was an active, well-established custom of Indian society, practiced among themselves and among strangers from other tribes, and very naturally extended to Europeans when they made their first appearance among them. Considering the number of the Spaniards often in military companies, and another fact which the aborigines were quick to notice, namely, that a white man consumed and wasted five times as much as an Indian required, their hospitality in many cases must have been grievously overtaxed.[1]

Attention has been called to this law of hospitality, and to its universality, for two reasons: firstly, because it implies the existence of common stores, which supplied the means for its practice; and secondly, because, wherever found, it implies communistic living in large households. It must be evident that this hospitality could not have been habitually practiced by the Iroquois and other northern tribes, and much less by the Village Indians of Mexico, Central and South America, with such uniformity, if the custom in each case had depended upon the voluntary contributions of single families. In that event it would have failed oftener than it would have succeeded. The law of hospitality, as administered by the American aborigines, indicates a plan of life among them which has not been carefully studied, nor have its effects been fully appreciated. Its explanation must be sought in the ownership of lands in common, the distribution of their products to households consisting of a number of families, and the practice of communism in living in the household. Common stores for large households, and possibly for the village, with which to maintain vil-

---

[1] "The appetite of the Spaniards appeared to the Americans insatiably voracious; and they affirmed that one Spaniard devoured more food in a day than was sufficient for ten Americans."— (Robertson's History of America, Lond. ed., 1856, i, p. 72.)

lage hospitality, are necessary to explain the custom. It could have been maintained on such a basis, and it is difficult to see how it could have been maintained on any other. The common and substantially universal practice of this custom, among the American Indian Tribes, at the period of their discovery, among whom the procurement of subsistence was their vital need, must be regarded as evidence of a generous disposition, and as exhibiting a trait of character highly creditable to the race.

CHAPTER III.

COMMUNISM IN LIVING.

We are now to consider the remaining usages and customs named in the last chapter.

THEIR COMMUNISM IN LIVING.

Communism in living had its origin in the necessities of the family, which, prior to the Later Period of barbarism, was too weak an organization to face alone the struggle of life. In savagery and in the Older and the Middle Period of barbarism the family was in the syndyasmian or pairing form, into which it had passed from a previous lower form.[1] Wherever the gentile organization prevailed, several families, related by kin, united as a rule in a common household and made a common stock of the provisions acquired by fishing and hunting, and by the cultivation of maize and plants. They erected joint tenement houses large enough to accommodate several families, so that, instead of a single family in the exclusive occupation of a single the house, large households as a rule existed in all parts of America in the aboriginal period. This community of provisions was limited to the household; but a final equalization of the means of subsistence was in some measure affected by the law of hospitality. To a very great extent communism in living was a necessary result of the condition of the Indian tribes. It entered into their plan of life and determined the character of their houses. In effect it was a union of effort to procure subsistence, which was the vital and commanding concern of life. The desire for individual accumulation had not been aroused in their minds to any sensible extent. It is made evident by a comparison of the conditions of barbarous tribes on

---

[1] Ancient Society, p. 459.

different continents that communism has widely prevailed among them, and that the influence of this ancient practice had not entirely disappeared among the more advanced tribes when civilization finally appeared.   The common meal-bin of the ancient and the common tables of the later Greeks seem to be survivals of an older communism in living.   This practice, though never investigated as a specialty, may be shown by the known customs of a number of Indian tribes, and may be confirmed by an examination of the plans of their houses.

Our first illustration will be taken from the usages of the Iroquois. In their villages they constructed houses, consisting of frames of poles covered with bark, thirty, fifty, eighty, and a hundred feet in length, with a passage-way through the center, a door at each end, and with the interior partitioned off at intervals of about seven feet.   Each apartment or stall thus formed was open for its entire width upon the passage-way.   These houses would accommodate five, ten, and twenty families, according to the number of apartments, one being usually allotted to a family.   Each household was made up on the principle of kin.   The married women, usually sisters, own or collateral, were of the same gens or clan, the symbol or totem of which was often painted upon the house, while their husbands and the wives of their sons belong to several other gentes.   The children were of the gens of their mother.   While husband and wife belonged to different gentes, the preponderating number in each household would be of the same gens, namely, that of their mothers.   As a rule the sons brought home their wives, and in some cases the husbands of the daughters were admitted to the maternal house.   Thus each household was composed of a mixture of persons of different gentes; but this would not prevent the numerical ascendency of the particular gens to whom the house belonged.   In a village of one hundred and twenty houses, as the Seneca village of Tiotohatton described by Mr. Greenbalgh in 1677,[1] there would be several such houses belonging to each gens.   It presented a general picture of Indian life in all parts of America at the epoch of European discovery.   Whatever was gained by any member of the household on hunting or fishing expeditions, or was raised by cultivation, was made a common stock.   Within the house

---

[1] Documentary History of New York, i, 13.

they lived from common stores. Each house had several fires, usually one for each four apartments, which was placed in the middle of the passage-way and without a chimney. Every household was organized under a matron who supervised its domestic economy. After the single daily meal was cooked at the several fires the matron was summoned, and it was her duty to divide the food, from the kettle, to the several families according to their respective needs. What remained was placed in the custody of another person until it was required by the matron. The Iroquois lived in houses of this description as late as A. D. 1700, and in occasional instances a hundred years later. An elderly Seneca woman[1] informed the writer, thirty years ago, that when she was a girl she lived in one of these joint tenement houses (called by them long-houses), which contained eight families and two fires, and that her mother and her grandmother, in their day, had acted as matrons over one of these large households. This mere glimpse at the ancient Iroquois plan of life, now entirely passed away, and of which remembrance is nearly lost, is highly suggestive. It shows that their domestic economy was not without method, and it displays the care and management of woman, low down in barbarism, for husbanding their resources and for improving their condition A knowledge of these houses, and how to build them, is not even yet lost among the Senecas. Some years ago Mr. William Parker, a Seneca chief, constructed for the writer a model of one of these long-houses, showing in detail its external and internal mechanism.

The late Rev. Ashur Wright, D. D., for many years a missionary among the Senecas, and familiar with their language and customs, wrote to the author in 1873 on the subject of these households, as follows: "As to their family system, when occupying the old long-houses, it is probable that some one clan predominated, the women taking in husbands, however, from the other clans; and sometimes, for a novelty, some of their sons bringing in their young wives until they felt brave enough to leave their mothers. Usually, the female portion ruled the house, and were doubtless clannish enough about it. The stores were in common; but woe to the luckless husband or lover who was too shiftless to do his share of the providing.

---

[1] The late Mrs. William Parker, of Tonawanda.

No matter how many children, or whatever goods he might have in the house, he might at any time be ordered to pick up his blanket and budge; and after such orders it would not be healthful for him to attempt to disobey; the house would be too hot for him; and unless saved by the intercession of some aunt or grandmother, he must retreat to his own clan, or as was often done, go and start a new matrimonial alliance in some other. The women were the great power among the clans, as everywhere else They did not hesitate, when occasion required, to 'knock off the horns,' as it was technically called, from the head of a chief and send him back to the ranks of the warriors   The original nomination of the chiefs also always rested with them."

The mother-right and gyneocracy among the Iroquois here plainly indicated is not overdrawn. The mothers and their children, as we have seen, were of the same gens, and to them the house belonged. It was a gentile house. In case of the death of father or mother, the apartments they occupied could not be detached from the kinship, but remained to its members. The position of the mother was eminently favorable to her influence in the household, and tended to strengthen the maternal bond. We may see in this an ancient phase of human life which has had a wide prevalence in the tribes of mankind, Asiatic, European, African, American, and Australian. Not until after civilization had begun among the Greeks, and gentile society was superseded by political society, was the influence of this old order of society overthrown. It left behind, at least among the Grecian tribes, deep traces of its previous existence.[1]

Among the Iroquois, those who formed a household and cultivated gardens gathered the harvest and stored it in their dwelling as a common stock. There was more or less of individual ownership of these products, and of their possession by different families. For example, the corn, after stripping back the husk, was braided by the husk in bunches and hung up in the different apartments; but when one family had exhausted its supply, their wants were supplied by other families so long as any remained. Each

---

[1] These statements illustrate the gyneocracy and mother-right among the ancient Grecian tribes discussed by Bachofen in "Das Mutterrecht." The phenomena discovered by Bachofen owes its origin, probably, to descent in the female line, and to the junction of several families in one house, on the principle of kin, as among the Iroquois.

hunting and fishing party made a common stock of the capture, of. which the surplus, on their return, was divided among the several families of each household, and, having been cured, was reserved for winter use. The village did not make a common stock of their provisions, and thus offer a bounty to imprudence. It was confined to the household. But the principle of hospitality then came in to relieve the consequences of destitution. We can speak with some confidence of the ancient usages and customs of the Iroquois ; and when any usage is found among them in a definite and positive form, it renders probable the existence of the same usage in other tribes in the same condition, because their necessities were the same.

In the History of Virginia, by Capt. John Smith, the houses of the Powhatan Indians are partially described, and are found to be much the same as those of the Iroquois. We have already quoted from this work the description of a house on Roanoke Island containing five chambers. Speaking of the houses in the vicinity of James River in 1606–1608, he remarks, "Their houses are built like our arbors, of small young sprigs bowed and tied, and so close covered with mats, or the bark of trees, very handsomely, that notwithstanding either wind, rain, or weather, they are as warm as stoves but very smoky ; yet at the top of the house there is a hole made for the smoke to go into right over the fire Against the fire they lie on little hurdles of reeds covered with a mat, borne from the ground a foot and more by a hurdle of wood. On these, round about the house, they lie, heads and points, one by the other, against the fire, some covered with mats, some with skins, and some stark naked lie on the ground, from six to twenty in a house * * * In some places are from two to fifty of these houses together, or but little separated by groves of trees."[1] The noticeable fact in this statement is the number of persons in the house, which shows a household consisting of several families. Their communism in living may be inferred. Elsewhere he speaks of "houses built after their manner, some thirty, some forty yards long ;"[2] and speaking of one of the houses of Powhatan he says, "This house is fifty or sixty yards in length;"[3] and again, at Pamunky, "A great fire was made in a long-house, a mat was spread on one side as on the other ; and on one side they caused him to

---

[1] Smith's History of Virginia, Richmond ed., 1819, i, 130.   [2] Ib., i, 143.   [3] Ib., i, 142.

sit."[1] We here find among the Virginia Indians at the epoch of their discovery long-houses very similar to the long-houses of the Iroquois, with
the same evidence of a large household. It may safely be taken as a rule
that every Indian household in the aboriginal period, whether large or small,
lived from common stores.

Mr. Caleb Swan, who visited the Creek Indians of Georgia in 1790,
found the people living in small houses or cabins, but in clusters, each
cluster being occupied by a part of a gens or clan. He remarks that "the
smallest of their towns have from ten to forty houses, and some of the
largest from fifty to two hundred, that are tolerably compact. These houses
stand in clusters of four, five, six, seven, and eight together.   *   *   *
Each cluster of houses contains a clan or family of relations *who eat and
live in common.*"[2] Here the fact of several families uniting on the principle of kin, living in a cluster of houses, and practicing communism, is
expressly stated.

James Adair, writing still earlier of the southern Indians of the United
States generally, remarks in a passage before quoted, as follows: "I have
observed, with much inward satisfaction, the community of goods that prevailed among them.   *   *   *   And though they do not keep one promiscuous common stock, yet it is to the very same effect, for every one has his
own family or tribe, and when any one is speaking either of the individuals
or habitations of his own tribe, he says, 'He is of my house,' or, 'It is my
house.'"[3] It is singular that this industrious investigator did not notice,
what is now known to be the fact, that all these tribes were organized in
gentes and phratries. It would have rendered his observations upon their
usages and customs more definite. Elsewhere he remarks further that "formerly the Indian law obliged every town to work together in one body, in
sowing or planting their crops, though their fields were divided by proper
marks, and their harvest is gathered separately. The Cherokees and Mus-
cogees [Creeks] still observe that old custom, which is very necessary for
such idle people."[4] They cultivated, like the Iroquois, three kinds of maize,

[1] Smith's Hist. Va., Richmond ed., 1819, i, 160.
[2] Schoolcraft's Hist. Cond. and Pros. of Indian Tribes, vol. v. 262.
[3] History of the American Indians, p. 17.
[4] Ib., p. 430.

an "early variety," the "hominy corn," and the "bread corn,"[1] also beans, squashes, pumpkins, and tobacco. Chestnuts, a tuberous root something like the potato but gathered in the marshes, berries, fish, and game, entered into their subsistence. Like the Iroquois, they made unleavened bread of maize flour, which was boiled in earthen vessels,[2] in the form of cakes, about six inches in diameter and an inch thick.

Among the tribes of the plains, who subsist almost exclusively upon animal food, their usages in the hunt indicate the same tendency to communism in food. The Blackfeet, during the buffalo hunt, follow the herds on horseback in large parties, composed of men, women, and children. When the active pursuit of the herd commences, the hunters leave the dead animals in the track of the chase to be appropriated by the first persons who come up behind. This method of distribution is continued until all are supplied. All the Indian tribes who hunt upon the plains, with the exception of the half-blood Crees, observe the same custom of making a common stock of the capture. It tended to equalize, at the outset, the means of subsistence obtained. They cut the beef into strings, and either dried it in the air or in the smoke of a fire. Some of the tribes made a part of the capture into pemmican, which consists of dried and pulverized meat mixed with melted buffalo fat, which is baled in the hide of the animal.

During the fishing season in the Columbia River, where fish are more abundant than in any other river on the earth, all the members of the tribe encamp together, and make a common stock of the fish obtained. They are divided each day according to the number of women, giving to each an equal share. At the Kootenay Falls, for example, they are taken by spearing, and in huge baskets submerged in the water below the falls. The salmon, during the spring run, weigh from six to forty pounds, and are taken in the greatest abundance, three thousand a day not being an unusual number. Father De Smet, the late Oregon missionary, informed the writer, in 1862, that he once spent several days with the Kootenays at these falls, and that the share which fell to him, as one of the party, loaded, when dried, thirty pack mules. The fish are split open, scarified, and dried on

---

[1] History of the American Indians, p. 430.　　[2] Ib., pp. 406, 408.

scaffolds, after which they are packed in baskets and then removed to their villages. This custom makes a general distribution of the capture, and leaves each household in possession of its share.[1]

Their communism in living is involved in the size of the household, which ranged from ten to forty persons. " The houses of the Sokulks are made of large mats of rushes, and are generally of a square or oblong form, varying in length from fifteen to sixty feet; the top is covered with mats, leaving a space of twelve or fifteen inches, the whole length of the house, for the purpose of admitting the light and suffering the smoke to pass through; the roof is nearly flat, * * * and the house is not divided into apartments, the fire being in the middle of the large room, and immediately under the hole in the roof. * * * On entering one of these houses he [Captain Clarke] found it crowded with men, women, and children, who immediately provided a mat for him to sit on, and one of the party immediately undertook to prepare something to eat."[2] Again: "He landed before five houses close to each other, but no one appeared, and the doors, which were of mats, were closed. He went towards one of them with a pipe in his hand, and pushing aside the mat entered the lodge, where he found thirty-two persons, chiefly men and women, with a few children, all in the greatest consternation."[3] And again: " This village being part of the same nation with the village we passed above, the language of the two being the same, and their houses being of the same form and materials, and calculated to contain about thirty souls."[4] In enumerating the people

---

[1] Alfred W. Howitt, F. G. S., of Bariusdale, Australia, mentions, in a letter to the author, the following singular custom of an Australian tribe concerning the distribution of food in the family group:

"A man catches seven river eels; they are divided thus (it is supposed that his family consists only of these named):

"1st eel. Front half himself; hind half his wife.

"2d eel. Front half his wife's mother; hind half his wife's sister.

"3d eel. Front half his elder sons; hind half his younger sons.

"4th eel. Front half his elder daughters; hind half his younger daughters.

"5th eel. Front half his brother's sons; hind half his brother's daughters.

"6th eel. One whole eel to his married daughter's husband.

"7th eel. One whole eel to his married daughter."

This custom may be supposed to show the ordinary household group, and the order of their relative nearness to *Ego*. It foots up himself and wife, wife's mother and sister, his sons and daughters, his brother's sons and daughter's, and his daughter's husband. It implies also other members of the household, who are obliged to take care of themselves; viz, his brothers and sisters.

[2] Lewis and Clarke's Travels, pp. 351–353.   [3] Ib., p. 357.   [4] Ib., p. 376.

Lewis and Clarke often state the number of inhabitants with the number of houses, thus:

"The Killamucks, who number fifty houses and a thousand souls."[1]

"The Chilts, who   *   *   *   are estimated at seven hundred souls and thirty-eight houses."

"The Clamoitomish, of twelve houses and two hundred and sixty souls."

"The Potoashees, of ten houses and two hundred souls."

"The Pailsk, of ten houses and two hundred souls."

"The Quinults, of sixty houses and one thousand souls."[1]

Speaking generally of the usages and customs of the tribes of the "Columbia plains," they make the following statements: "Their large houses usually contain several families, consisting of the parents, their sons and daughters-in-law and grandchildren, among whom the provisions are common, and whose harmony is scarcely ever interrupted by disputes. Although polygamy is permitted by their customs, very few have more than a single wife, and she is brought immediately after the marriage into the husband's family, where she resides until increasing numbers oblige them to seek another house   In this state the old man is not considered the head of the family, since the active duties, as well as the responsibility, fall on some of the younger members.   As these families gradually expand into bands, or tribes, or nations, the paternal authority is represented by the chief of each association.   This chieftain, however, is not hereditary."[2]   Here we find among the Columbian tribes, as elsewhere, communism in living, but restricted to large households composed of several families.

A writer in Harper's Magazine, speaking of the Aleutians, remarks: "When first discovered this people were living in large yourts, or dirt houses, partially underground,   *   *   *   having the entrances through a hole in the top or centre, going in and out on a rude ladder.   Several of these ancient yourts were very large, as shown by the ruins, being from thirty to eighty yards long and twenty to forty in width.   *   *   *   In these large yourts the primitive Aleuts lived by fifties and hundreds for the double object of protection and warmth."[3]

---

[1] Lewis and Clarke's Travels, pp. 426–428.   [2] Ib., p. 443.
[3] Harper's Magazine, vol. 55, p. 806.

Whether these tribes at this time were organized in gentes and phratries is not known.   At the time of the Wilkes expedition (1838–1842) the gentile organization did not exist among them ; neither does it now exist ; but it is still found among the tribes of the Northwest Coast, and among the Indian tribes generally.   The composition of the household, as here described, is precisely like the household of the Iroquois prior to A. D. 1700.

The Mandan village contained at the time of Catlin's visit (1832), as elsewhere stated, about fifty houses and about fifteen hundred people. "These cabins are so spacious," Catlin remarks, "that they hold from twenty to forty persons—a family and all their connections.   *   *   * From the great numbers of the inmates in these lodges they are necessarily very spacious, and the number of beds considerable.   It is no uncommon thing to see these lodges fifty feet in diameter inside (which is an immense room), with a row of these curtained beds extending quite around their sides, being some ten or twelve of them, placed four or five feet apart, and the space between them occupied by a large post, fixed quite firmly in the ground, and six or seven feet high, with large wooden pegs or bolts in it, on which are hung or grouped, with a wild and startling taste, the arms and armor of the respective proprietors."[1]   The household, according to the cutsom of the Indians, was a large one.   The number of inhabitants divided among the number of houses would give an average of thirty persons to each house. It is evident from several statements of Catlin before given that the household practiced communism in living, and that it was formed of related families, on the principle of gentile kin, as among the Iroquois.   Elsewhere he intimates that the Mandans kept a public store or granary as a refuge for the whole community in a time of scarcity.[2]

In like manner Carver, speaking generally of the usages and customs of the Dakota tribes and of the tribes of Wisconsin, remarks that "they will readily share with any of their own tribe the last part of their provisions, and even with those of a different nation, if they chance to come in when they are eating.   Though they do not keep one common store, yet that community of goods which is so prevalent among them, and their gen-

---

[1] North American Indians, Philadelphia ed., 1857, i, 139.
[2] Ib., i, 210.

erous disposition, render it nearly of the same effect."[3] What this author seems to state is that community of goods existed in the household, and that it was lengthened out to the tribe by the law of hospitality. Elsewhere, speaking of the large village of the Sauks, he says: " This is the largest Indian town I ever saw. It contains about ninety houses, each large enough for several families."[1] In a previous chapter (*supra* p. 49.) Hecke-welder's observations upon hospitality among the Delawares and Munsees, implying the principle of communism, have been given He remarks further that " there is nothing in an Indian's house or family without its particular owner. Every individual knows what belongs to him, from the horse or cow down to the dog, cat, kitten, and little chicken. * * * For a litter of kittens or a brood of chickens there are often as many different owners as there are individual animals. In purchasing a hen with her brood one frequently has to deal for it with several children. Thus, while the principle of community of goods prevails in the State, the rights of property are acknowledged among the members of the family. This is attended with a very good effect, for by this means every living creature is properly taken care of."[2] I do not understand what Heckewelder means by the remark that "the principle of community of goods prevails in the state," unless it be that the rule of hospitality was so all-pervading that it was tantamount to a community of goods, while individual property was everywhere recognized until it was freely surrendered. This may be the just view of the result of their communism and hospitality, but it is a higher one than I have been able to take.

The household of the Mandans consisting of from twenty to forty persons, the households of the Columbian tribes of about the same number, the Shoshonee household of seven families, the households of the Sauks, of the Iroquois, and of the Creeks each composed of several families, are fair types of the households of the Northern Indians at the epoch of their discovery. The fact is also established that these tribes constructed as a rule large joint tenement houses, each of which was occupied by a large household composed of several families, among whom provisions were in common, and who practiced communism in living in the household.

---

[3] Travels, etc., p. 171.   [1] Travels, etc., Phila. ed. 1796, p. 29.   [2] Indian Nations, p. 158.

Among the Village Indians of New Mexico a more advanced form of house architecture appears, and their joint tenement character is even more pronounced. They live in large houses, two, three, and four stories high, constructed of adobe brick, and of stone imbedded in adobe mortar, and containing fifty, a hundred, two hundred, and in some cases five hundred apartments in a house. They are built in the terraced form, with fireplaces and chimneys added since their discovery, the first story closed up solid, and is entered by ladders, which ascend to the platform-roof of the first story. These houses are fortresses, and were erected as strongholds to resist the attacks of the more barbarous tribes by whom they were perpetually assailed. Each house was probably occupied by a number of household groups, whose apartments were doubtless separated from each other by partition walls. In a subsequent chapter the character of these houses will be more fully shown.

Our knowledge of the plan of life in these houses in the aboriginal period is still very imperfect. They still practice the old hospitality, own their lands in common, but with allotments to individuals and to families, and are governed by a cacique or sachem and certain other officers annually elected. An American missionary to the Laguna Village Indians, Rev. Samuel Gorman, in an address before the Historical Society of New Mexico in 1869, remarks as follows: "They generally marry very young, and the son-in-law becomes the servant of the father-in-law, and very often they all live together in one family for years, even if there be several sons-in-law; and this clannish mode of living is often, if not generally, a fruitful source of evil among this people. Their women generally have control over the granary, and they are more provident than their Spanish neighbors about the future. Ordinarily they try to have one year's provisions on hand. It is only when they have two years of scarcity succeeding each other that pueblos as a community suffer hunger."[1] The usages of these Indians have doubtless modified in the last two hundred years under Spanish influence; they have decreased in numbers, and the family group is probably smaller than formerly. But it is not too late to recover the aboriginal plan of life among them if the subject were

---

[1]Address, p. 14.

intelligently investigated. It is to be hoped that some one will undertake this work.

The Spanish writers do not mention the practice of communism in living as existing among the Village Indians of Mexico or Central America. They are barren of practical information concerning their mode of life; but we have the same picture of large households composed of several families, whose communism in the household may reasonably be inferred.

We have also the striking illustration of "Montezuma's Dinner," hereafter to be noticed, which was plainly a dinner in common by a communal household. Beside these facts we have the ownership of lands in common by communities of persons. Moreover, the ruins of ancient houses in Central and South America, and in parts of Mexico, show very plainly their joint tenement character. From the plans of these houses the communism of the people by households may be deduced theoretically with reasonable certainty.

Yucatan, when discovered, was occupied by a number of tribes of Maya Indians. The Maya language spread beyond the limits of Yucatan. This region, with Chiapas, Guatemala, and a part of Honduras, contained and still contains evidence, in the ruins of ancient structures, of a higher advancement in the arts of life than any other part of North America The present Maya Indians of Yucatan are the descendants of the people who occupied the country at the period of the Spanish conquest, and who occupied the massive stone houses now in ruins, from which they were forced by Spanish oppression.

We have a notable illustration of communism in living among the present Maya Indians, as late as the year 1840, through the work of John L. Stephens. At Nohcacab, a few miles east of the ruins of Uxmal, Mr Stephens, having occasion to employ laborers, went to a settlement of Maya Indians, of whom he gives the following account: "Their community consists of a hundred labradores, or working men; their lands are held and wrought in common, and the products are shared by all. Their food is prepared at one hut, and every family sends for its portion, which explains a singular spectacle we had seen on our arrival, a procession of women and children, each carrying an earthen bowl containing a quantity of smoking hot broth, all coming down the same road, and disappearing among the different huts.   Every member belonging to the community, down to the smallest pappoose, contributing in turn a hog.   From our ignorance of the language, and the number of other and more pressing matters claiming our attention, we could not learn all the details of their internal economy, but it seemed to approximate that improved state of association which is some-times heard of among us; and as theirs has existed for an unknown length of time, and can no longer be considered merely experimental, Owen or Fourier might perhaps take lessons from them with advantage."[1]   A hundred working men indicate a total of five hundred persons, who were then depend-ing for their daily food upon a single fire, the provisions being supplied from common stores, and divided from the caldron.   It is, not unlikely, a truth-ful picture of the mode of life of their forefathers in the "House of the Nuns," and in the "Governor's House" at Uxmal, at the epoch of the Span-ish conquest.

It is well known that Spanish adventurers captured these pueblos, one after the other, and attempted to enforce the labor of the Indians for per-sonal ends, and that the Indians abandoned their pueblos and retreated into the inaccessible forests to escape enslavement, after which their houses of stone fell into decay, the ruins of which, and all there ever was of them, still remain in all parts of these countries

It is hardly supposable that the communism here described by Mr. Stephens was a new thing to the Mayas; but far more probable that it was a part of their ancient mode of life, to which these ruined houses were emi-nently adapted.   The subject of the adaptation of the old pueblo houses in Yucatan and Central America to communism in living will be elsewhere considered.

When Columbus first landed on the island of Cuba, he sent two men into the interior, who reported that "they travelled twenty-two leagues, and found a village of fifty houses, built like those before spoken of, and they contained about one thousand persons, because a whole generation lived in a house; and the prime men came out to meet them, led them by the arms, and lodged them in one of these new houses, causing them to sit down on

---

[1] Incidents of Travel in Yucatan, ii, 14.

seats; * * * and they gave them boiled roots to eat, which tasted like chestnuts."[1] One of the first expeditions which touched the main land on the coast of Venezuela in South America found much larger houses than these last described. "The houses they dwelt in were common to all, and so spacious that they contained one hundred and sixty persons, strongly built, though covered with palm-tree leaves, and shaped like a bell."[2] Herrera further remarks of the same tribe, that "they observed no law or rule in matrimony, but took as many wives as they would, and they as many husbands, quitting one another at pleasure, without reckoning any wrong done on either part. There was no such thing as jealousy among them, all living as best pleased them, without taking offense at one another."[3] This shows communism in husbands as well as wives, and rendered communism in food a necessity of their condition Elsewhere the same author speaks of the habitations of the tribes on the coast of Carthagena. "Their houses were like long arbors, with several apartments, and they had no beds but hammocks."[4] Many similar statements are scattered through his work.

Among the more advanced tribes of Peru the lands were divided, and allotted to different uses; one part was for the support of the government, another for the support of religion, and another for the support of individuals. The first two parts were cultivated by the people under established regulations, and the crops were placed in public storehouses. This is the statement of Garcilasso.[5] Herrera, however, says generally that the people lived from common stores "The Spaniards drawing near to Caxamalca begun to have a view of the Inca army lying near the bottom of a mountain. * * * They were pleased to see the beauty of the fields, most regularly cultivated, for it was an ancient law among these people that all should be fed from common stores, and none should touch the standing corn."[6] The discrepancy between Herrera and Garcilasso may perhaps be explained by the reservation of the crops grown on lands set apart for the government and for religion.

The reason for presenting the foregoing observations of different authors concerning the households, the houses, and the practice of communism in

---

[1] Herrera, i, 55.   [2] Ib., 216.   [3] Ib., i, 216.   [4] Ib., 348.
[5] Royal Com. l. c., pp. 154, 157.   [6] Herrera, iv, 249.

food, has been to show, firstly, that the household of the Indian tribes was a large one, composed of several families; secondly, that their houses were constructed to accommodate several families; and thirdly, that the household practiced communism in living. These are the material facts, and they have been sufficiently illustrated. The single family of civilized society live from common stores, yet it is not communism; but where several families coalesce in one common household and make a common stock of their provisions, and this is found to be a general rule in entire tribes, it is a form of communism important to be noticed. It is seen to belong to a society in a low stage of development, where it springs from the necessities of their condition. These usages and customs exhibit their plan of life, and reveal the wide difference between their condition and that of civilized society; between the Indian family, without individuality, and the highly individualized family of civilization.

CHAPTER IV.

USAGES AND CUSTOMS WITH RESPECT TO LANDS AND TO FOOD

THE OWNERSHIP OF LANDS IN COMMON.

Among the Iroquois the tribal domain was held and owned by the tribe in common. Individual ownership, with the right to sell and convey in fee-simple to any other person, was entirely unknown among them. It required the experience and development of the two succeeding ethnical periods to bring mankind to such a knowledge of property in land as its individual ownership with the power of alienation in fee-simple implies. No person in Indian life could obtain the absolute title to land, since it was vested by custom in the tribe as one body, and they had no conception of what is implied by a legal title in severalty with power to sell and convey the fee. But he could reduce unoccupied land to possession by cultivation, and so long as he thus used it he had a possessory right to its enjoyment which would be recognized and respected by his tribe. Gardens, planting-lots, apartments in a long-house, and, at a later day, orchards of fruit were thus held by persons and by families. Such possessory right was all that was needed for their full enjoyment and for the protection of their interest in them. A person might transfer or donate his rights to other persons of the same tribe, and they also passed by inheritance, under established customs, to his gentile kin. This was substantially the Indian system in respect to the ownership of lands and apartments in houses among the Indian tribes within the areas of the United States and British America in the Lower Status of barbarism. In later times, when the State or National Government acquired Indian lands, and made compensation therefor, payment for the lands went to the tribe, and for improvements to the individual who had the possessory right. At the Tonawanda Reservation of the

Seneca-Iroquois, a portion of the lands are divided into separate farms, which are fenced and occupied in severalty, while the remainder are owned by the tribe in common. When a young man marries and has no land on which to subsist, the chiefs may allot him a portion of these reserved lands. The title to all these lands, occupied and unoccupied, remains in the tribe in common. Individuals may sell or rent their possessory rights to each other, or rent them to a white man. No white man can now acquire a title from an Indian to Indian lands in any part of the United States. A person could transfer his possessions to another, but apartments in a house must remain to his gentile kindred. In the time of James II the right to acquire lands was vested in the Crown exclusively as a royal prerogative, to which prerogative our State and National Governments succeeded.

The same usages prevail on the Tuscarora Reservation, near the Niagara River, where this Iroquois tribe owns in common about 8,000 acres of fine agricultural land in one body. A part of this reservation has long been parceled out to individuals in small farms, fenced, and cultivated by the possessors. The remainder is unparceled and under the control of the chiefs. The people are allowed to remove from the wood-land of the reserve the dead wood and litter, but are not permitted to touch the standing timber. When a young man marries, if he has no land, the chiefs allot him forty acres to cultivate for his subsistence; but, before giving him possession, the lot is first open to all the tribe to cut off the timber for fire-wood. Thus, the double object is gained of supplying the people with fire-wood and of clearing the land for cultivation for the new family. These possessory rights pass by inheritance to the recognized heirs. A person may transfer or rent his possession to another person; he may rent to a white man, but in no case can he sell to a white man.

And here I may be allowed a brief digression, to notice a recent opinion of the late Secretary of the Interior, Hon. Carl Schurz, shared in to some extent by the National Government, in relation to the division of our Indian reservations into lots or tracts, and their conveyance in severalty to the Indians themselves, with power of alienation to white men after a short period, say twenty-five years. It is to be hoped that this policy will never be adopted by any National Administration, as it is fraught with nothing but mischief to the Indian tribes. The Indian is still, as he always has been, and will remain for many years to come, entirely incapable of meeting the white man, with safety to himself, in the field of trade and of resisting the arts and inducements which would be brought to bear upon him. He is incapable of steadily attaching that value to the ownership of land which its importance deserves, or of knowing how far the best interests of himself and family are involved in its continued possession. The result of individual Indian ownership, with power to sell, would unquestionably be, that in a very short time he would divest himself of every foot of land and fall into poverty. The case of the Shawnee tribe of Kansas affords a perfect illustration of this pernicious policy. The Shawnees were removed to Kansas under the Jackson policy, so called, and occupied a splendid reservation on the Kansas River, where they were told they were to make their home forever. But after a few years of undisturbed possession, our people, in the natural flow of population, reached Kansas, where they found the Shawnees in possession of the best part of what has since been the State of Kansas Our people at once wanted these Indian lands, and they determined to root out the Shawnees in the interest of civilization and progress. They accomplished this result in the most speedy and scientific manner, using as their proposed lever this identical plan since adopted by Mr. Schurz. First, the government was induced to re-purchase a part of the reservation on the ground that they had more land than they needed for cultivation; and, secondly, the government induced the Indians to have the remainder divided up into farms and conveyed to heads of families in severalty, with power of alienation. In 1859, when this scheme was being worked out, I visited Kansas, and found the Shawnees cultivating and improving their farms, some of which embraced a thousand acres, and owning them, too, like other farmers. When next in Kansas, ten years later, the work was done. There was not a Shawnee in Kansas, but American farmers were in possession of all these lands. It was this individual ownership with power to sell that had done the work.

In managing the affairs of our Indian tribes, we must apply a little common sense to their condition. In their brains they are in the same stage of growth and development with our remote forefathers when they learned to domesticate animals, and came to rely upon a meat and milk subsistence. The next condition of advancement at which the Indian would naturally reach is the pastoral, the raising of flocks and herds of domestic animals. The Indian has taught himself to raise the horse in herds, and some of the tribes raise sheep and goats. A few of them raise cattle. If the government could assist them in this until they were started, they would soon become expert herdsmen; would make a proper use of the unoccupied prairie area in the interior of the continent as well as of the reservations, and would become prosperous and abundant in their resources.

Among the sedentary Village Indians of New Mexico, who were in the Middle Status of barbarism, the land system is much the same in principle, but with special usages adapted to a more advanced condition At Taos, the pueblo lands are held under a Spanish grant of 1689, covering four Spanish square leagues. This grant was afterward confirmed, as I am informed by David J. Miller, esq. of the surveyor-general's office at Santa Fé, by letters patent of the United States. It is, of course, to the Taos Indians in common as a tribe, and without the power of alienation except among themselves These lands have been allotted from time to time to individuals, and held in severalty for cultivation; but these allotments, so to call them, are verbal, and the rights of persons to their possession are settled and adjusted by the chiefs in case of disputes. Mr. Miller wrote me from Taos, under date of December 5, 1877, that "A land-owner cannot, under any circumstance, sell to any but a Pueblo Indian, and one of this (Taos) pueblo If he should do so he would be banished the pueblo, and the sale be treated as void. There is an instance now in this pueblo of a San Juan Indian man married here, but he is not allowed to acquire land in the pueblo premises. His wife has lands which he cultivates. A piece of land belonging to a man may or may not be utilized by him, but it is recognized and treated as his in fee until he sell it or dies. If a lad grows up and marries, and his father or father-in-law has no land to give him, he may purchase in the pueblo, or the pueblo may assign him land, whereby the title in fee as private property remains in him until he sells or dies. When he dies it is divided equally among widow and children. If the children are small, his brother or other relatives cultivate the land for them until they can do it for themselves; but the right of property is in the children. When a piece of land is sold it is done in the presence of witnesses, if it is so desired. Oftener the sale and transfer are made by and between the parties themselves No documents are used. This is so in all the pueblos. The rules and customs in the sale and delivery of rooms in a house and of personal property, such as animals, are the same. There is no preference, as to males or females, in the descent of property rights and titles There is a corn-field at each pueblo, cultivated by all in common, and when grain is scarce the poor take from this store after it is housed. It is in the charge of, and at the disposal of, the cacique (called the governor). Land cannot be sold to an alien; but an Indian coming from another pueblo to live at this may acquire land to subsist upon, though such immigration is rare. It is not allowed at any of the pueblos that a white person acquire property therein. An Indian woman is not allowed to marry a Mexican and live at the pueblo. A piece of land held and recognized as belonging to a person is his property, whether he utilizes it or not, and he may sell or donate it absolutely at his will to persons within the community.

"At Jemes and Zia (other pueblos in New Mexico), when a woman dies her property goes into the control of her husband; if a widow, it descends to her children; if she has no children, it goes to her brothers and sisters equally; and if none survive her, then to her nearest relatives; if she has no relatives, then to such friends as attend her in her last illness. It never reverts to the pueblo, which as a corporate community owns no land."

What Mr. Miller refers to as property rights and titles, and ownership in fee of land, is sufficiently explained by the possessory right found among the Northern tribes. The limitations upon its alienation to an Indian from another pueblo or to a white man, not to lay any stress upon the absence of written conveyances of titles made possible by Spanish and American intercourse, show quite plainly that their ideas respecting the ownership of the ultimate title to land, with power to alienate in fee, were entirely below this conception of property in land. The more important ends of individual ownership were obtained through the possessory right, while the ultimate title remained in the tribe for the protection of all. That the pueblo now owns no land, as Mr. Miller states, must be understood to mean that all the lands of the original grant have been parcelled out.   The further statement of Mr. Miller, that if a father dies his land is divided between his widow and children, and that if a mother dies, leaving no husband, her land is divided equally between her sons and daughters, is important, because it shows an inheritance by the children from both father and mother, a total departure from the principles of gentile inheritance. While visiting the Taos pueblo in the summer of 1878 I was unable to find among them the gentile organization, and from lack of sufficient time could not inquire into their rules of descent and inheritance.

My friend, Mr. Ad. F. Bandelier, now recognized as our most eminent scholar in Spanish American history, has recently investigated the subject of the tenure of lands among the ancient Mexicans with great thoroughness of research.   The results are contained in an essay published in the Eleventh Annual Report of the Peabody Museum of Archæology and Ethnology, p. 385 (Cambridge, 1878).   It gives me great pleasure to incorporate verbatim in this chapter, and with his permission, so much of this essay as relates to the kinds or classes of land recognized among them, the manner in which they were held, and his general conclusions.

In the pueblo of Mexico (Tenochtitlan), he remarks: "Four quarters had been formed by the localizing of four relationships composing them respectively, and it is expressly stated that each one 'might build in its quarter (barrio) as it liked.'[1]   The term for these relationships, in the Nahuatl tongue, and used among all the tribes speaking it, was 'calpulli.' It is also used to designate a great hall or house, and we may therefore infer that, originally at least, all the members of one kinship *dwelt under one common roof*.[2]   The ground thus occupied by the 'calpulli' was NOT, as

---

[1] Durán (Cap. V, p. 42).   Acosta (Lib. VII, cap. VII, p. 467).   Herrera (Dec. III, Lib. II, cap. XI, p. 61).

[2] Torquemada (Lib. II, cap. LXVIII, p. 194.   "Estaba de ordinario, recogido en una grande Sala (ó calpul)."   (Lib. III, cap. XXVII, p. 305.   Lib. IV, cap. XIX, p. 396 (que asi llaman las Salas grandes de Comunidad, ú de Cabildo).   We find, under the corrupted name of "galpon," the "calpulli" in Nicaragua among the Niquirans, which speak a dialect of the Mexican (Nahuatl) language.   See E. G. Squier ("Nicaragua," Vol. II, p. 342).   "The council-houses were called grepons, surrounded by broad corridors called galpons, beneath which the arms were kept, protected by a guard of young men").   Mr. Squier evidently bases upon Oviedo ("Hist. general," Lib. XLII, cap. III, p. 52.   "Esta casa de cabildo llaman galpon . . . ."   It is another evidence in favor of our statements, that the kinship formed the original unit of the tribe, and at the same time a hint that, as in New Mexico, originally an entire kin inhabited a single large house.   See Molina's Vocab. (p. 11).

Torquemada admits, *assigned* to it *by a higher power; the tribal government itself held* NO DOMAIN which it might apportion among subdivisions or to individuals, either gratuitously or on condition of certain prestations, or barter against a consideration.[1] The tribal territory was distributed, at the time of its occupancy, *into possessory rights held by* the KINDRED GROUPS AS SUCH, by common and tacit consent, as resulting *naturally* from their *organization* and *state of culture*.[2]

"The patches of solid ground, on which these 'quarters' settled, were gradually built over with dwellings, first made out of canes and reeds, and latterly, as their means increased, of turf, 'adobe,' and light stone   These houses were of *large size*, since it is stated that even at the time of the conquest 'there were seldom less than two, four, and six dwellers in one house; thus there were infinite people (in the pueblo) since, as there was no other way of providing for them, many aggregated together as they might please.' *Communal living*, as the idea of the 'calpulli' implies, seems, therefore, to have prevailed among the Mexicans *as late as the period of their greatest power*.[3]

---

[1] The division into "quarters" is everywhere represented as resulting from common consent. But nowhere is it stated that the *tribal government or authority* assigned locations to any of its fractions. This is only attributed to the chiefs, on the supposition that they, although *elective*, were still hereditary monarchs.

[2] There is no evidence of any tribute or prestation due by the quarters to the tribe. The custom always remained, that the "calpulli" was sovereign within its limits. See Alonzo de Zurita ("Rapport sur les différentes classes de chefs de la Nouvelle-Espagne," pp. 51–65). Besides, Ixtlilxochitl says: ("Hist. des Chichim," cap. XXXV, p. 242), "Other fields were called Calpolalli or Altepetlalli." Now calpulalli (from "calpulli," quarter or kinship, and "tlalli," soil), means soil of the kin, and altepetlalli ("altepetl," tribe), soil of the tribe. Clavigero even says that the lands called "altepetlalli," belonging to the communities "of the towns and villages, were divided into so many parts as there were quarters in the town, each quarter *having its own, without the least connection wi'h the other*." (Lib. VII, cap. XIV.) This indicates plainly that the kinships *held the soil*, whereas the tribe occupied the territorial expanse. The *domain*, either as pertaining to a "lord," or to a "state," was unknown among the Indians in general. Even among the Peruvians, who were more advanced than the Mexicans in that respect, there was no domain of the tribe.

[3] See Torquemada (Lib. II, cap. XI, and Lib. III, cap XXII). Durán (cap. V). The quotation is from Herrera (Dec. II, Lib. VII, cap. XIII, p. 190), and is confirmed by Torquemada (Lib. III, cap. XXIII, p. 291), and especially by Gomara ("Conquista de Méjico," p. 443. Vedia, I). "Many married people ("muchos casados") live in one house, either on account of the brothers and relations being together, as they do not divide their grounds ("heredades"), or on account of the limited space of the pueblos; although the pueblos are large, and even the houses." Peter Martyr of Angleria ("De Novo Orbe," translated by Richard Eden and Michael Lok, London, 1612, Dec. V, cap. X, p. 228), says: "But the common houses themselves as hygh as a mannes Girdle, were also built of stone, by reason of the swellyng of the lake through the floode, or washing flote of the Ryvers fallying into it. Vpon those greate foundations, they builde the reste of the house, with Bricke dryed, or burned in the sunne, intermingled with Beames of Tymber, and the common houses have but one floore or planchin." We are

"The soil built over by each 'calpulli' probably remained 'for some time the only *solid* expanse held by the Mexicans. Gradually, however, the necessity was felt for an increase of this soil. Remaining unmolested 'in the midst of canes and reeds,' their numbers had augmented, and for residence as well as for food a greater area was needed. Fishing and hunting no longer satisfied a people whose original propensities were horticultural; they aspired to cultivate the soil as they had once been accustomed to, and after the manner of the kindred tribes surrounding them. For this purpose they began throwing up *little artificial garden beds*, 'chinampas,' on which they planted Indian corn and perhaps some other vegetables. Such plots are still found, as 'floating gardens,' in the vicinity of the present city of Mexico, and they are described as follows by a traveler of this century:

"'They are artificial gardens, about fifty or sixty yards long, and not more than four or five wide. They are separated by ditches of three or four yards, and are made by taking the soil from the intervening ditch and throwing it on the chinampa, by which means the ground is raised generally about a yard, and thus forms a small fertile garden, covered with the finest culinary vegetables, fruits, and flowers. * * *'

"Each consanguine relationship thus gradually surrounded the surface on which it dwelt with a number of garden plots sufficient to the wants of its members. The aggregate area thereof, including the abodes, formed the '*calpullalli*'—soil of the 'calpulli'[1]—*and was held by it as a unit;* the *single tracts*, however, being tilled and used for the benefit of the *single families.* The mode of tenure of land among the Mexicans at that period was therefore very simple. The tribe claimed its *territory*, 'ALTEPETLALLI,' an undefined expanse over which it *might extend*—the 'calpules,' however, *held* and *possessed within that territory* such portions of it as were *productive;* each

---

forcibly reminded here of the houses of Itza on Lake Peten, which were found in 1695. "Hist. de la Conq. de los Itzaex," Lib. VIII, cap. XII, p. 494." "It was all filled with houses, some with stone walls more than one rod high, and higher up of wood, and the roofs of straw, and some only of wood and straw. There lived in them all the Inhabitants of the Island brutally together, one relationship occupying a single house." See also the highly valuable Introduction to the second Dialogue of Cervantes-Salázar ("Mexico in 1554") by my excellent friend Sr. Icazbalceta (pp. 73 and 74).

[1] Alonzo de Zurita (p. 51). Ixtlilxochitl ("Hist. des Chichim," cap. XXXV, p. 242). Torquemada (Lib. XIV, cap. VII, p. 545). Bustamante ("Tezcoco en los ultimos Tiempos de sus antiguas Reyes," p. 232).

'calpulli' being *sovereign* within its limits, and assigning to its individual members *for their use* the minor tracts into which the soil was parcelled in consequence of their mode of cultivation. If, therefore, the terms 'altepet-lalli' and 'calpulalli' are occasionally regarded as *identical*, it is because the former indicates the *occupancy*, the latter *the distribution* of the soil. We thus recognize in the calpulli, or kindred group, the unit of tenure of whatever soil the Mexicans deemed worthy of definite possession. Further on we shall investigate how far individuals, as members of this communal unit, participated in the aggregate tenure.

" In the course of time, as the population further increased, *segmentation* occurred within the four original 'quarters,' new 'calpulli' being formed.[1] For *governmental* purposes this segmentation produced a new result by leaving, more particularly in military affairs, the first four clusters as *great subdivisions*.[2] But these, as soon as they had disaggregated, *ceased* to be any longer *units* of territorial possession, their original areas being held thereafter by the 'minor quarters' (as Herrera, for instance, calls them), who exercised, each one within its limits, the same sovereignty which the original 'calpulli' formerly held over the whole.[3] A further consequence of this disaggrega-

---

[1] This successive formation of new "calpulli" is nowhere explicitly stated, but it is implied by the passage of Durán which we have already quoted (Cap. V, p. 42). It also results from their military organization as described in the "Art of War" (p. 115). With the increase of population, the original kinships necessarily disaggregated further, as we have seen it to háve occurred among the Qquiché (see "Popol-Vuh," quoted in our note 7), forming smaller groups of consanguinei. After the successful war against the Tecpanecas, of which we shall speak hereafter, we find at least twenty chiefs, representing as many kins (Durán, cap. XI, p. 97), besides three more, adopted then from those of Culhuacan (Id., pp. 98 and 99). This indicates an increase.

[2] "Art of War, etc.," pp. 115 and 120.

[3] Torquemada (Lib. III, cap. XXIV, p. 295): " I confess it to be truth that this city of Mexico is divided into four principal quarters, each one of which contains others, smaller ones, included, and all, in common as well as in particular, have their commanders and leaders . . . ." Zurita ("Rapport," p. 58–64). That the smaller subdivisions were those who held the soil, and not the four original groups, must be inferred from the fact that the ground was attached to the calpulli. Says Zurita (p. 51), "They (the lands) do not belong to each inhabitant of the village, but to the calpulli, which possèsses them in common." On the other hand, Torquemada states (Lib. XIV, cap. VII, p. 545), "That in each pueblo, according to the number of people, there should be (were) clusters ('parcialidades') of diverse people and families . . . . These clusters were distributed by calpules, which are quarters ('barrios'), and it happened that one of the aforesaid clusters sometimes contained three, four, and more calpules, according to the population of the place ('pueblo') or tribe." The same author further affirms: "These quarters and streets were all assorted and leveled with so much accuracy that those of one quarter or street could not take a palm of land from those of another, and the same was with the streets, their lots running (being scattered) all over the pueblo." Consequently there were no communal lands allotted to the four great quarters of Mexico as such, but each one of the kinships (calpules) held its part of the original aggregate. Compare Gomara (Vedia, Vol. I, "Conq. de Méjico," p. 434: "Among tributaries it is a custom, etc., etc." Also p. 440). Clavigero (Lib. VII, cap. XIV): " Each quarter has its own tract, without the least connection with the others."

tion was (by removing the tribal council farther from the calpules) the necessity for an *official building*, exclusively devoted to the business of the *whole* tribe alone.[1]

"This building was the '*teepan*' called, even by Torquemada, 'house of the community'; it was, therefore, since the council of chiefs was the highest authority in the government, the 'council house' proper. It was erected near the center of the 'pueblo,' and fronting the open space reserved for public celebrations. But, whereas formerly occasional, gradually merging into *regular*, meetings of the chiefs were sufficient, constant daily attendance at the "teepan' became required, even to such an extent that a permanent *residence* of the head-chief *there* resulted from it and was *one of the duties of the office*. Consequently the 'tlacatecuhtli,' his family, and such assistants as he needed (like runners), dwelt at the 'official house.' But this occupancy was in no manner connected with a possessory right by the occupant, whose family relinquished the abode as soon as the time of office expired through death of its incumbent. The 'teepan' was occupied by the head warchiefs only as long as they exercised the functions of that office.[2] * * *

"Of those tracts whose products were exclusively applied to the governmental needs of the pueblo or tribe itself (taken as an independent unit) there were, as we have already seen, two particular classes:

"The first was the 'teepan-tlalli,' land of the house of the community, whose crops were applied to the sustenance of such as employed themselves in the construction, ornamentation, and repairs of the public house. Of these there were sometimes several within the tribal area. They were tilled in common by special families who resided on them, using the crops in compensation for the work they performed on the official buildings.

---

[1]Compare Durán (Cap. XI, p. 87). Acosta (Lib. VII, cap, XXXI, p. 470). It appears as if the "teepan" had not been constructed previous to the middle of the 14th century, the meetings of the tribe being previously called together by priests, and probably in the open space around the main house of worship. The fact of the priests calling the public meetings is proved by Durán (Cap. IV, p. 42). Acosta (Lib. VII, cap. VII, p. 468). Veytia (Lib. II, cap. XVIII, pp. 156,159. Cap. XXI, p. 186). Acosta first mentions "unos palacios, aunque harto pobres." (Lib. VII, cap. 8, p. 470), on the occasion of the election of the first regular "tlacatecuhtli:" Acamapichtli—Torquemada says (Lib. XII, cap. XXII, p. 290) that they lived in miserable huts of reeds and straw, erected around the open space where the altar or place of worship of Huitzilopochtli was built. The public building was certainly their latest kind of construction.

[2]Nearly every author who attempts to describe minutely the "chief-house" (teepan) mentions it as containing great halls (council-rooms). See the description of the teepan of Tezcuco by Ixtlilxochitl ("Hist. des Chichiméques," cap. XXXVI, p. 247).

"The second class was called 'tlatoca-tlalli,' land of the speakers. Of these there was but one tract in each tribe, which was to be 'four hundred of their measures long on each side, each measure being equal to three Castilian rods.'[1] The crops raised on such went exclusively to the requirements of the household at the 'teepan,' comprising the head-chief and his family with the assistants. The tract was worked in turn by the other members of the tribe, and it remained always public ground, reserved for the same purposes.[2]

"Both of these kinds were often comprised in one, and it is even not improbable that the first one may have been but a variety of the general tribute-lands devoted to the benefit of the conquering confederates. Still the evidence on this point is too indefinite to warrant such an assumption.

"While the crops raised on the 'teepan-tlalli,' as well as on the 'tlatoca-tlalli,' were consumed exclusively by the official houses and households of the tribe, the soil itself which produced these crops was neither claimed nor possessed by the chiefs themselves or their descendants. It was simply, as far as its products were concerned, official soil.[3]

"The establishing and maintaining of these areal subdivisions was very simple with the tribes of the mainland, since they all possessed ample territories for their wants and for the requirements of their organizations. *Their* soil formed a contiguous unit. It was not so, however, with the Mexicans proper. With all their industry in adding artificial sod to the patch on which they had originally settled, the solid surface was eventually much too small for their numbers, and they themselves put an efficient stop to

---

[1] Ixtlilxochitl ("Hist. des Chichim," cap. XXXV, p. 242). Vedia (Lib. III, cap. VI, p. 195). "This had to be four hundred of their measures in square ('encuadro,' each side long), each one of these being equal to three Castilian rods . . . ." See "Art of War" (p. 944, note 183). "The rod" (vara) is equal to 2.78209 feet English (Guyot).

[2] Veytia (Lib. III, cap. VI, p. 195). It is superfluous to revert to the erroneous impression that the chiefs might dispose of it.

[3] "Patrimonial Estates" are mentioned frequently, but the point is, where are they to be found? Neither the "teepan-tlalli" nor the "tlatoca-tlalli," still less the "calpulalli," show any trace of individual ownership. "Eredad" (heirloom) is called indiscriminately "milli" and "cuemitl" (Molina, Parte Ia, p. 57). The latter is also rendered as "tierra labrada, ó camellon" (Molina, Parte IIa, p. 26). It thus reminds us of the "chinamitl" or garden-bed (as the name "camellon" also implies), and reduces it to the proportion of an ordinary cultivated lot among the others contained within the area of the calpulli. It is also called "tlalli," but that is the general name for soil or ground. "Tierras o eredades de particulares, juntas en alguna vega," is called "tlalmilli." This decomposes into "tlalli" soil and "milli." But "vega" signifies a fertile tract or field, and thus we have again the conception of communal lands, divided into lots improved by particular families, as the idea of communal tenure necessarily implies.

further growth thereof by converting, as we have seen elsewhere, for the
purpose of defence, their marshy surroundings into water-sheets, through
the construction of extensive causeways.[1] While the remnants of the original 'teepantlalli' and of the 'tlatocatlalli' still remained visible in the gardens, represented to us as purely ornamental, which dotted the pueblo of
Mexico,[2] the substantial elements wherewith to fulfill a purpose for which
they were no longer adequate had, in course of time, to be drawn from the
mainland.   But it was not feasible, from the nature of tribal condition, to
extend thither by colonization.   The soil was held there by other tribes,
whom the Mexicans might well overpower and render tributary, but whom
they could not incorporate, since the kinships composing these tribes could
not be fused with their own.   Outposts, however, were established on the
shores, at the outlets of the dykes, at Tepeyacac on the north, at Iztapalapan, Mexicaltzinco, and at Huitzilopocheo to the south, but these were only
military positions, and beyond them the territory proper of the Mexicans
never extended.[3]   *Tribute*, therefore, had to furnish the means for sustaining
their governmental requirements in the matter of food, and the *tribute lands*
had to be distributed and divided, so as to correspond minutely to the details
of their home organization   For this reason we see, after the overthrow of
the Tecpanecas, lands assigned apparently to the head war-chiefs, to the
military chiefs of the quarters, 'from which to derive some revenue for their
maintenance and that of their children [4] These tracts were but 'official
tracts,' and they were apart from those reserved for the special use of the
kinships.   The latter may have furnished that *general* tribute which, although

---

[1] "Art of War" (pp. 150 and 151). L. H. Morgan ("Ancient Society," Part II, cap. VII, pp. 190
and 191).

[2] Humboldt ("Essai politique sur la Nouvelle Espagne," Vol. II, Lib. III, cap. VIII, p. 50):
Nearly all the old authors describe the public buildings as surrounded by pleasure-grounds or ornamental gardens.   It is very striking that, the pueblo having been founded in 1325, and nearly a century
having been spent in adding sufficient artificial sod to the originally small solid expanse settled, the
Mexicans could have been ready so soon to establish purely decorative parks within an area, every inch
of which was valuable to them for subsistence alone!

[3] The Mexican tribe proper clustered exclusively within the pueblo of Tenuchtitlan. The settlements at Iztapalapan, Huitzilopochco, and Mexicaltzinco were but military stations—outworks, guarding
the issues of the causeways to the South. Tepeyacac (Guadalupe Hidalgo) was a similar position—
unimportant as to population—in the north. Chapultepec was a sacred spot, not inhabited by any number of people, and only held by the Mexicans for burial purposes, and on account of the springs furnishing fresh water to their pueblo.

[4] Tezozomoc (Cap. XV, p. 24).

given nominally to the head war-chief, still was 'for all the Mexicans in common.'

"The various classes of lands which we have mentioned were, as far as their tenure is concerned, included in the 'calpulalli' or lands of the kinships. Since the kin, or 'calpulli,' was the unit of governmental organization, it also was the unit of *landed tenure*. Clavigero says: 'The lands called altepetlalli, that is, those who belonged to the communities of the towns and villages, were divided into as many parts as there were quarters in a town, and each quarter held its own for itself, and without the least connection with the rest. Such lands could in no manner be alienated.'[1] These 'quarters' were the 'calpulli'; hence it follows *that the consanguine groups* held the altepetlalli or *soil of the tribe*.

"We have, therefore, in Mexico the identical mode of the tenure of lands which Polo de Ondogardo had noted in Peru and reported to the King of Spain, as follows: * * * 'Although the crops and other produce of these lands were devoted to the tribute, the land itself belonged to the people themselves. Hence a thing will be apparent which has not hitherto been properly understood. When any one wants land, it is considered sufficient if it can be shown that it belonged to the Inca or to the sun. But in this the Indians are treated with great injustice; for in those days they paid the tribute, and *the land was theirs*.'[2] * * *

"The expanse held and occupied by the calpulli, and therefore called 'calpulalli' was possessed by the kin in *joint* tenure.[3] It could neither be

---

[1] "Storia del Messico" (Lib. VII, cap. XVI).

[2] "Narratives of the Rites and Laws of the Yncas, translated from the original Spanish manuscripts, and edited by Clement R. Markham." Publication of the "Hackluyt Society," 1873. "Report of Polo de Ondegardo," who was "Regidor" of Cuzco in 1560, and a very important authority (see Prescott, "History of the Conquest of Peru," note to Book I, cap. V). Confirmed by Garcia ("El Origen de los Indios," Lib. IV, cap. XVI, p. 162).

[3] Zurita ("Rapport," etc., etc., p. 50): "The chiefs of the second class are yet called calpullec in the singular and chinancallec in the plural. (This is evidently incorrect, since the words 'calpulli' and 'chinancalli' can easily be distinguished from each other. "Chinancalli," however, after Molina means 'cercado de seto' (Parte IIa, p. 21), or an inclosed area, and if we connect it with the old original 'chinamitl' we are forcibly carried back to the early times, when the Mexicans but dwelt on a few flakes of more or less solid ground. This is an additional evidence in favor of the views we have taken of the growth of landed tenure among the Mexican tribe. We must never forget that the term is 'Nahuatl,' and as such recognized by all the other tribes, outside of the Mexicans proper. The interpretation as 'family' in the QQuiché tongue of Guatemala, which we have already mentioned, turns up here as of further importance; th. is chiefs of an old race or family, from the word calpulli or chinancalli, which is the same, and signifies a quarter (barrio), inhabited by a family known, or of old

alienated nor sold ; in fact, there is no trace of barter or sale of land previous to the conquest.[1] If, however, any calpulli weakened, through loss of numbers from any cause whatever, it might farm out its area to another similar group, deriving subsistence from the rent.[2] If the kinship died out, and its lands therefore became vacant, then they were either added to those of another whose share was not adequate for its wants or they were distributed among all the remaining calpulli.'[3] The calpulli was a democratic organization. Its business lay in the hands of elective chiefs—'old men' promoted to that dignity, as we intend to prove in a subsequent paper, for their merits and experience, and after severe religious ordeals. These chiefs formed the council of the kin or quarter, but their authority was not absolute, since on all important occasions a general meeting of the kindred was convened.[4] The council in turn selected an executive, the 'calpullec' or 'chinancallec,' who in war officiated as 'achcacauhtin' or 'teachcauhtin'

---

origin, which possesses since long time a territory whose limits are known, and whose members are of the same lineage." " The calpullis, families or quarters, are very common in each province. Among the lands which were given to the chiefs of the second class there were also calpullis. These lands are the property of the people in general ('de la masse du peuple') from the time the Indians reached this land. Each family or tribe received a portion of the soil for perpetual enjoyment. They also had the name of calpulli, and until now this property has been respected. They do not belong to each inhabitant of the village in particular, but to the calpulli, which possesses them in common." Don Ramirez de Fuenleal, letter dated Mexico, 3 Nov., 1532 ("Recueil de pièces," etc., Ternaux-Compans, p. 253): "There are very few people in the villages which have lands of their own ; *   *   *   the lands are held in common and cultivated in common." Herrera (Dec. III, Lib. IV, cap. XV, p. 135) confirms, in a condensed form, the statements of Zurita, " and they are not private lands of each one, but held in common." Torquemada (Lib. XIV, cap. VII, p. 545.) Veytia (Lib III, cap. VI, p. 196). "Finally, there were other tracts of lands in each tribe, called calpulalli, which is land of the calpules (barrios), which also were worked in common." Oviedo (Lib. XXXII, cap. LI, pp. 536 and 537). Clavigero (Lib. VII, cap. XIV). Bustamante ("Tezcoco," etc., Parte IIIa, cap. V. p. 232).

[1] Zurita (p. 52): "He who obtained them from the sovereign has not the right to dispose of them." Herrera (Dec. III, Lib. IV, cap. XV, p. 135): " He who possessed them could not alienate them, although he enjoyed their use for his lifetime." Torquemada (Lib. XIV, cap. VII, p. 545): "Disputes about lands are frequently mentioned, but they refer to the enjoyment and possession, and not the transfer of the land. Baron Humboldt ("Vues des Cordillères et monuments indigènes des peuples de l'Amérique," Vol. I, Tab. V) reproduces a Mexican painting representing a litigation about land. But this painting was made subsequent to the conquest, as the fact that the parties contending are Indians and Spaniards sufficiently asserts. Occasional mention is made that certain lands "could be sold." All such tracts, however, like the " pallali," have been shown by us to be held in communal tenure of the soil, their *enjoyment* alone being given to individuals and their families.

[2] Zurita (p. 93): "In case of need it was permitted to farm out the lands of a calpulli to the inhabitants of another quarter." Herrera (Dec. III. lib. IV, cap. XV, p. 134): "They could be rented out to another lineage."

[3] Zurita (p. 52): "When a family dies out, its lands revert to the calpulli, and the chief distributes them among such members of the quarter as are most in need of it."

[4] Zurita (pp. 60, 61, 62). Ramirez de Fuenleal ("Letter," etc., Ternaux-Compans, p. 249).

(elder brother).[1]   This office was for life or during good behavior.[2]   It was one of his duties to keep a reckoning of the soil of the calpulli, or ' calpulalli,' together with a record of its members, and of the areas assigned to each family, and to note also whatever changes occurred in their distribution.[3]   Such changes, if unimportant, might be made by him; more important ones, or contested cases, had to be referred to the council of the kinship, which in turn often appealed to a gathering of the entire quarter.[4]

"The ' calpulalli' was divided into lots or arable beds, ' tlalmilli.'[5] These were assigned each to one of the married males of the kinship, to be worked by him for his use and that of his family.   If one of these lots remained unimproved for the term of two consecutive years, it fell back to the quarter for redistribution.   The same occurred if the family enjoying its possession removed from the calpulli.   But it does not appear that the cultivation had always to be performed by the holders of the tract themselves.   The fact of improvement under the *name* of a certain tenant was only required to insure this tenant's rights.[6]

---

[1] Zurita (p. 60): The calpulli have a chief taken necessarily from among the tribe; he must be one of the principal inhabitants, an able man who can assist and defend the people.   The election takes place among them.   *   *   *   The office of this chief is not hereditary; when any one dies, they elect in his place the most respected old man.   *   *   *   If the deceased has left a son who is able the choice falls upon him, and a relative of the former incumbent is always preferred" (Id., pp. 50 and 222). Simancas M. S. S. ("De l'ordre de succession," etc.; "Recueil," p. 225): As to the mode of regulating the jurisdiction and election of the alcaldes and regidors of the villages, they nominated men of note who had the title of achcacaulitin.   *   *   *   There were no other elections of officers."   *   *   *   "Art of War," etc. (pp. 119 and 120).

[2] Zurita (pp. 60 and 61).   Herrera (Dec. III, Lib. IV, cap. XV, cap. 125): "I le elegian entre si y tenian por maior."

[3] Zurita (pp. 61 and 62): "This chief has charge of the lands of the calpulli.   It is his duty to defend their possession.   He keeps paintings showing the tracts, the names of their holders, the situation, the limits, the number of men tilling them, the wealth of private individuals, the designations of such as are vacant, of others that belong to the Spaniards, the date of donation, to whom and by whom they were given.   These paintings he constantly renews, according to the changes occurring, and in this they are very skillful."   It is singular that Motolinia, in his "Epistola proémial" ("Col. de Doc."; Icazbalceta, Vol. I, p. 5), among the five "books of paintings" which he says the Mexicans had, makes no mention of the above.   Neither does he notice it in his letter dated Cholula, 27 Aug., 1554 ("Recueil de pièces," etc., Ternaux-Compans).

[4] Zurita "Rapport," etc., pp. 56 and 62).   We quote him in preference, since no other author known to us has been so detailed.

[5] "Tlalmilli" "tierras, ú heredades de particulares, que estan juntas en alguna vega" (Molina, Part II a, p. 124).

[6] Each family, represented by its male head, obtained a certain tract or lot for cultivation and use, Zurita (p. 55).   "The party (member of the calpulli, because no member of another one had the right to settle within the area of it—see Id., p. 53), who has no lands applies to the chief of the calpulli, who, upon the advice of the other old men, assigns to him such as corresponds to his ability and wants.   These lands go to his heirs."   *   *   *   Id., p. 56).   "The proprietor who did not cultivate during two years, either through his own fault or through negligence, without just cause,   *   *   *   he

"Therefore the chiefs and their families, although they could not, from the nature of their duties, till the land themselves, still could remain entitled to their share of 'tlalmilpa' as members of the calpulli. Such tracts were cultivated by others for their use. They were called by the specific name of 'pillali' (lands of the chiefs or of the children, from 'piltontli,' boy, or 'piltzintli,' child), and those who cultivated them carried the appellation of 'tlalmaitl'—hands of the soil.[1]

"The 'tlalmilpa,' whether held by chiefs or by ordinary members of the kin ('macehuales'), were, therefore, the only tracts of land possessed for use by individuals in ancient Mexico. They were so far distinguished from the 'tecpantlalli' and 'tlatocatlalli' in their mode of tenure as, whereas the latter two were dependent from a certain office, the incumbent of which changed at each election, the 'tlalmilli' was assigned to a certain family, and its possession, therefore, connected with *customs* of *inheritance*.

"Being thus led to investigate the customs of Inheritance of the ancient Mexicans, we have to premise here, that the personal effects of a deceased can be but slightly considered. The rule was, in general, that whatever a man held descended to his offspring.[2] Among most of the

---

was called upon to improve them, and if he failed to do so they were given to another the following year." Bustamante (Tezcoco, etc., Parte IIIa, p. 190, cap I): "The fact that any holder of a 'tlalmilli' might *rent* out his share, if he himself was occupied in a line precluding him from actual work on it, results from the lands of the 'calpulli' being represented alternately treated as communal and again as private lands. Besides, it is said of the traders who, from the nature of their occupation, were mostly absent, that they were also members and participants of a 'calpulli' (Zurita, p. 223. Sahagun, Lib. VIII, cap III, p. 349): "Now, as every Mexican belonged to a kinship, which held lands after the plan exposed above, it follows that such as were not able to work themselves, on account of their performing other duties subservient to the interests of the community, still preserved their tracts by having others to work them for their benefit. It was not the right of tenancy which authorizes the improvement, but the fact of improvem ent for a certain purpose and benefit, which secured the possession or tenancy."

[1] From "tlalli" soil, and "maitl' hand. Hands of the soil. Molina (Parte IIa, p. 124) has: "tlalmaitl"—"labrador, ò gañan." This name is given in distinction of the "macehuales" or people working the soil in general. The tlalmàites are identical with the "mayeques." (See Zurita, p. 224): "tlalmaites or mayeques, which signifies tillers of the soil of others." * * * He distinguishes them plainly from the "teccallec," which are the "tecpanpouhque" or "tecpantlaca" formerly mentioned as attending to a class of official lands (p. 221, Zurita). Herrera (Dec. III, Lib. IV, cap. XVII, p. 138): "These mayeques could not go from one tract to another, neither leave those which they cultivated, and they paid a rent to its masters according as they agreed upon ('en lo que se concertaban') in what they raised. They paid tribute to nobody else but the master of the land." This tends to show that there existed not an established obligation, a serfdom, but a voluntary contract, that the "tlalmaites' were not serfs, but simply renters.

[2] Motolinia (Tratado II, cap. V, p. 120): "But they left their houses and lands to their children . . ." Gomara (p. 434): "Es costumbre de pecheros que el hijo mayor herede al padre en toda la hacienda raiz y mueble, y que tenga y mantenga todos los hermanos y sobrinos, con tal que hagan

northern Indians a large cluster participated.[1] In conformity with the organization of society based upon kin, when in the first stage of its development, the kindred group inherited, and the common ancestor of this kin being considered a female, it follows that if a man died, not his children, still less his wife, but his mother's descendants, that is, his brothers, sisters, in fact the entire consanguine relationship from which he derived on his mother's side, were his heirs.[2] Such may have been the case even among the Muysca of New Granada.[3] It was different, however, in Mexico, where we meet with traces of a decided progress. Not only had descent been changed to the male line,[4] but heirship was limited, to the exclusion of the kin and of the agnates themselves, to the children of the male sex.[5] Whatever personal effects a father left, which were not offered up in sacrifice at the ceremonies of his funeral,[6] they were distributed among his male off-

ellos lo que el les mandare." Clavigero (Lib. VII, cap. XIII) : "In Mexico, and nearly the entire realm, the royal family excepted as already told, the sons succeeded to the father's rights; and if there were no sons, then the brothers, and the brothers' sons inherited." Bustamante ("Tezcoco," etc., p. 219) : In all these cases, Bustamante only speaks of chiefs; but the quotations from Motolinia and Gomara directly apply to the people in general.

[1] Mr. L. H. Morgan has investigated the customs of inheritance, not only among the northern Indians, but also among the pueblo Indians of New Mexico. He establishes the fact, that the "kinship" or "gens," which we may justly consider as the unit of organization in American aboriginal society, participated in the property of the deceased. He proves it among the Iroquois ("Ancient Society," Part II, cap. II, pp. 75 and 76). Wyandottes, Id., cap. VII, p. 153. Missouri-tribes, p. 155. Winnebagoes, p. 157. Mandans, p. 158. Minnitarees, p. 159. Creeks, p. 161. Choctas, p. 162. Chickasas, p. 163. Ojibwas, p. 167; also Potowattomies and Crees, Miamis, p. 168. Shawnees, p. 169. Sauks, Foxes, and Menominies, p. 170. Delawares, p. 172. Munsees and Mohegans, p. 173. Finally, the pueblo Indians of New Mexico are shown to have, if not the identical at least a similar mode of inheritance. It would be easy to secure further evidence, from South America also.

[2] "Ancient Society" (Part II, cap. II, p. 75; Part IV, cap. I, pp. 528, 530, 531, 536, and 537).

[3] Gomara ("Historia de las Indios," Vedia I, p. 201). Garcia ("Origen de los Indios," Lib. IV, cap. 23, p. 247). Piedrahita (Parte 1, Lib. I, cap. 5, p. 27). Joaquin Acosta ("Compendio historico del Descumbrimiento y Colonisazion de la Nueva-Granada," Cap. XI, p. 201). Ternaux-Compans ("L'ancien Cundinamarca," pp. 21 and 38).

[4] Motolinia (Trat. II, cap. V, p. 120). Gomara (p. 434). Clavigero (Lib. VII, cap. XIII). Zurita (pp. 12 and 43).

[5] Letter of Motolinia and Diego d'Olarte, to Don Luis de Velasco, Cholula, 27 Aug., 1554 ("Recueil," etc., etc., p. 407): "The daughters did not inherit; it was the principal, wife's son . . . ." Besides, nearly every author designates but a son, or sons, as the heirs. There is no mention made of daughters at all. In Tlaxcallan, it is expressly mentioned that the daughters did not inherit (Torquemada, Lib. XI, cap. XXII, p. 348). In general, the position of woman in ancient Mexico was a very inferior one, and but little above that which it occupies among Indians in general. (Compare the description of Gomara, p. 440, Vedia I, with those of Sahagun. Lib. X, cap. I, p. 1; cap. XIII, pp. 30, 31, 32, and 33. The fact is generally conceded). H. H. Bancroft, "Native Races," Vol. II, cap. VI, p. 224, etc.

[6] Motolinia (Trat. II, cap. V, p. 120). Torquemada (Lib. XIII, cap. XLII to XLVIII, pp. 515 to 529). Acosta (Lib. V, cap. VIII, pp. 320, 321, and 322). Gomara (pp. 436 and 437, Vedia, I). Mendieta (Lib. II, cap. XL, pp. 162 and 163). Clavigero (Lib. VI, cap. XXXIX). "They burnt the clothes, arrows, and a portion of the household utensils . . . . "

springs, and if there were none, they went to his brothers. Females held nothing whatever, beyond their wearing apparel and some few ornaments for personal use.

"The 'tlalmilli' itself, at the demise of a father, went to his oldest son, with the obligation to improve it for the benefit of the entire family until the other children had been disposed of by marriage [1] But the other males could apply to the chief of the calpulli for a 'tlalmilli' of their own;[2] the females went with their husbands. Single blessedness, among the Mexicans, appears to have occurred only in case of religious vows, and in which case they fell back for subsistence upon the part allotted to worship, or in case of great infirmities, for which the calpulli provided.[3] No mention is made of the widow participating in the products of the 'tlalmilli,' still it is presumable that she was one of those whom the oldest son had to support. There are indications that the widow could remarry, in which case her husband, of course, provided for her.

"The customs of Inheritance, as above reported, were the same with chiefs as well as with the ordinary members of the tribe. Of the personal effects very little remained, since the higher the office was which the deceased had held, the more display was made at his cremation, and consequently the more of his dresses, weapons, and ornaments were burnt with the body. Of lands, the chiefs only held each their 'tlalmilli' in the usual way, as members of their kin, whereas the other 'official' lots went to the new incumbents of the offices. It should always be borne in mind that none of these offices were hereditary themselves. Still, a certain 'right of succession' is generally admitted as having existed. Thus, with the Tezcucans, the office of head war-chief might pass from father to son,[4] at Mexico from

---

[1] Gomara ("Conq. de Mèjico, p. 434): "It is customary among tributary classes that the oldest son shall inherit the father's property, real and personal, and shall maintain and support all the brothers and nephews, provided they do what he commands them. The reason why they do not partition the estates is in order not to decrease it through such a partition . . . . " Simancas M. S. S. ("Recueil," etc., etc., p. 224): "Relative to the calpulalli . . . . the sons mostly inherited."

[2] Zurita (p. 55): "He who has no land applies to the chief of the tribe (calpulli), who, upon the advice of the other old men, assigns to him a tract suitable for his wants, and corresponding to his abilities and to his strength." Herrera (Dec. III, Lib. IV, cap. XV, p. 135).

[3] Such unmarried females were the "nuns" frequently mentioned by the old writers. We shall have occasion to investigate the point in our paper on "The ancient Mexican priesthood." As attendants to worship, they participated in the tributes furnished towards it by each calpulli, of which we have spoken.

[4] Zurita (p. 12). Gomara (Vedia I, p. 434). Torquemada (Lib. IX, cap. IV, p. 177; Lib. XI, cap. 27, p. 356, etc. etc.).

brother to brother, and from uncle to nephew.[1] This might, eventually, have tended to *perpetuate* the office in the *family*, and with it also the possession of certain lands, attached to that officer's functions and duties. But it is quite certain too that this stage of development had not yet been reached by any of the tribes of Mexico at the time of its conquest by the Spaniards. The principal idea had not yet been developed, namely, that of the *domain*, which, in eastern countries at least, gradually segregated into individually hereditary tenures and ownerships.

"Out of the scanty remains thus left of certain features of aboriginal life in ancient Mexico, as well as out of the conflicting statements about that country's early history, we have now attempted to reconstruct the conceptions of the Mexican aborigines about tenure of lands, as well as their manner of distribution thereof. Our inquiries seem to justify the following conclusions:

"1. The notion of abstract ownership of the soil, either by a nation or state, or by the head of its government, or by individuals, was unknown to the ancient Mexicans.

"2. Definite possessory right was vested in the kinships composing the tribe; but the idea of sale, barter, or conveyance or alienation of such by the kin had not been conceived.

"3. Individuals, whatever might be their position or office, without any exception, held but the right to use certain defined lots for their sustenance, which right, although hereditary in the male line, was nevertheless limited to the conditions of residence within the area held by the kin, and of cultivation either by or in the name of him to whom the said lots were assigned.

"4. No possessory rights to land were attached to any office or chieftaincy. As members of a kin, each chief had the use of a certain lot, which he could rent or farm to others, for his benefit.

"5. For the requirements of tribal business, and of the governmental features of the kinships (public hospitality included), certain tracts were set apart as official lands, out of which the official households were supplied and sustained; but these lands and their products were totally independent from the persons or families of the chiefs themselves.

---

[1] This fact is too amply proven to need special references. We reserve it for final discussion in our proposed paper on the chiefs of the Mexicans, and the duties, powers and functions of their office.

"6. Conquest of any tribe by the Mexicans was not followed by an annexation of that tribe's territory, nor by an apportionment of its soil among the conquerors. Tribute was exacted, and, for the purpose of raising that tribute (in part), special tracts were set off; the crops of which were gathered for the storehouses of Mexico.

"7. Consequently, as our previous investigations (of the warlike institutions and customs of the ancient Mexicans) have disproved the generally received notion of a military despotism prevailing among them, so the results of his review of Tenure and distribution of lands tend to establish 'that the principle and institution of feudality did not exist in aboriginal Mexico.'"

Among the Peruvians their land system was probably much the same as among the ancient Mexicans. But according to Garcilapo de la Vega, they had carried their system with respect to lands a little farther. Their lands, he remarks, were "divided into three parts and applied to different uses. The first was for the Sun, his priests and ministers; the second was for the King, and for the support and maintenance of his governors and officers. * * * And the third was for the natives and sojourners of the provinces, which was divided equally according to the needs which each family required."[1]

While these several statements may not present the exact case in all respects in Peru, Mexico, or among the Northern Indian tribes, they sufficiently indicate the ownership of land by communities of persons, larger or smaller, with a system of tillage that points to large households. Neither the Peruvians, nor the Aztecs, nor any Indian tribe had attained to a knowledge of the ownership of land in severalty in fee simple at the period of their discovery. This knowledge belongs to the period of civilization. There is not the slightest probability that any Indian, whether Iroquois, Mexican, or Peruvian, owned a foot of land that he could call his own, with power to sell and convey the same in fee simple to whomsoever he pleased.

---

[1] Royal Commentaries of Peru, Lond. ed., 1688. Rycaut, trans., p. 154.

THE CUSTOM OF HAVING BUT ONE PREPARED MEAL EACH DAY—A DINNER—AND THEIR SEPARATION AT MEALS, THE MEN EATING FIRST, AND THE WOMEN AND CHILDREN AFTERWARDS.

This was the usage among the Indian tribes in the Lower Status of barbarism. In the Middle Status there seems to have been more method and regularity of life, but no change in their customs with respect to food, so marked in character that we are forced to recognize a new plan of domestic life among them. The Iroquois had but one cooked meal each day. It was as much as their resources and organization for housekeeping could furnish, and was as much as they needed. It was prepared and served usually before the noon-day hour, ten or eleven o'clock, and may be called a dinner. At this time the principal cooking for the day was done. After its division at the kettle, among the members of the household, it was served warm to each person in earthen or wooden bowls. They had neither tables, nor chairs, nor plates, in our sense, nor any room in the nature of a kitchen or a dining room, but ate each by himself, sitting or standing, and where most convenient to the person. They also separated as to the time of eating, the men eating first and by themselves, and the women and children afterwards and by themselves. That which remained was reserved for any member of the household when hungry. Towards evening the women cooked hominy, the maize having been pounded into bits the size of a kernel of rice, which was boiled and put aside to be used cold as a lunch in the morning or evening, and for the entertainment of visitors. They had neither a formal breakfast nor a supper Each person, when hungry, ate of whatever food the house contained. They were moderate eaters. This is a fair picture of Indian life in general in America, when discovered. After intercourse commenced with whites, the Iroquois gradually began to adopt our mode of life, but very slowly. One of the difficulties was to change the old usage and accustom themselves to eat together. It came in by degrees, first with the breaking up of the old plan of living together in numbers in the old long-houses, and with the substitution of single houses for each family, which ended communism and living in the large household, and substituted the subsistence of a single family through individual effort. After many years came the use of the table and chairs among the more advanced families of the Iroquois tribes. There are still upon the Iroquois reservations in this State many log houses or cabins with but a single room on the ground floor, and a loft above, with neither a table or chair in their scanty furniture. A portion of them still live very much in the old style, with perhaps two regular meals daily instead of one. That they have made this much of change in the course of two centuries must be accounted remarkable, for they have been compelled, so to speak, to jump one entire ethnical period, without the experience or training of so many intervening generations, and without the brain-growth such a change of the plan of domestic life implies, when reached through natural individual experience There is a tradition still current among the Seneca-Iroquois, if the memory of so recent an occurrence may be called traditional, that when the proposition that man and wife should eat together, which was so contrary to immemorial usage, was first determined in the affirmative, it was formally agreed that man and wife should sit down together at the same dish and eat with the same ladle, the man eating first and then the woman, and so alternately until the meal was finished.

The testimony of such writers as have noticed the house-life of the Indian tribes is not uniform in respect to the number of meals a day. Thus Catlin remarks, "As I have before observed, these men (the Mandans) generally eat but twice a day, and many times not more than once, and these meals are light and simple * * * The North American Indians, taking them in the aggregate, even when they have an abundance to subsist on, eat less than any civilized population of equal numbers that I have ever travelled among."[1] And Heckewelder, speaking of the Delawares and other tribes, says: "They commonly make two meals every day, which they say is enough. If any one should feel hungry between meal-times, there is generally something in the house ready for him.[2] Adair contents himself with stating of the Chocta and Cherokee tribes that "they have no stated meal time."[3] There was doubtless some variation in different localities, and even in the same household; but as a general rule, from what is known of

---

[1] North American Indians, Philadelphia ed., 1857, i, 203.
[2] Indian Nations, 193.
[3] History of the American Indian, Lond. ed., 1775, p. 17.

their mode of life, one prepared meal each day expresses very nearly all the people in this condition of society can do for the sustenance of mankind.

Although the sedentary Village Indians were one ethnical period in advance of the Northern Indians, there can be but little doubt that their mode of life in this respect was substantially the same. Among the Aztecs or ancient Mexicans a dinner was provided about midday, but we have no satisfactory account of a breakfast or a supper habitually and regularly prepared. Civilization, with its diversified industries, its multiplied products, and its monogamian family, affords a breakfast and supper in addition to a dinner. It is doubtful whether they are older than civilization; and even if they can be definitely traced backward into the older period of barbarism, there is little probability of their being found in the Middle period. Clavigero attempts to invest the Aztecs with a breakfast, but he was unable to find any evidence of a supper. "After a few hours of labor in the morning," he observes, "they took their breakfast, which was most commonly *atolli*, a gruel of maize, and their dinner after midday; but among all the historians we can find no mention of their supper."[1] The "gruel of maize" here mentioned as forming usually the Aztec breakfast suggests the "hominy of the Iroquois," which, like it, was not unlikely kept constantly prepared in every Mexican house as a lunch for the hungry. Two meals each day are mentioned by other Spanish authors, but as the Aztecs, as well as the tribes in Yucatan and Central America, were ignorant of the use of tables and chairs in eating their food, divided their food from the kettle, placing the dinner of each person usually in a separate bowl, and separated at their meals, the men eating first and by themselves, and the women and children afterwards, this similarity of usage renders it probable they were not far removed from the Iroquois in respect to the time and manner of taking their food. Montezuma's dinner, witnessed by Bernal-Diaz and others, and elaborately described by a number of authors, shows that the Aztecs had a smoking hot dinner each day, prepared regularly, and on a scale adequate to a large household; that the dinner of each person was placed in one bowl, and all these bowls to the number of several hundred were brought in and set down together upon the floor of one room,

---

[1] History of Mexico, ii, 262.

where they were taken up one by one by the male members of the household, and the contents eaten sitting down upon the floor or standing in the open court, as best suited them. The breakfast that preceded it, and the supper that follows, are not mentioned, from which we infer that there was neither a breakfast nor a supper for these inquisitive observers to see. Neither is the subsequent dinner of the women and children of the household mentioned, from which it may be inferred that as the men ate their dinner first in a particular hall by themselves, the women and children took their dinner later in another hall, not seen by the Spaniards.

In the accounts of Montezuma's dinner a cook-house or kitchen is mentioned, in which the dinner for the large household of the "Tecpan" or "official house," so fully explained above by Mr. Bandelier, was prepared. This kitchen, and the use of another room, where the bowls containing the dinner of each person separately were set down on the floor in a mass by themselves—an incipient dining-room—make their first appearance in the Middle Status of barbarism. But, as will be noticed, they are but rude realizations of the kitchen and dining-room of civilized man. The pueblo houses in Yucatan and Chiapas, now in ruins, are without chimneys, from which it may be inferred that no cooking was done within them. At Uxmal we recognize in the Governor's House the Tecpan or official-house, and in the House of the Nuns, and other structures which formed the pueblo, the joint-tenement houses in which the body of the tribe resided. If the truth of the matter is ever ascertained, it will probably be found that the dinner for each household group, consisting of several families, was prepared in a common cook-house outside of the main structure, and that it was divided at the kettle to the individuals of each household.

The separation of the sexes at their meals has been sufficiently referred to among the Iroquois. Robertson states the usage as general: "They must approach their lords with reverence; they must regard them as more exalted beings, and are not permitted to eat in their presence"[1] Catlin the same: "These women, however, although graceful and civil, and ever so beautiful, or ever so hungry, are not allowed to sit in the same group with the men while at their meals. So far as I have yet travelled in the

---

[1] History of America, New York ed., 1856, 178.

Indian country, I have never seen an Indian woman eating with her husband. Men form the first group at the banquet, and women and children and dogs all come together at the next."[1]   And Adair "for the men feast by themselves and the women eat the remains."[2]   Herrera remarks that "the woman of Yucatan are rather larger than the Spanish, and generally have good faces, * * * but they would formerly be drunk at their festivals, though they did eat apart"[3]   And Sahagun, speaking of the ceremony of baptism among the Aztecs, observes that "to the women, who ate apart, they did not give cacao to drink."[4]   With these general references to the universality of the practice on the part of the men of eating first, and leaving the women and children to come afterwards, according to the manners of barbarism, we leave the subject.

---

[1] North American Indians, i, 202.   [2] History of the American Indians, p. 140.
[3] History of America, iv, 175.   [4] Historia General, lib. iv, 36.

CHAPTER V.

The growth of the idea of house architecture in general is a subject more comprehensive than the scope of this volume. But there is one phase of this growth, illustrating as it does the condition of society and of the family in savagery and in barbarism, to which attention will be invited. It is found in the domestic architecture of the American aborigines, considered as a whole, and as parts of one system. As a system it stands related to the institutions, usages, and customs presented in the previous chapters. There is not only abundant evidence in the collective architecture of the Indian tribes of the gradual development of this great faculty or aptitude of the human mind among them, through three ethnical periods, but the structures themselves, or a knowledge of them, remain for comparison with each other. A comparison will show that they belong to a common indigenous system of architecture. There is a common principle running through all this architecture, from the hut of the savage to the commodious joint-tenement house of the Village Indians of Mexico and Central America, which will contribute to its elucidation.

The indigenous architecture of the Village Indians has given to them, more than aught else, their position in the estimation of mankind. The facts of their social condition in other respects, which, unfortunately, are obscure, have been much less instrumental in fixing their status than existing architectural remains. The Indian edifices in Mexico and Central America of the period of the Conquest may well excite surprise and even admiration; from their palatial extent, from the material used in their construction, and from the character of their ornamentation, they are highly creditable to their skill in architecture. But a false interpretation has, from the first, been put upon this architecture, as I think can be shown, and

104

inferences with respect to the social condition and the degree of advancement of these tribes have been constantly drawn from it both fallacious and deceptive, when the plain truth would have been more creditable to the aborigines. It will be my object to give an interpretation of this architecture in harmony with the usages and customs of the Indian tribes. The houses of the different tribes, in ground-plan and mechanism, will be considered and compared, in order to show wherein they represent one system.

A common principle, as before stated, runs through all this architecture, from the "long-house" of the Iroquois to the "pueblo houses" of New Mexico, and to the so-called "palace" at Palenque, and the "House of the Nuns" at Uxmal. It is the principle of adaptation to *communism in living*, restricted in the first instance to household groups, and extended finally to all the inhabitants of a village or encampment by *the law of hospitality*. Hunger and destitution were not known at one end of an Indian village while abundance prevailed at the other. Joint-tenement houses, each occupied by one large household, as among the Iroquois, or by several household groups, as in Yucatan, were the natural and inevitable result of their usages and customs. Communism in living and the law of hospitality, it seems probable, accompanied all the phases of Indian life in savagery and in barbarism. These and other facts of their social condition embodied themselves in their architecture, and will contribute to its elucidation.

The house architecture of the Northern tribes is of little importance, in itself considered; but, as an outcome of their social condition and for comparison with that of the Southern Village Indians, it is highly important. An attempt will be made to show, firstly, that the known communism in living of the former tribes entered into and determined the character of their houses, which are communal; and, secondly, that wherever the structures of the latter class are obviously communal, the practice of communism in living at the period of discovery may be inferred from the structures themselves, although many of them are now in ruins, and the people who constructed them have disappeared. Some evidence, however, of the communism of the Village Indians has been presented.

COMMUNAL HOUSES OF TRIBES IN SAVAGERY.

Mr. Stephen Powers, in his recent and instructive work on the " California Tribes,"[1] enumerates seven varieties of the lodge constructed by these tribes, adapted to the different climates of the State. One form was adapted to the raw and foggy climate of the California coast, constructed of redwood poles over an excavated pit; another to the snow-belt of the Coast Range and of the Sierras; another to the high ranges of the Sierras; another to the warm coast valleys; another, limited to a small area, constructed of interlaced willow poles, the interstices being open; another to the woodless plains of the Sacramento and the San Joaquin, dome-shaped and covered with earth; and another to the hot and nearly rainless region of the Kern and Tulare valleys, made of tule. Four of these varieties are given below, the illustrations being taken from his work.

"In making a wigwam, they excavated about two feet, banked up the earth enough to keep out the water, and threw the remainder on the roof dome-shaped. With the Lolsel the bride often remains in the father's house, and her husband comes to live with her, whereupon half the purchase money is returned. Thus there will be two or three families in one lodge. They are very clannish, especially the mountain tribes, and family influence is all potent."[2] Elsewhere he remarks upon this form of house as follows: " On the great woodless plains of the Sacramento and San Joaquin, the savages naturally had recourse to earth for a material. The round, domed-shaped, earth-covered lodge is considered the characteristic one of California ; and probably two-thirds of its immense aboriginal population lived in dwellings of this description. The doorway is sometimes directly on top, sometimes on the ground, at one side. I have never been able to ascertain whether the amount of rain-fall of any given locality had any influence in determining the place of the door."[3] This mode of entrance reappears in the more artistic house of the Pueblo Indians of New Mexico, where the rooms are entered by means of a trap-door in the roof, the de-

---

[1] Powell's Geographical Survey, &c., of the Rocky Mountain Region, Contributions to American Ethnology, vol. iii, Powers' Tribes of California, p. 436.

[2] Ib., p. 221.

[3] Ib., p. 437.

FIG. 1.—Earth Lodges in the Sacramento Valley.

FIG. 2.—Gallinomero Thatched Lodge.

scent being made by a ladder, The "immense aboriginal population" of California, claimed by Mr. Powers, is too strong a statement.

"This wigwam is in the shape of the capital letter L, made up of slats leaning up to a ridge-pole and heavily thatched. All along the middle of it the different families or generations have their fires, while they sleep next the walls, lying on the ground, underneath rabbit-skins and other less elegant robes, and amid a filthy cluster of baskets, dogs, and all the wretched trumpery dear to the aboriginal heart. There are three narrow holes for dens, one at either end and one at the elbow."[1] This is Mr. Powers' fifth variety of the lodge.

"In the very highest region of Sierra, where the snow falls to such an enormous depth that the fire would be blotted out and the whole open side snowed up, the dwelling retains substantially the same form and materials, but the fire is taken into the middle of it, and one side of it (generally the east one) slopes down more nearly horizontal than the other, and terminates in a curved way about three feet high and twice as long."[3] Half a dozen such houses make an Indian village, with the addition of a "dome-shaped assembly or dance house" in the middle space. "One or more acorn-granaries of wicker-work stand around each lodge, much like hogsheads in shape and size, either on the ground or mounted on posts as high as one's head, full of acorns and capped with thatch."[1]

In Southern California, where the climate is both dry and hot, the natives constructed a wigwam entirely different from those found in other parts of the State. "In the Yokut nation," Mr. Powers remarks, "there appears to be more political solidarity, more capacity in the petty tribes of being grouped into large and coherent masses than is common in the State. This is particularly true of those living on the plains, who display in their encampments a military precision and regularity which are remarkable. Every village consists of a single row of wigwams, conical or wedge-shaped, generally made of tule, and just enough hollowed out within so that the inmates may sleep with the head higher than the feet, all in perfect alignment, and with a continuous awning of brushwood stretching along in front. In one end-wigwam lives the village captain; on the other the

---

[1] Powers' Tribes of Cal., p. 284.

shaman or *si-se'-ro*. In the mountains there is some approach to this mar-
tial array, but it is universal on the plains."[1]

As a rule these houses were occupied by more families than one, as is
shown by the same author. In the northern part of the State "the Tatu
wigwams do not differ essentially from those of the vicinal tribes. They
are constructed of stout willow wicker-work, dome-shaped, and thatched
with grass. Sometimes they are very large and oblong, with sleeping-room
for thirty or forty persons."[2] The Yo-kai'-a inhabit a section of the northwest part of the State. "Their style of lodge is the same which prevails
generally along Russian River, a huge frame-work of willow poles covered
with thatch, and resembling a large flattish haystack. Though still pre-
serving the same style and materials, since they have adopted from the
Americans the use of boards they have learned to construct all around the
wall of the wigwam a series of little state rooms, if I may so call them,
which are snugly boarded up and furnished with bunks inside. This enables
every family in these immense patriarchal lodges to disrobe and retire with
some regard to decency, which could not be done in the one common room
of the old-style wigwam."[3] Again: "The *Se-nel*, together with three other
petty tribes, mere villages, occupy that broad expanse of Russian River
Valley on one side of which now stands the American village of Senel.
Among them we find unmistakably developed that patriarchal system which
appears to prevail all along Russian River. They construct immense dome-
shaped or oblong lodges of willow poles an inch or two in diameter, woven
in square lattice-work, securely lashed and thatched.   In each one of these
live several families, sometimes twenty or thirty persons, including all who
are blood relations.   Each wigwam, therefore, is a *pueblo*, a law unto itself;
and yet these lodges are grouped in villages, some of which formerly contained hundreds of inhabitants.[4] I cannot find that Mr. Powers mentions
the practice of communism in these households, but the fact seems probable.
Their usages in the matter of hospitality are much the same as in the other
tribes. Their principal food was salmon, acorn-flour bread, game, kamas,
and berries. They were, without pottery, cooked in ground ovens, and
also in water-tight baskets by means of heated stones.

---

[1] Powers' Tribes of Cal., p. 370.   [2] Ib., p. 139.   [3] Ib., p. 163.   [4] Ib., p. 168.

FIG. 3. Maidu Lodge in the High Sierra.

Fig. 4.—Yókuts Tule Lodges.

A brief reference may be made to the skin lodge of the Kŭtchĭn or Louchoux of the Yukon and Peel Rivers.

This simple structure, the ground plan and elevation of which were taken from the Smithsonian Report,[1] is thus described by Mr. Strachan

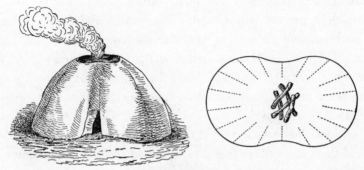

FIG. 5.—Kŭtchĭn Lodge.

Jones: " Deer-skins are dressed with the hair on, and sewed together, forming two large rolls, which are stretched over a frame of bent poles. The lodge is nearly elliptical, about twelve or thirteen feet in diameter and six feet high, very similar to a tea-cup turned over. The door is about four feet high, and is simply a deer-skin fastened above and hanging down. The hole to allow the smoke to escape is about four feet in diameter. Snow is heaped up outside the edges of the lodge and pine brush spread on the ground inside, the snow having been previously shoveled off with snow-shoes. The fire is made in the middle of the lodge, and one or more families, as the case may be, live on each side of the fire, every one having his or her particular place."[2] He further remarks that "they have no pottery," and that they boil water " by means of stones heated red hot and thrown into the kettle."[3] The principal fact to be noticed is that the lodge is comparted into stalls open on the central space, in the midst of which is the fire-pit, evidently for the accommodation of more families than one. This arrangement of the interior will reappear in numerous other cases. The Kŭtchĭn must be classed as savages, although near the close of that condition.

---

[1] Report for 1866, p. 321.   [2] Ib., p. 322.   [3] Ib., p. 321.

The tribes of the valley of the Columbia lived more or less in villages, but, like the tribes of California, were without horticulture and without pottery. But they found an abundant subsistence in the shell-fish of the coast, and in the myriads of fish in the Columbia and its tributaries. They also subsisted upon kamash and other bread roots of the prairies, which they cooked in ground ovens, and upon berries and game. They were expert boatmen and fishermen, manufactured water-tight baskets, implements of wood, stone, and bone, and used the bow and arrow. As another quite remarkable fact, they used plank in their houses, made by splitting logs with stone and elk-horn chisels. Like the Kŭtchĭn, they were in the Upper Status of savagery.

When Lewis and Clarke visited the Columbia River district (1805–1806) they found the Indian tribes living in houses of the plainest communal type, and some of them approaching in ground dimensions and in the number of their occupants the pueblo houses in New Mexico. They speak of a house of the Chopunish (Nez Percés) as follows: "This village of Tumachemootool is in fact only a single house one hundred and fifty feet long, built after the Chopunish fashion, with sticks, straw and dried grass. It contains twenty-four fires, about double that number of families, and might perhaps muster a hundred fighting men."[1] This would give five hundred people in a single house. The number of fires probably indicates the number of groups practicing communism in living among themselves, though for aught we know it may have been general in the entire household.

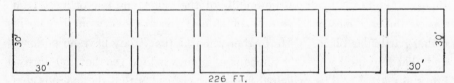

30'   30'
30'   226 FT.   30'

FIG. 6—Ground-plan of Ncerchokioo.

Another great house, Ncerchokioo, is thus described: "This large building is two hundred and twenty-six feet in front, entirely above ground, and may be considered a single house, because the whole is under one roof, otherwise it would seem more like a range of buildings, as it is divided into

---

[1] Travels, etc., l. c., p. 548.

seven distinct apartments, each thirty feet square, by means of broad boards set up on end from the floor to the roof. The apartments are separated from each other by a passage or alley four feet wide, extending through the whole depth of the house, and the only entrance is from the alley through a small hole about twenty inches wide and not more than three feet high. The roof is formed of rafters and round poles laid on horizontally. The whole is covered with a double roof of bark of white cedar."[1] The apartments, as in the previous case of the fires, may be supposed to indicate the number of groups into which the great household was subdivided for the practice of communism.

Elsewhere, speaking of the houses of the Clahclellahs, they remark: "These houses are uncommonly large; one of them measured one hundred and sixty by forty feet, and the frames are constructed in the usual manner. * * * Most of the houses are built of boards and covered with bark, though some of the more inferior kind are constructed wholly of cedar bark, kept smooth and flat by small splinters fixed crosswise through the bark, at the distance of twelve or fourteen inches apart."[2]

The houses of the coast tribes (Clatsops and Chinooks) are also described. "The houses in this neighborhood are all large wooden buildings, ranging in length from twenty to sixty feet, and from fourteen to twenty in width. They are constructed in the following manner: two posts of split timber or more, agreeable to the number of partitions, are sunk in the ground, above which they rise to the height of fourteen or eighteen feet. They are hollowed at the top, so as to receive the end of a round beam or pole (ridge-pole) stretching from one to the other, and forming the upper point of the roof for the whole extent of the building. On each side of this range is placed another, which forms the eaves of the house, and is about five feet high; and as the building is often sunk to the depth of four or five feet, the eaves come very near the surface of the earth. Smaller pieces of timber are now extended by pairs, in the form of rafters, from the lower to the upper beams, where they are attached at both ends with cords of cedar bark. On these rafters two or three ranges of small poles are placed horizontally, and secured in the same way with strings of cedar bark. The

---

[1] Lewis and Clarke's Travels, p. 503.   [2] Ib., p. 515.

sides are now made, with a range of white boards, sunk a small distance into the ground, with upper ends projecting above the poles at the eaves. * * * The gable end and partitions are formed in the same way. * * * The roof is then covered with a double range of thin boards, except an aperture of two or three feet in the center, for the smoke to pass through. The entrance is by a small hole, cut out of the boards, and just large enough to admit the body. The very largest houses only are divided by partitions, for though three or four families reside in the same room, there is quite space enough for all of them. In the center of each room is a space six or eight feet square, sunk to the depth of twelve inches below the rest of the floor, and inclosed by four pieces of square timber. Here they make the fire, for which purpose pine bark is generally preferred. Around the fireplace mats are placed, and serve as seats during the day, and very frequently as beds at night. There is, however, a more permanent bed made by fixing, in two or sometimes three sides of the room, posts reaching from the roof to the ground, and at the distance of four feet from the wall. From these posts to the wall itself, one or two ranges of boards are placed so as to form shelves, in which they either sleep or there stow away their various articles of merchandise."[1]

These explorers found the houses of the Indian tribes throughout the Columbia Valley occupied by several families, the smallest of them containing from twenty to forty persons, and the largest five hundred. The presence of large households is fully shown as the rule in their house-life. The practice of communism by the household, as stated by these authors, has already (*supra*, p. 71) been presented. This tendency to aggregation in groups, for subsistence and for mutual protection, reveals the weakness of the single family in the presence of the hardships of life. Communism in living was very plainly a necessity of their condition.

In a recent description (1869) of the modern houses of the Makah Indians of Cape Flattery, Washington Territory, by Mr. James G. Swan, the old usage which led to joint-tenement houses still asserts itself. Speaking of the manner of building these houses in detail, he remarks that "they are designed to accommodate several families, and are of various dimen-

---

[1] Lewis and Clarke's Travels, p. 431.

sions; some of them being sixty feet long by thirty wide, and from ten to fifteen feet high."[1] The houses were made of split boards on a frame of timber.

COMMUNAL HOUSES OF TRIBES IN LOWER STATUS OF BARBARISM.

Among the Indian tribes in the Lower Status of barbarism some diversity existed in the plans of the lodge and house. Fig. 7, which is taken from Schoolcraft's work on the Indian tribes, shows the frame of an Ojibwa cabin or lodge of the best class, as it may still be seen on the south shore of Lake Superior. Its mechanism is sufficiently shown by the frame of elastic poles exhibited by the figure. It is covered with bark, usually canoe-birch, taken off in large pieces and attached with splints. Its size on the ground va-

FIG. 7.—Frame of Ojibwa Wig-e-wam.

ried from ten to sixteen feet, and its height from six to ten. Twigs of spruce or hemlock were strewn around the border of the lodge on the ground floor, upon which blankets and skins were spread for beds. The fire-pit was in the center of the floor, over which, in the center of the roof, was an opening for the exit of the smoke. Such a lodge would accommodate, in the aboriginal plan of living, two and sometimes three married pairs with their children. Several such lodges were usually found in a cluster, and the several households consisted of related families, the principal portion being of the same gens or clan. I am not able to state whether or not the households thus united by the bond of kin practiced communism in living in ancient times, but it seems probable. Carver, who visited an Ojibwa village in Wisconsin in 1767, makes it appear that each house was occupied by several families. "This town," he remarks, "contains about forty houses, and can send out upwards of a hundred warriors, many of whom are fine young men."[2] This would give, by the usual rule

---

[1] Smithsonian Contributions to Knowledge, No. 220, p. 5.   [2] Travels, etc., p. 65.

of computation, five hundred persons, and an average of twelve persons to a house.

When first discovered the Dakotas lived in houses constructed with a frame of poles and covered with bark, each of which was large enough for

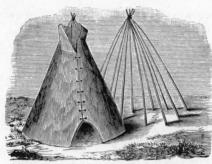

several families. They dwelt principally in villages in their original area on the head-waters of the Mississippi, in the present State of Minnesota. Forced upon the plains by an advancing white population, but after they had become possessed of horses, they invented a skin tent eminently adapted to their present nomadic condition.

FIG. 8.—Dakota wä-ká-yo, or Skin Tent.

It is superior to any other in use among the American aborigines from its roominess, its portable character, and the facility with which it can be erected and struck. The frame consists of thirteen poles from fifteen to eighteen feet in length, which, after being tied together at the small ends, are raised upright with a twist so as to cross the poles above the fastening. They are then drawn apart at the large ends and adjusted upon the ground in the rim of a circle usually ten feet in diameter. A number of untanned and tanned buffalo skins, stitched together in a form adjustable to the frame, are drawn around it and lashed together, as shown in the figure. The lower edges are secured to the ground with tent-pins. At the top there is an extra skin adjusted as a collar, so as to be open on the windward side to facilitate the exit of the smoke. A low opening is left for a doorway, which is covered with an extra skin used as a drop. The fire-pit and arrangements for beds are the same as in the Ojibwa lodge, grass being used in the place of spruce or hemlock twigs. When the tent is struck, the poles are attached to a horse, half on each side, like thills, secured to the horse's neck at one end, and the other dragging on the ground. The skin-covering and other camp-equipage are packed upon other horses and even upon their dogs, and are thus transported from place to place on the plains. This tent is so well adapted to their mode of life that it has spread far and wide among the Indian tribes of the prairie region.   I have seen it in use among seven or eight Dakota sub-tribes, among the Iowas, Otoes, and Pawnees, and among the Black-feet, Crows, Assiniboines, and Crees.   In 1878 I saw it in use among the Utes of Colorado.   A collection of fifty of these tents, which would accommodate five hundred persons, make a picturesque appearance. Under the name of the "Sibley tent" it is now in use, with some modifica-tions of plan, in the United States Army, for service on the plains.

Sir Richard Grenville's expedition in 1585 visited the south part of the original colony of Virginia, now included in North Carolina.   They landed at Roanoke Island, and also ascended a section of Albemarle Sound as far as the villages of Pomeiock and Secotan.   An artist, John Wyth, be-fore mentioned, was a member of this expedition, and we are indebted to him for a number of valuable sketches—the two villages named among the number, of which copies are given, together with representa-tions of the people and of their in-dustrial arts   The description of Pomeiock is as follows: "The towns in Virginia are very like those of Florida, not, however, so well and

FIG. 9.—Village of Pomeiock.

firmly built, and are enclosed by a circular palisade with a narrow entrance. In the town of Pomeiock, the buildings are mostly those of the chiefs and men of rank.   On one side is the Temple (council-house) (A) of a circular shape, apart from the rest, and covered with mats on every side, without windows, and receiving no light except through the entrance.   The resi-dence of their chief (B) is constructed of poles fixed in the ground, bound together and covered with mats, which are thrown off at pleasure, to admit as much light and air as they may require.   Some are covered with the boughs of trees.   The natives, as represented in the plate, are indulging in their sports.   When the spring or pond is at a distance from the town, they dig a ditch from it that supplies them with water."[1]

The village consisted of seventeen joint-tenement houses and a council-house, arranged around a central open space, and surrounded with a palisade.   Here the Algonkin lodge, unlike that of the Ojibwas, is a long, round-roofed house, apparently from fifty to eighty feet in length, covered with movable matting in the place of bark, and large enough to accommodate several families.   The suggestion of this author, that "the buildings were mostly those of chiefs and men of rank," embodies the precise error which has repeated itself from first to last with respect to the houses of American aborigines.   Because the houses at Pomeiock were large, they were the residences of chiefs; and because the House of the Nuns at Uxmal was of palatial extent, it was the exclusive residence of an Indian potentate—conclusions opposed to the whole theory of Indian life and institutions. Indian chiefs, the continent over, were housed with the people, and no better, as a rule, than the poorest of them.

"Some of their towns," says the same author, "are not enclosed with a palisade and are much more pleasant; Secotan, for example, here drawn from nature.   The houses are more scattered and a greater degree of comfort and cultivation is observable, with gardens in which tobacco (E) is cultivated, woods filled with deer, and fields of corn.   In the fields they erect a stage (F), in which a sentry is stationed to guard against the depredations of birds and thieves.   Their corn they plant in rows (H), for it grows so large, with thick stalk and broad leaves, that one plant would stint the other and it would never arrive at maturity.   They have also a curious place (C) where they convene with their neighbors at their feasts, as more fully shown on Plate 20, and from which they go to the feast (D) On the opposite side is their place of prayer (B), and near to it the sepulchre of their chiefs (A).   *   *   *   They have gardens for melons (I), and a place (K) where they build their sacred fires.   At a little distance from the town is the pond (L) from which they obtain their water."[2]

The houses of the Powhatan Indians of Virginia proper, as described

[1] Wyth's Sketches of Virginia, first published by De Bry, 1690, Langly's ed., 1841, Plate 21.
[2] Sketches, etc., of Virginia, description of Plate 22.

FIG. 10.—Village of Secotan.

by Captain John Smith, were precisely like those of Pomeiock and Secotan.
A part of the interior of the house in which Smith was received by Powhatan as a prisoner is engraved upon his map of Virginia, of which the
following is a copy:

"Their houses are
built," Smith remarks, "like
our arbors, of small young
sprigs, bowed and tied, and
so close covered with mats,
or the bark of trees, very
handsomely, that notwith-
standing either wind, rain,
or weather, they are as
warm as stoves, but very
smoky; yet, at the top of
the house there is a hole
made for the smoke to go
into right over the fire.
Against the fire they lie on
little hurdles of reeds covered with a mat, borne from
the ground a foot or more
by a hurdle of wood. On
these, round about the house,
they lie, heads and points,

POWHATAN
*Held this state & fashion when Capt. Smith
was delivered to him prisoner
1607*

FIG. 11.—Interior of House of Virginia Indians.

one by the other against the fire, some covered with mats, some with skins,
and some stark naked lie on the ground, from six to twenty in a house."[1]

The engraving is probably an improvement upon the original house in
the symmetry of the structure, but it is doubtless a truthful representation
of its mechanism. It seems likely that a double set of upright poles were
used, one upon the outside and one on the inside, between which the mat-
tings of canes or willows were secured, as the houses at Pomeiock and Secotan are ribbed externally at intervals of about eight feet, showing four, five,

---

[1] History of Virginia, i, 130.

and six sections. Each house, on this hypothesis, would be from twenty-four to forty-eight feet long. A reference (*supra*, p 67) has been made to the size of the houses of the Virginia Indians, from which their communistic character may be inferred.

In the "Journal of a Voyage to New York," in 1679–'80, by Jasper Dankers and Peter Sluyter, edited and translated by Hon. Henry C. Murphy, there is a careful description of a house of the Nyack Indians of Long Island, an Algonkin tribe, affiliated linguistically with the Virginia Indians. The Nyack house corresponds very closely with those last named. "We went from hence to her habitation," these authors remark, "where we found the whole troop together, consisting of seven or eight families, and twenty or twenty-two persons, I should think. Their house was low and long, about sixty feet long and fourteen or fifteen feet wide. The bottom was earth; the sides and roof were made of reed and the bark of chestnut trees; the posts or columns were limbs of trees stuck in the ground, and all fastened together The top or ridge of the roof was open about half a foot wide, from one end to the other, in order to let the smoke escape, in the place of a chimney. On the sides or walls of the house, the roof was so low that you could hardly stand under it. The entrance, or doors, which were at both ends, were so small and low that they had to stoop down and squeeze themselves to get through them. The doors were made of reed or flat bark. In the whole building there was no lime, stone, iron, or lead They build their fires in the middle of the floor, according to the number of families which live in it, so that from one end to the other each of them boils its own pot, and eats when it likes, not only the families by themselves, but each Indian alone, according as he is hungry, at all hours, morning, noon, and night. By each fire are the cooking utensils, consisting of a pot, a bowl or calabash, and a spoon, also made of a calabash. These are all that relate to cooking. They lie upon mats with their feet towards the fire, on each side of it. They do not sit much upon anything raised up, but, for the most part, sit on the ground or squat on their ankles. Their other household articles consist of a calabash of water, out of which they drink, a small basket in which to carry and keep their maize and small beans, and a knife. * * * All who live in one house are generally of one stock or descent, as father and mother with their offspring. Their bread is maize pounded on a block by a stone, but not fine. This is mixed with water and made into a cake, which they bake under the hot ashes. They gave us a small piece when we entered, and although the grains were not ripe, and it was half baked and coarse grains, we nevertheless had to eat it, or, at least, not throw it away before them, which they would have regarded as a great sin, or a great affront."[1]

There is nothing in these statements forbidding the supposition that the household described practiced communism in living. The composition of the household shows that it was formed on the principle of gentile kin, while the several families cooked at the different fires, which was the usual practice in the different tribes; the stores were probably common, and the household under a matron. It will be noticed also that they gave him maize bread when he first entered the house. He little supposed that it was in obedience to a law or usage universal in the Indian family.

Fig. 12.—Ho-de'-no-sote of the Seneca-Iroquois.

During the greater part of the year the Iroquois resided in villages. The size of the village was estimated by the number of the houses, and the size of the house by the number of fires it contained. One of the largest of the Seneca-Iroquois villages, situated at Mendon, near Rochester, N. Y., is thus described by Mr. Greenbalgh, who visited it in 1677 : "Tiotohatton is on the brink or edge of a hill, has not much cleared ground, is near the river Tiotohatton [outlet of Honeoye Lake], which signifies *bending*.

[1] Journal, etc., p. 124.

It lies to the westward of Canagora (Canandaigua) about thirty miles, contains about 120 houses, being the largest of all the houses we saw, the ordinary being fifty to sixty feet long, with twelve and thirteen fires in one house. They have a good store of corn growing to the northward of the town."[1]

The "long-house" of the Iroquois, from which they called themselves, as one confederated people, Ho-de'-no-sau-nee (People of the Long-House), was from fifty to eighty and sometimes one hundred feet long. It consisted of a strong frame of upright poles set in the ground, which were strengthened with horizontal poles attached with withes, and surmounted with a triangular, and in some cases with a round roof. It was covered over, both sides and roof, with large strips of elm bark tied to the frame with strings or splints. An external frame of poles for the sides and of rafters for the roof were then adjusted to hold the bark shingles between them, the two frames being tied together.

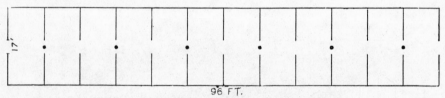

FIG. 13.—Ground-plan of Seneca-Iroquois Long-House.

The interior of the house was comparted at intevals of six or eight feet, leaving each chamber entirely open like a stall upon the passage way which passed through the center of the house from end to end. At each end was a doorway covered with suspended skins. Between each four apartments, two on a side, was a fire-pit in the center of the hall, used in common by their occupants. Thus a house with five fires would contain twenty apartments and accommodate twenty families, unless some apartments were reserved for storage. They were warm, roomy, and tidily-kept habitations. Raised bunks were constructed around the walls of each apartment for beds. From the roof-poles were suspended their strings of corn in the ear, braided by the husks, also strings of dried squashes and pumpkins. Spaces were contrived here and there to store away their accu-

---

[1] Documentary History of New York, vol. i, p. 13.

mulations of provisions. Each house, as a rule, was occupied by related families, the mothers and their children belonging to the same gens, while their husbands and the fathers of these children belonged to other gentes; consequently the gens or clan of the mother largely predominated in the household. Whatever was taken in the hunt or raised by cultivation by any member of the household, as has elsewhere been stated, was for the common benefit. Provisions were made a common stock within the household.

Here was communism in living carried out in practical life, but limited to the household, and an expression of the principle in the plan of the house itself Having found it in one stock as well developed as the Iroquois, a presumption of its universality in the Indian family at once arises, because it was a law of their condition. Evidence of its general prevalence has elsewhere been presented.

In a previous chapter the usages of the Iroquois in regard to eating have been given. It came practically to one cooked meal each day. The separate fires in each house were for convenience in cooking, all the stores in the house being common The plan of life within them was studied and economical. This is shown by the presence of a matron in each household, who made a division of the food from the kettle to each family according to their needs, and reserved what remained for future disposal. It shows system and organization in their long-houses, with a careful supervision of their stores, and forethought as well as equity in the management and distribution of their food. In these households, formed on the principle of kin, was laid the foundation for that "mother power" which was even more conspicuous in the tribes of the Old World, and which Professor Bachofen was the first to discuss under the name of gyneocracy and mother-right [1] Since the mothers who dwelt together were usually sisters, own or collateral, and of the same gens, and since their children were also of the gens of their mother, the preponderating number in the household would be of gentile kin. The right and the influence of the mother were protected and strengthened through the maternal as well as the gentile bond. The husbands were in the minority as to kindred. In case of separation it was the

---

[1] Das Mutterrecht, Stuttgart, 1861.

husband and not the wife who left the house. But this influence of the woman did not reach outward to the affairs of the gens, phratry, or tribe, but seems to have commenced and ended with the household. This view is quite consistent with the life of patient drudgery and of general subordination to the husband which the Iroquois wife cheerfully accepted as the portion of her sex. Among the Grecian tribes descent had been changed to the male line at the commencement of the historical period. It thus reversed the position of the wife and mother in the household; she was of a different gens from her children, as well as her husband; and under monogamy was now isolated from her gentile kindred, living in the separate and exclusive house of her husband. Her new condition tended to subvert and destroy that power and influence which descent in the female line and the joint-tenement houses had created. It is, therefore, the more surprising that so many traces of this anterior condition should have remained in the Grecian and other tribes, which Professor Bachofen has pointed out, since gyneocracy and mother-right, as discussed by him, must have originated among these tribes when under the gentile organization, and with descent in the female line.

The "Joint Undivided Family" of the Hindus at the present time, "joint in food, worship, and estate," brought to our notice by Sir Henry Maine,[1] is a similar but probably more numerous household than that of the Iroquois. As soon as special investigation is made, joint-tenement houses and communism in living are found to be persistent features of barbarous life in the Old World as well as the New, but limited to the household. Strabo informs us that the Gauls lived in great houses, constructed of planks and wicker, with dome roofs covered with heavy thatch.[2] Wherever such houses existed there is at least a presumption that they were occupied by several families, who formed a single household and practiced communism.

The Iroquois long-houses disappeared before the commencement of the present century. Very little is now remembered by the Indians themselves of their form and mechanism, or of the plan of life within them. Some knowledge of these houses remains among that class of Indians who

---

[1] Early History of Institutions, Holt's ed., pp. 100 and 106.   [2] Lib. iv, c. 4, s. 3.

are curious about their ancient customs. It has passed into the traditionary form, and is limited to a few particulars. A complete understanding of the mode of life in these long-houses will not, probably, ever be recovered. In 1743 Mr. John Bartram attended a council at Onondaga, and kept a journal, afterwards published, in which he inserted a ground plan of the long-house in which they were quartered. It is the first ground plan of one of these houses ever published, so far as the author is aware, and the only one prior to the appearance of Johnson's Cyclopædia in 1875.

FIG. 14.—Bartram's ground-plan and cross-section of Onondaga Long-House, in 1743.

It should be noted that in 1696 Count Frontenac invaded Onondaga with a large French and Indian force, and that the Onondagas destroyed their principal village and retired. "The cabins of the Indians," says the relator, "and the triple palisade which encircled their fort were found entirely burnt."[1] The new village visited by Mr. Bartram was probably quite near the site of the old. He says, "The town in its present state is about two or three miles long, yet the scattered cabins on both sides of the water are not above forty in number; many of them hold two families, but all stand single, so that the whole town is a strange mixture of cabins, interspersed with great patches of high grass, bushes and shrubs, some of peas, corn, and squashes. * * * We alighted at the council-house, where the chiefs were already assembled to receive us, which they did with a grave, cheerful complaisance according to their custom. They showed us where to lay our luggage, and repose ourselves during our stay with them, which was in the two end apartments of this large house. The Indians that came with us were placed over against us. This cabin is about eighty feet long and seventeen broad, the common passage six feet wide, and the apartments on each side five feet, raised a foot above the passage by a long

---

sapling hewed square, and fitted with joists that go from it to the back of the house.   On these joists they lay large pieces of bark, and on extraordinary occasions spread mats made of rushes, which favor we had.   On these floors they set or lye down every one as he will.   The apartments are divided from each other by boards or bark six or seven feet long from the lower floor to the upper, on which they put their lumber.   When they have eaten their hominy, as they set in each apartment before the fire, they can put the bowl over head, having not above five foot to reach.   They set on the floor sometimes at each end, but mostly at one.   They have a shed to put their wood into in the winter, or in the summer to set, converse or play, that has a door to the south.   All the sides and roof of the cabin is made of bark, bound fast to poles set in the ground, and bent round on the top, or set aflat for the roof as we set our rafters; over each fire-place they leave a hole to let out the smoke, which in rainy weather they cover with a piece of bark, and this they can easily reach with a pole to push it on one side or quite over the hole.   After this manner are most of their cabins built."[1] The end section shows a round roof, as in the houses of the Virginia Indians, and the ground plan agrees in all respects with the old long-houses of the Seneca-Iroquois as described by them to the author before he had seen Mr. Bartram's plan.

In the Documentary History of New York (vol. iii, p. 14) there is a remarkable picture of the principal village of the Onondagas which was visited or rather attacked by Champlain in 1615.   The location of this village was not established until 1877, when General John S Clarke, of Auburn, by means of Champlain's map and sketch of the village, and his relation of the particulars of the expedition, found the site of the village in the town of Fenner, some miles northeast of the Onondaga Valley.

It was situated upon the edge of a natural pond, covering ten acres of land, and between a small brook which emptied into the pond on the left and the outlet of the pond which passed it on the right.   The space covered by the village site was about six acres of land, strongly fortified by a series of palisades.   Champlain states in his relation that " their village was enclosed with strong quadruple palisades of large timber, thirty feet high,

---

[1] Observations, etc.; Travels to Onondaga, Lond. ed., 1751, pp. 40, 41.

Fig. 15.—Palisaded Onondaga Village.

interlocked the one with the other, with an interval of not more than half a foot between them, with galleries in the form of parapets, defended with double pieces of timber, proof against our arquebuses, and on one side they had a pond with a never-failing supply of water, from which proceeded a number of gutters which they had laid along the intermediate space, throwing the water without, and rendering it effectual inside for the purpose of extinguishing the fire.   Such was their mode of fortification and defence, which was much stronger than the villages of the Attigouatuans (Hurons) and others."[1]

Although Champlain attacked this place with fire-arms, then first heard by the Onondagas, and by means of a rude tower of his invention, and with a considerable force of French and Indians, he was unable to capture it, and retired.   The use of water, with gutters to flood the ground upon an outer palisade when attacked with fire, as imperfectly shown in the engraving, was certainly ingenious.   General Clarke has investigated the defensive works of the Iroquois, and it is to be hoped that he will soon give the results to the public.

Knowing, as we now do, that the space inclosed within the palisades was about six acres of land, the houses are not only seen to be log houses, but arranged or constructed side by side in blocks, and the whole thrown together in the form of a square, with an open space in the center.   The houses seem to be in threes and fours, and even sixes, side by side, and from sixty to one hundred feet in length; but if this conclusion is fairly warranted by the engraving, it might well be that each house was separated from its neighbor by a narrow open space or lane.   It is the only representation I have ever seen of a palisaded village of the Iroquois of the period of their discovery.   It covered about fifty-four acres of land.

The Mandans and Minnetarees of the Upper Missouri constructed a timber-framed house, superior in design and in mechanical execution to to those of the Indians north of New Mexico.   In 1862 I saw the remains of the old Mandan village shortly after its abandonment by the Arickarees, its last occupants.   The houses, nearly all of which were of the same model, were falling into decay—for the village was then deserted of inhabitants—

---

[1] Doc. Hist. New York, iii, 14.

but some of them were still perfect, and the plan of their structure easily made out.   The above ground-plan of the village was taken from the work of Prince Maximilian, and the remaining illustrations are from sketches and measurements of the author.   It was situated upon a bluff on the west side

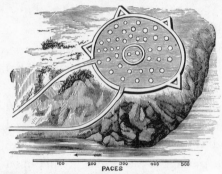

FIG. 16.—Mandan Village Plot.

of the Missouri, and at a bend in the river which formed an obtuse angle, and covered about six acres of land. The village was surrounded with a stockade made of timbers set vertically in the ground, and about ten feet high, but then in a dilapidated state.

The houses were circular in external form, the walls being about five feet high, and sloping inward and upward from the ground, upon which rested an inclined roof, both the exterior wall and the roof being plastered over with earth a foot and a half thick.   For this reason they have usually been called "dirt lodges."

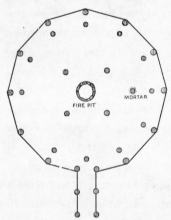

FIG. 17.—Ground-plan of a Mandan House.

These houses are about forty feet in diameter, with the floor sunk a foot or more below the surface of the ground, six feet high on the inside at the line of the wall, and from twelve to fifteen feet high at the center.   Twelve posts, six or eight inches in diameter, are set in the ground, at equal distances, in the circumference of a circle, and rising about six feet above the level of the floor.   String-pieces, resting in forks cut in the ends of these posts, form a polygon at the base and also upon the ground floor.   Against these an equal number of braces are sunk in the ground about four feet distant, which, slanting upward, are adjusted by means of depressions cut in the ends, so as to hold both the posts and the stringers firmly in their places.   Slabs of wood are then set in the spaces between the braces at the same inclination, and resting against the stringers, which when completed surrounded the lodge with a wooden wall. Four round posts, each six or eight inches in diameter, are set in the ground near the center of the floor, in the angles of a square, ten feet apart, and rising from ten to fifteen feet above the ground floor. These again are connected by stringers resting in forks at their tops, upon which and the external wall the rafters rest.

The engraving exhibits a cross-section, as described. Poles three or four inches in diameter are placed as rafters from the external wall to the string-pieces above the central parts, and near enough together to give the requisite strength to support the earth covering placed upon the roof.

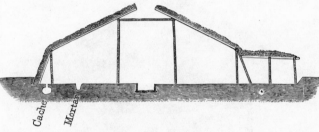

FIG. 18.—Cross-section of House.

These poles were first covered over with willow matting, upon which prairie grass was overspread, and over all a deep covering of earth. An opening was left in the center, about four feet in diameter, for the exit of the smoke and for the admission of light. The interior was spacious and tolerably well lighted, although the opening in the roof and a single doorway were the only apertures through which light could penetrate. There was but one entrance, protected by what has been called the Eskimo doorway; that is, by a passage some five feet wide, ten or twelve feet long, and about six feet high, constructed with split timbers, roofed with poles, and covered with earth. Buffalo-robes suspended at the outer and inner entrances supplied the place of doors. Each house was comparted by screens of willow matting or unhaired skins suspended from the rafters, with spaces between for storage. These slightly-constructed apartments opened towards the central fire like stalls, thus defining an open central area around the fire-pit, which was the gathering place of the inmates of the lodge. This fire-pit was about five feet in diameter, a foot deep, and encircled with flat stones set up edgewise. A hard, smooth, earthen floor completed the interior. Such a lodge would accommodate five or six families, embracing thirty or forty persons.

It was a communal house, in accordance with the usages and institutions of the American aborigines, and growing naturally out of their mode of life. I counted forty-eight houses, which would average forty feet in diameter, all constructed upon this plan, besides several rectangular log houses of later erection and of the American type.

These houses, of which a representation is given in Fig. 19, were

FIG. 19.—Mandan house.

thickly studded together to economize the space within the stockade, so that in walking through the village you passed along some circular foot-paths. There was no street, and it was impossible to see in any direction, except for short distances. In the center there was an open space, where their religious rites and festivals were observed [1]

Not the least interesting fact connected with these creditable structures was the quantity of materials required for their erection and the amount of labor required for their transportation for long distances down the river, and to fashion them, with the aid of fire and stone implements, into such comfortable dwellings. The trees are here confined to the bottom lands between the banks of the river, the river being bordered for miles by open prairies, and the trees growing in patches at long distances apart. To cut the timber without metallic implements, and to transport it without animal power, indicate a degree of persevering industry highly creditable to a people who, at this stage of progress, are averse to labor on the part of the males. Habitual male industry makes its first appearance in the next or the Middle Status of barbarism. The men here did the heavy work.

In the spaces between the lodges were their drying-scaffolds (Fig. 20), one for each lodge, which were nearly as conspicuous in the distance as the

---

[1] The war post, which stood in the center, and a number of stone and bone implements I brought away with me, as mementoes of the place. They are now in my collection.

houses themselves. They were about twenty feet long, twelve feet wide, and seven feet high to the flooring, made of posts set upright, with cross-pieces resting in forks   Other poles were then placed longitudinally, upon which was a flooring of willow mats   These scaffolds, mounted with ladders (Fig. 21), were used for drying their skins, and also their maize, meat, and vegetables.

The Indians knew the use of the ladder, and some of them made an excellent article before the discovery of America. When Coronado visited and captured the seven so-called cities of Cibola in 1540–1542, he found the people living in seven or eight large joint-tenement

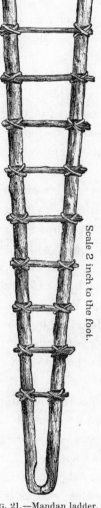

Scale 2 inch to the foot.

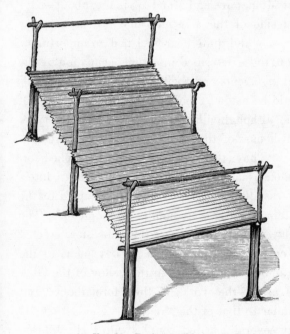

FIG. 20.—Drying-scaffold.

FIG. 21.—Mandan ladder.

houses, each capable of holding about a thousand persons. These houses were without entrances from the ground, but they mounted to the first ter-race by means of ladders, and so to each successive story above. "The ladders which they have for their houses," Coronado says in his relation, "are all in a manner movable and portable as ours be."[1]   The ladders at the Mandan village were made of two limbs growing nearly parallel and severed below the junction, as shown in the figure, and set with the forked end upon the ground, and the ends against the scaffold.   Depressions were sunk in the rails to receive the rounds, which were secured by rawhide strings.   They were usually from ten to twelve feet long, and one or two at each scaffold.

Situated thus picturesquely on a bluff, at an angle of the river, with houses of this peculiar model, and with such an array of scaffolds rising up among them, the village was strikingly conspicuous for some distance both above and below on the river, and presented a remarkable appearance.

Afterwards, at the present Minnetaree and Mandan village, about sixty-five miles above on the east side of the Missouri, and also at the new Arickaree village on the west side, and quite near it, I had an opportunity to see houses precisely similar to those described in actual occupation by the Indians, with their interior arrangements and their mode of life.

A reference, at least, should be made to the Maricopas and Mohaves of the Lower Colorado River, who, although village Indians of the pueblo type, still live in ordinary communal houses of the northern type, which are thus described by General Emory: "They (the Maricopas) occupy thatched cottages thirty or forty feet in diameter, made of twigs of cottonwood trees, interwoven with straw of wheat, cornstalks, and cane."[2]   Those occupied by the Mohaves, as described by Captain Sitgreave, are similar in character.[3]   The Pimas of the Gila River, on the contrary, claim that their ancestors erected houses of adobe brick, and cultivated by irrigation.   They point to the remains of ancient structures and of old acequias in the valley of the Gila, as Captain Crossman informs us, as the works of their forefathers.   But now their condition is very similar to that of the Mohaves.   The last-named writer remarks that "generally several married couples with their children live in one hut."[4]

---

[1] Hakluyt, Coll. of Voyages, London ed., 1812, vol. 5, p. 498.
[2] Notes, &c., New Mexico, p. 132. See also Bartlet's Personal Narrative, p. 230.
[3] Expedition, &c., Zuñi and Colorado, p. 19.
[4] Smithsonian Report for 1871, p. 415.

The first two tribes, although their antecedent history is little known, seem to be in a transitional stage from the Lower to the Middle Status of barbarism, having passed into the horticultural and sedentary condition without being far enough advanced to imitate their near neighbors in the use of adobe brick and of stone in their houses. They seem to be existing examples of that ever-recurring advancement of ruder tribes in past ages, through which the Village Indians of the pueblo type were constantly replenished from the more barbarous tribes. The present Taos Indians are another example.

It is made reasonably plain, I think, from the facts stated, that in the Upper Status of savagery, and also in the Lower Status of barbarism, the Indian household was formed of a number of families of gentile kin; that they practiced communism in living in the household, and that this principle found expression in their house architecture and predetermined its character.

CHAPTER VI.

HOUSES OF THE SEDENTARY INDIANS OF NEW MEXICO.

We are next to consider the houses and mode of life of the Sedentary Village Indians, among whom architecture exhibits a higher development, with the use of durable materials, and with the defensive principle super-added to that of adaptation to communism in living. It will not be difficult to discover and follow this latter principle, as one of the chief characteristics of this architecture in the pueblo houses in New Mexico, and in the region of the San Juan River, and afterwards in those of Mexico and Central America. Throughout all these regions there was one connected system of house architecture, as there was substantially one mode of life.

In New Mexico, going southward, the Indians, at the epoch of discovery, were met in a new dress and in an improved condition. They had advanced out of the Lower and into the Middle Status of barbarism; the houses in which they dwelt were of adobe brick or of stone, two, three, four, and sometimes five and six stories in height, and containing from fifty to five hundred apartments. They cultivated maize and plants by means of irrigating canals. The water was drawn from a running stream, taken at a point above the pueblo and carried down and through a series of garden beds. They wore mantles of cotton,[1] as well as garments of skin.[2] The present Pueblo Indians of New Mexico are in the main their descendants. They live, some of them, in the same identical houses their forefathers occupied at the time of Coronado's expedition to New Mexico in 1541–1542, as

---

[1] "They have no cotton-wool growing, because the country is cold, yet they wear mantles thereof, as your honor may see by the show thereof; and true it is, that there was found in their houses certain yarn made of cotton-wool."—Coronado's Relation, Hakluyt's Coll. of Voyages, London ed., 1600, iii, 377.

[2] "Their garments were of cotton and deer skins, and the attire, both of men and women, was after the manner of Indians of Mexico. * * * Both men and women wore shoes and boots, with good soles of neat's leather—a thing never seen in any part of the Indies."—Voyages to New Mexico, by Friar Augustin Rueyz, a Franciscan, in 1581, and Antonio de Espejo in 1583. Explorations for Railroad Route, &c., Report Indian Tribes, vol. iii, p. 114.

at Acoma, Jemez, and Taos, and although their plan and mode of life have changed in some respects in the interval, it is not unlikely that they remain to this day a fair sample of the life of the Village Indians from Zuñi to Cuzco as it existed in the sixteenth century.

The Indians north of New Mexico did not construct their houses more than one story high, or of more durable materials than a frame of poles or of timber covered with matting or bark, or coated over with earth. A stockade around their houses was their principal protection. In New Mexico, going southward, are met for the first time houses constructed with several stories. Sun-dried brick must have come into use earlier than stone. The practice of the ceramic art would suggest the brick sooner or later. At all events, what are supposed to be the oldest remains of architecture in New Mexico, such as the *Casas Grandes* of the Gila and Salinas rivers, are of adobe brick. They also used cobble-stone with adobe mortar, and finally thin pieces of tabular sandstone, prepared by fracture, which made a solid and durable stone wall. Some of the existing pueblo houses in New Mexico are as old as the expedition of Coronado (1540–1542). Others, constructed since that event, and now occupied, are of the aboriginal model. There are at present about twenty of these pueblos in New Mexico, inhabited by about 7,000 Village Indians, the descendants of those found there by Coronado. They are still living substantially under their ancient organization and usages. Besides these, there are seven pueblos of the Mokis, near the Little Colorado, occupied by about 3,000 Indians, who have remained undisturbed to the present time, except by Roman Catholic missionaries, and among whom the entire theory of life of the Sedentary Village Indians may yet be obtained. These Village Indians represent at the present moment the type of life found from Zuñi to Cuzco at the epoch of the Discovery, and, while they are not the highest, they are no unfit representatives of the entire class.

The Yucatan and Central American Indians were, in their architecture, in advance of the remaining aborigines of North America. Next to them, probably, were the Aztecs, and some few tribes southward. Holding the third position, though not far behind, were the Village Indians of New Mexico. All alike they depended upon horticulture for subsistence, and cultivated by irrigation; cotton being superadded to the maize, beans, squashes, and tobacco, cultivated by the northern tribes. Their houses, with those previously described, represent together an original indigenous architecture, which, with its diversities, sprang out of their necessities. Its fundamental communal type, I repeat, is found not less clearly in the houses about to be described, and in the so-called palace at Palenque, than in the long-house of the Iroquois. An examination of the plan of the structures in Mexico, New Mexico, and Central America will tend to establish the truth of this proposition.

New Mexico is a poor country for civilized man, but quite well adapted to Sedentary Indians, who cultivate about one acre out of every hundred thousand. This region, and the San Juan, immediately north of it, possessed a number of narrow fertile valleys, containing together, possibly, 50,000 inhabitants, and it is occupied now by their descendants (excepting the San Juan) in manner and form as it was then. Each pueblo consisted either of a single great house, or of three or four such houses grouped together; and what is more significant, the New Mexican pueblo is a fair type of those now found in ruins in Yucatan, Chiapas, Guatemala, and Honduras, in general plan and in situation. All the people lived together in these great houses on terms of equality, for their institutions were essentially democratical. Common tenements for common Indians around these structures were not found there by Coronado in 1541, neither have any been found there since. There is not the slightest ground for supposing that any such tenements ever existed around those in Yucatan and Central America. Every structure was in the nature of a fortress, showing the insecurity in which they lived.

Since the year 1846, the date of the conquest of New Mexico, a number of military reconnaissances, under the direction of the War Department, have been made in various parts of the Territory. The army officers in charge devoted their chief attention to the physical geography and resources of the regions traversed; but, incidentally, they investigated the pueblos in ruins, and the present condition of the Pueblo Indians. The admirable manner in which they have executed the work is shown by the series of reports issued from time to time by the government. More recently, the Geological and Geographical Survey of the Territories, under Prof. F. V. Hayden, geologist in charge, and also the Geographical and Geological Survey of the Rocky Mountain Region, Maj. J. W. Powell, geologist in charge, have furnished a large amount of additional information concerning the ruins on the San Juan and its tributaries, the Cliff Houses on the Mancos River and elsewhere, and the Moki Pueblos. Valuable as this information is to us, it falls short of a full exposition of these several subjects.

At the time of Coronado's expedition to capture the Seven Cities of Cibola, so called in the relations of the period, the aborigines of New Mexico manufactured earthen vessels of large size and excellent workmanship, wove cotton fabrics with spun thread, cultivated irrigated gardens, were armed with the bow, arrow, and shield, wore deer-skins and buffalo robes and also cotton mantles as external garments, and had domesticated the wild turkey."[1] "They had hardly provisions enough for themselves," remarks Jaramillo of the Cibolans, "and what they had consisted of maize, beans, and squashes."[2] What was true of the Cibolans in this respect was doubtless true of the Sedentary Indians in general. Each pueblo was an independent organization under a council of chiefs, except as several contiguous pueblos, speaking dialects of the same language, were confederated for mutual protection, of which the seven Cibolan pueblos, situated probably in the valley of the Rio Chaco, within an extent of twelve miles, afford a fair example. The degree of their advancement is more conspicuously shown in their house architecture.

The present Village Indians of New Mexico, or at least some of them, still manufacture earthen vessels, and spin and weave cotton fabrics in the aboriginal manner, and live in houses of the ancient model. Some of them, as the Mokis and Lagunas, are organized in gentes, and governed by a council of chiefs, each village being independent and self-governing. They observe the same law of hospitality universally practiced by the Northern Indians. Upon this subject, Mr. David J. Miller, of Santa Fé, writes as follows to the author: "A visitor to one of their houses is invariably ten-

---

[1] "We found here Guinea cocks [turkeys], but few. The Indians tell me in all these seven cities that they eat them not, but that they keep them only for their feathers. I believe them not, for they are excellent good, and greater than those of Mexico."—Coronado Rel., Hakluyt, iii, 377.

[2] Relation of Capt. Juan Jaramillo, Coll. Terneaux-Compans, ix, 369.

dered its hospitality in the form of food placed before him.   A failure to
tender it is deemed a grave breach of hospitality and an insult; and a
declension to partake of it would be regarded as a breach of etiquette.   As
among us, they have their rich and their poor, and the former give to the
latter cheerfully and in due plenty."   Here we find a nearly exact repetition
of the Iroquois and Mandan rules of hospitality before given.   Whether
or not they formerly practiced communism in household groups, I am not
informed.   Their houses are adapted to this mode of life, as will presently
be shown; and upon that fact and their stage of social advancement, the
deduction of the practice must for the present rest.

JOINT TENEMENT HOUSES OF VILLAGE INDIANS IN NEW MEXICO.

Santo Domingo is composed of several structures of adobe brick
grouped together, as shown in the engraving, Fig. 22.   Each is about two
hundred feet long, with two parallel rows of apartments on the ground, of
which the front row is carried up one story, and the back two; the flat roof of
the first story forming a terrace in front of the second.   The first story is
closed up solid for defensive reasons; with the exception of small window
openings.   The first terrace is reached by means of ladders from the ground;
the rooms in the first story are entered through trap-doors in the floors, and in
the second through doors opening upon the terrace, and also through trap-
doors through the floors which form the roof.   These structures are typical of
all the aboriginal houses in New Mexico.   They show two principal features:
first, the terraced form of architecture, common also in Mexico, with the
house tops as the social gathering places of the inmates; and, second, a
closed ground story for safety.   Every house, therefore, is a fortress.   Lieutenant Abert remarks upon one of the houses of this pueblo, of which he gives
an elevation, that "the upper story is narrower than the one below, so that
there is a platform or landing along the whole length of the building.   To
enter, you ascend to the platform by means of ladders that could easily be
removed; and, as there is a parapet wall extending along the platform, these

Fig. 22.—Pueblo of Santo Domingo.

houses could be converted into formidable forts."[1]   The number of apartments in each house is not stated.   The different houses at that time were
inhabited by eight hundred Indians.   Chimneys now appear above the roofs,
the fire-place being at the angle of the chamber in front.   These were evidently of later introduction.   The defensive element, so prominent in this
architecture, was not so much to protect the Village Indians from each other,
as from the attacks of migrating bands flowing down upon them from the
North.   The pueblos now in ruins throughout the original area of New
Mexico, and for some distance north of it, testify to the perpetual struggle
of the former to maintain their ground, as well as prove the insecurity in
which they lived.   It could be shown that the second and additional stories
were suggested by the defensive principle.

Zuñi, Fig. 23, is the largest occupied pueblo in New Mexico at the present time.   It probably once contained five thousand inhabitants, but in 1851
the number was reduced to fifteen hundred   The village consists of several
structures, most of them accessible to each from their roof terraces.   They
are constructed of adobe brick, and of stone embedded in adobe mortar, and
plastered over.

In the summer of 1879, Mr. James Stevenson, in charge of the field
parties under Major Powell, made an extended visit to Zuñi and the neighboring pueblos, for the purpose of making collections of their implements,
utensils, etc., during which time the photographs from which the accompanying illustrations of the pueblos were made.   His wife accompanied him,
and she has furnished us the following description of that pueblo :

"Zuñi is situated in Western New Mexico, being built upon a knoll
covering about fifteen acres, and some forty feet above the right bank of
the river of the same name.

"Their extreme exclusiveness has preserved to the Zuñians their strong
individuality, and kept their language pure.   According to Major Powell's
classification, their speech forms one of four linguistic stocks to which may
be traced all the pueblo dialects of the southwest.   In all the large area
which was once thickly dotted with settlements, only thirty-one remain,
and these are scattered hundreds of miles apart from Taos, in Northern New

---

[1] Ex. Doc. No. 41, 1st session 30th Congress, 1848, p. 462.

Mexico, to Isleta, in Western Texas. Among these remnants of great native tribes, the Zuñians may claim perhaps the highest position, whether we regard simply their agricultural and pastoral pursuits, or consider their whole social and political organization.

"The town of Zuñi is built in the most curious style. It resembles a great beehive, with the houses piled one upon another in a succession of terraces, the roof of one forming the floor or yard of the next above, and so on, until in some cases five tiers of dwellings are successively erected, though no one of them is over two stories high. These structures are of stone and 'adobe.' They are clustered around two plazas, or open squares, with several streets and three covered ways through the town.

"The upper houses of Zuñi are reached by ladders from the outside. The lower tiers have doors on the ground plan, while the entrances to the others are from the terraces. There is a second entrance through hatchways in the roof, and thence by ladders down into the rooms below. In many of the pueblos there are no doors whatever on the ground floor, but the Zuñians assert that their lowermost houses have always been provided with such openings   In times of threatened attack the ladders were either drawn up or their rungs were removed, and the lower doors were securely fastened in some of the many ingenious ways these people have of barring the entrances to their dwellings. The houses have small windows, in which mica was originally used, and is still employed to some extent; but the Zuñians prize glass highly, and secure it, whenever practicable, at almost any cost   A dwelling of average capacity has four or five rooms, though in some there are as many as eight   Some of the larger apartments are paved with flagging, but the floors are usually plastered with clay, like the walls   Both are kept in constant repair by the women, who mix a reddish-brown earth with water to the proper consistency, and then spread it by hand, always laying it on in semicircles. It dries smooth and even, and looks well. In working this plaster the squaw keeps her mouth filled with water, which is applied with all the dexterity with which a Chinese laundryman sprinkles clothes. The women appear to delight in this work, which they consider their special prerogative, and would feel that their rights were infringed upon were men to do it. In building, the men lay the stone foundations and set in place the huge logs that serve as beams to support the roof, the spaces between these rafters being filled with willow-brush; though some of the wealthier Zuñians use instead shingles made by the carpenters of the village The women then finish the structure. The ceilings of all the older houses are low; but Zuñi architecture has improved, and the modern style gives plenty of room, with doors through which one may pass without stooping. The inner walls are usually whitened. For this purpose a kind of white clay is dissolved in boiling water and applied by hand. A glove of undressed goat-skin is worn, the hand being dipped in the hot liquid and then passed repeatedly over the wall.

"In Zuñi, as elsewhere, riches and official position confer importance upon their possessors. The wealthy class live in the lower houses, those of moderate means next above, while the poorer families have to be content with the uppermost stories. Naturally no one will climb into the garret who has the means of securing more convenient apartments, under the huge system of " French flats," which is the way of living in Zuñi. Still there is little or no social distinction in the rude civilization, the whole population of the town living almost as one family. The Alcalde, or Lieutenant-Governor, furnishes an exception to the general rule, as his official duties require him to occupy the highest house of all, from the top of which he announces each morning to the people the orders of the Governor, and makes such other proclamation as may be required of him.

"Each family has one room, generally the largest in the house, where they work, eat, and sleep together. In this room the wardrobe of the family hangs upon a log suspended beneath the rafters, only the more valued robes, such as those worn in the dance, being wrapped and carefully stored away in another apartment. Work of all kinds goes on in this large room, including the cookery, which is done in a fire-place on the long side, made by a projection at right angles with the wall, with a mantel-piece on which rests the base of the chimney. Another fire-place in a second room is from six to eight feet in width, and above this is a ledge shaped somewhat like a Chinese awning. A highly-polished slab, fifteen or twenty inches in size, is raised a foot above the hearth. Coals are heaped beneath this slab, and upon it the *Waiavi* is baked. This delicious kind of bread is made of meal ground finely and spread in a thin batter upon the stone with the naked hand. It is as thin as a wafer, and these crisp, gauzy sheets, when cooked, are piled in layers and then folded or rolled. Light bread, which is made only at feast times, is baked in adobe ovens outside the house When not in use for this purpose the ovens make convenient kennels for the dogs and play-houses for the children. Neatness is not one of the characteristics of the Zuñians. In the late autumn and winter months the women do little else than make bread, often in fanciful shapes, for the feasts and dances which continually occur. A sweet drink, not at all intoxicating, is made from the sprouted wheat. The men use tobacco, procured from white traders, in the form of cigarettes from corn-husks; but this is a luxury in which the women do not indulge.

"The Pueblo mills are among the most interesting things about the town. These mills, which are fastened to the floor a few feet from the wall, are rectangular in shape, and divided into a number of compartments, each about twenty inches wide and deep, the whole series ranging from five to ten feet in length, according to the number of divisions. The walls are made of sandstone. In each compartment a flat grinding stone is firmly set, inclining at an angle of forty-five degrees. These slabs are of different degrees of smoothness, graduated successively from coarse to fine. The squaws, who alone work at the mills, kneel before them and bend over them as a laundress does over the wash-tub, holding in their hands long stones of volcanic lava, which they rub up and down the slanting slabs, stopping at intervals to place the grain between the stones. As the grinding proceeds the grist is passed from one compartment to the next until, in passing through the series, it becomes of the desired fineness. This tedious and laborious method has been practiced without improvement from time immemorial, and in some of the arts the Zuñians have actually retrograded"

The living-rooms are about twelve by eighteen feet and about nine feet high, with plastered walls and an earthen floor, and usually a single window opening for light. To form a durable ceiling round timbers about six inches in diameter are placed three or four feet apart from the outer to the inner wall. Upon these, poles are placed transversely in juxtaposition. A deep covering of adobe mortar is placed upon them, forming the roof terrace in front, and the floor in the apartments above in the receding second story. Water-jars of their own manufacture, of fine workmanship, and holding several gallons, closely woven osier baskets of their own make,

FIG. 24.—Room in Zuñi House.

and blankets of cotton and wool, woven by their own hand-looms, are among the objects seen in these apartments. They are neatly kept, roomy and comfortable, and differ in no respect from those in use at the period of the conquest, as will elsewhere be shown. The mesa elevation upon which the old town of Zuñi was situated is seen in the background of the engraving, Fig. 23.

It should be noticed that this architecture, and the necessities that gave it birth, led to a change in the mode of life from the open ground to the terraces or flat roofs of these great houses. When not engaged in tillage, the terraces were the gathering and living places of the people. During the greater part of the year they lived practically in the open air, to which the climate was adapted, and upon their housetops, first for safety and afterwards from habit.

Elevations of the principal pueblos of New Mexico have from time to time been published. They agree in general plan, but show considerable diversity in details. Rude but massive structures, they accommodated all the people of the village in security within their walls.

The Moki Pueblos are supposed to be the towns of Tusayan, visited by a detachment of Coronado's expedition in 1541. Since the acquisition of New Mexico they have been rarely visited, because of their isolation and distance from American settlements.

The accompanying illustration of Wolpi, Fig. 25, one of these pueblos, is from a photograph taken by Major Powell's party.

In 1858 Lieut. Joseph C. Ives, in command of the Colorado Exploring Expedition, visited the Moki Pueblos, near the Little Colorado. They are seven in number, situated upon mesa elevations within an extent of ten miles, difficult of access, and constructed of stone. Mi-shong'-i-ni'-vi, the first one entered, is thus described. After ascending the rugged sides of the mesa by a flight of stone steps, Lieutenant Ives remarks : "We came upon a level summit, and had the walls of the pueblo on one side and an extensive and beautiful view upon the other. Without giving us time to admire the scene, the Indians led us to a ladder planted against the front face of the pueblo. The town is nearly square, and surrounded by a stone wall fifteen feet high, the top of which forms a landing extending around the whole. Flights of stone steps led from the first to a second landing, upon which the doors of the houses open. Mounting the stairway opposite to the ladder, the chief crossed to the nearest door and ushered us into a low apartment, from which two or three others opened towards the interior of the dwelling. Our host courteously asked us to be seated upon some skins spread along the floor against the wall, and presently his wife brought in a vase of water and a tray filled with a singular substance (tortillas), that looked more like a sheet of thin blue wrapping paper than anything else I had ever seen.   I learned afterwards that it was made from corn meal, ground very fine, made into a gruel, and poured over a heated stone to be baked.   When dry it has a surface slightly polished, like paper.   The sheets are folded and rolled together, and form the staple article of food of the Moki Indians. As the dish was intended for our entertainment, and looked clean, we all partook of it.   It has a delicate fresh-bread flavor, and was not at all un-palatable, particularly when eaten with salt.   *   *   *   The room was fifteen feet by ten; the walls were made of adobes; the partitions of sub-stantial beams; the floors laid with clay.   In one corner were a fire-place and chimney.   Everything was clean and tidy.   Skins, bows and arrows, quivers, antlers, blankets, articles of clothing and ornament were hanging upon the walls or arranged upon the shelves.   At the other end was a trough divided into compartments, in each of which was a sloping stone slab, two or three feet square, for grinding corn upon.   In a recess of an inner room was piled a goodly store of corn in the ear.   *   *   *   Another inner room appeared to be a sleeping apartment, but this being occupied by females we did not enter, though the Indians seemed to be pleased rather than otherwise at the curiosity evinced during the close inspection of their dwelling and furniture.   *   *   *   Then we went out upon the landing, and by another flight of steps ascended to the roof, where we beheld a mag-nificent panorama.   *   *   *   We learned that there were seven towns. *   *   *   Each pueblo is built around a rectangular court, in which we suppose are the springs that furnish the supply to the reservoirs.   The exterior walls, which are of stone, have no openings, and would have to be scaled or battered down before access could be gained to the interior.   The successive stories are set back, one behind the other.   The lower rooms are reached through trap-doors from the first landing.   The houses are three rooms deep, and open upon the interior court.   The arrangement is as strong and compact as could well be devised, but as the court is common, and the landings are separated by no partitions, it involves a certain community of residence."[1]

This account leaves a doubt whether the stories receded from the inclosed court outward, or from the exterior inward. Lieutenant Ives does not state that he passed through the building into the court and ascended to the first platform from within, and yet the remainder of the description seems to imply that he did, and that the structure occupied but three sides of the court, since he states that "the houses are three rooms deep and open upon the interior court." The structure was three stories high.

FIG. 26.—Room in Moki House.

The above engraving was prepared for an article by Maj. Powell, on these Indians. Two rooms are shown together, apparently by leaving out the wooden partition which separated them, showing an extent of at least thirty feet. The large earthen water-jars are interesting specimens of Moki

[1] Colorado Exploring Expedition, p. 121.

pottery. At one side is the hand mill for grinding maize. The walls are ornamented with bows, quivers, and the floor with water-jars, as described by Lieutenant Ives.

In places on the sides of the bluffs at this and other pueblos, Lieutenant Ives observed gardens cultivated by irrigation. "Between the two," he remarks, "the faces of the bluff have been ingeniously converted into terraces. These were faced with neat masonry, and contained gardens, each surrounded with a raised edge so as to retain water upon the surface. Pipes from the reservoirs permitted them at any time to be irrigated."[1]

Fig. 27 shows one of two large adobe structures constituting the pueblo of Taos, in New Mexico. It is from a photograph taken by the expedition under Major Powell. It is situated upon Taos Creek, at the western base of the Sierra Madre Range, which forms the eastern border of the broad valley of the Rio Grande, into which the Taos stream runs. It is an old and irregular building, and is supposed to be the Braba of Coronado's expedition.[2] Some ruins still remain, quite near, of a still older pueblo, whose inhabitants, the Taos Indians affirm, they conquered and dispossessed. The two structures stand about twenty-five rods apart, on opposite sides of the stream, and facing each other. That upon the north side, represented in the above engraving, is about two hundred and fifty feet long, one hundred and thirty feet deep, and five stories high; that upon the south side is shorter and deeper, and six stories high. The present population of the pueblo, about four hundred, are divided between the two houses, and they are a thrifty, industrious, and intelligent people. Upon the east side is a long adobe wall, connecting the two buildings, or rather protecting the open space between them. A corresponding wall, doubtless, closed the space on the opposite side, thus forming a large court between the buildings, but, if so, it has now disappeared. The creek is bordered on both sides with ample fields or gardens, which are irrigated by canals, drawing water from the stream. The adobe is of a yellowish-brown color, and the two structures make a striking appearance as they are approached. Fire-places and chimneys have been added to the principal room of each family; but it is evident

---

[1] Colorado Exploring Expedition, p. 120.
[2] Relation of Castenada, Coll. H. Ternaeux-Compans. ix, 138. Trans. of American Ethnological Society.

Fig. 27.—North Pueblo of Taos.

Fig. 28.—Room in Pueblo of Taos.

that they are modern, and that the suggestion came from Spanish sources. They are constructed in the corner of the room. The first story is built up solid, and those above recede in the terraced form. Ladders planted against the walls show the manner in which the several stories are reached, and, with a few exceptions, the rooms are entered through trap-doors by means of ladders. Children and even dogs run up and down these ladders with great freedom. The lower rooms are used for storage and granaries, and the upper for living rooms; the families in the rooms above owning and controlling the rooms below. The pueblo has its chiefs.

The measurements of the two edifices were furnished to the writer in 1864 by Mr. John Ward, at that time a government Indian agent, by the procurement of Dr. M. Steck, superintendent of Indian affairs in New Mexico. Among further particulars given by Mr. Ward are the following: " The thickness of the walls of these houses depends entirely upon the size of the *adobe* and the way in which it is laid upon the wall ; that is, whether lengthwise or crosswise. There is no particular standard for the size of the *adobes*. On the buildings in question the *adobes* on the upper stories are laid lengthwise, and will average about ten inches in width, which gives the thickness of the walls. On the first story or ground rooms the *adobes* are in most places laid crosswise, thus making the thickness of these walls just the length of the *adobe*, which averages about twenty inches. The width of an *adobe* is usually one-half its length, and the thickness will average about four inches. The floors and roofs are coated with mud mortar from four to six inches thick, which is laid on and smoothed over with the hand. This work is usually performed by women. When the right kind of earth can be obtained the floor can be made very hard and smooth, and will last a very long time without needing repairs. The walls both inside and out are coated in the same manner. On the inside, however, more care is taken to make the walls as even and smooth as possible, after which they are whitewashed with *yesso* or gypsum."

Several rooms on the ground floor were measured by Mr. Ward and found to be, in feet, 14 by 18, 20 by 22, and 24 by 27, with a height of ceiling averaging from 7 to 8 feet. In the second story they measured, in feet, 14 by 23, 12 by 20, and 15 by 20, with a height of ceiling varying from 7 to $7\frac{1}{4}$ feet.   The rooms in the third, fourth, and fifth stories were found to diminish in size with each story.   There is probably a mistake here, as the main longitudinal partition walls must have been carried up upon each other from bottom to top.   A few of the doorways were measured and found to range from $2\frac{1}{2}$ feet wide by $4\frac{1}{2}$ feet high and $2\frac{1}{3}$ feet wide by $4\frac{10}{12}$ feet high.   The scuttles or trap-doors in the floors, through which they descended into these rooms by means of ladders, were 3 feet by $2\frac{1}{2}$, 3 feet by 2, and $1\frac{10}{12}$ by $2\frac{1}{2}$ feet; and the window openings through the walls were, in inches, 14 by 14, 8 by 16, 16 by 20, and 18 by 18.

Mr. Ward then proceeds: "No room has more than two windows; very few have more than one.   The back rooms usually have one or more round holes made through the walls from six to eight inches in diameter.   These openings furnish the apartments with a scanty supply of light and air.   The first story or the ground rooms are usually without doors or windows, the only entrance being through the scuttle-holes or doors in the roof, which are within the rooms comprising the story immediately above.   These basement rooms are used for store-rooms.   Those in the upper stories are the rooms mostly inhabited.   Those located in the front part of the building receive their light through the doors and windows before described.   The back rooms have no other light than that which goes in through the scuttle-holes and the partition walls leading from the front rooms; that is, where a room is so situated as to have both.   Others again have no other light than that which enters through the holes already described.   Such rooms are always gloomy.   Some families have as many as four or five rooms, one of which is set apart for cooking, and is furnished with a large fire-place for the purpose.   Those who have only two or three rooms usually cook and sleep in the same apartment, and in such cases they cook in the usual fire-place, which stands in one corner of the room.   No perceptible addition has been made to either of the buildings for many years; and it is evident that after the death or removal of their owners they were entirely neglected.   Those in good condition are still occupied.   From the best information attainable the original buildings were not erected all at one time, but were added to from time to time by additional rooms, including the second, third, and more stories.   There are no regular terraces, the roof of the rooms below answering that purpose.   Thus it is that no entire circuit can be made around any one of these stories, the only thing that can be called a terrace being the narrow space left in front of some of the rooms from the roofs of the lower rooms."

Mr. Ward seems to object to the word "terrace" in defining the platform left in front of each story as a means of access to its apartments and to the successive stories.   It was used by the early Spanish writers to explain the same peculiarity found in many of the great houses in the pueblo of Mexico and elsewhere over Mexico, the roofs being flat and the stories receding from each other.   While this platform is not in strictness a terrace, the term expresses this architectural feature with sufficient clearness.   The two structures at Taos are large enough to accommodate five hundred persons in each, the inmates living in the Indian fashion.   They were occupied in 1864 by three hundred and sixty-one Taos Indians.

"Each terrace is reached," remarks Mr. Miller before mentioned, speaking of the pueblos in general, "by a wooden ladder, first from the ground and afterward from the one below; and ingress and egress to and from the rooms below is on the inside in the room above through trap-doors and upon ladders.   It is wonderful to see with what agility the Indian children and the dogs run up and down these ladders.   Nowhere is there any side communication between the rooms in the great building, and but one family occupy each series of rooms situated one above the other."   This last statement is too broadly made, as we have seen that Mr. Ward has given the measurements of doors through partition walls.   Such doors will also be shown in a subsequent engraving.   But there is no doubt of the fact that the number of lateral rooms communicating with each other was small, and that the families or groups, if such existed, united in a communal household, were separated from each other by solid partition walls, a fact which will reappear in the house-architecture of Yucatan.

In 1877, David J. Miller, esq., of Santa Fé, visited the Taos Pueblo at my request, to make some further investigations.   He reports to me the following facts: The government is composed of the following persons, all of whom, except the first, are elected annually: 1. A cacique or principal sachem. 2. A governor or alcalde.   3. A lieutenant-governor.   4. A war captain, and a lieutenant war captain.   5. Six fiscals or policemen.   " The cacique," Mr. Miller says, "has the general control of all officers in the performance of their duties, transacts the business of the pueblo with the surrounding whites, Indian agents, etc., and imposes reprimands or severer punishments upon delinquents.   He is keeper of the archives of the pueblo; for example, he has in his keeping the United States patent for the tract of four square leagues on which the pueblo stands, which was based upon the Spanish grant of 1689; also deeds of other purchased lands adjoining the pueblo.   He holds his office for life.   At his death, the people elect his successor.   The cacique may, before his death, name his successor, but the nomination must be ratified by the people represented by their principal men assembled in the estufa."   In this cacique may be recognized the sachem of the northern tribes, whose duties were purely of a civil character.   Mr. Miller does not define the duties of the governor.   They were probably judicial, and included an oversight of the property rights of the people in their cultivated lands, and in rooms or sections of the pueblo houses.   "The lieutenant-governor," he remarks, "is the sheriff to receive and execute orders.   The war captain has twelve subordinates under his command to police the pueblo, and supervise the public grounds," such as grazing lands, the cemetery, estufas, &c.   The lieutenant war captain executes the orders of his principal, and officiates for him during his absence, or in case of his disability.   The six fiscals are a kind of town police.   It is their duty to see that the catechism (Catholic) is taught in the pueblo, and learned by the children, and generally to keep order and execute the municipal regulations of the pueblo under the direction of the governor, who is charged with the duty of seeing to their execution."

"The regular time for meeting in the estufa is the last day of December, annually, for the election of officers for the ensuing year.   The cacique, governor, and principal men nominate candidates, and the election decides. There may also be a fourth nomination of candidates, that is, by the people. In the election, all adult males vote; the officers first, and then the general public.   The officers elected are at the present time sworn in by the United States Territorial officials."

In this simple government we have a fair sample, in substance and in spirit, of the ancient government of the Pueblo Indians of New Mexico. Some modification of the old system may be detected in the limitation of officers below the grade of cacique to one year. From what is known of the other pueblos in New Mexico, that of Taos is a fair example of all of them in governmental organization at the present time. They are, and always were, essentially republican, which is in entire harmony with Indian institutions. I may repeat here what I have ventured to assert on previous occasions, that the whole theory of governmental and domestic life among the Village Indians of America from Zuñi to Cuzco can still be found in New Mexico.

The representation of a room in this pueblo, Fig. 28, is from a sketch by Mr. Galbraith, who accompanied Major Powell's party to New Mexico.

What Mr. Miller refers to as "property rights and titles" and "ownership in fee" of land, is sufficiently explained by the possessory right which is found among the northern Indian tribes. The limitations upon its alienation to an Indian from another pueblo, or to a white man, not to lay any stress upon the absence of written titles or conveyances of land which have been made possible by Spanish and American intercourse, show very plainly that their ideas respecting the ownership of the absolute title to land, with power to alienate to whomsoever the person pleased, were entirely above their conception of property and its uses. All the ends of individual ownership and of inheritance were obtained through a mere right of possession, while the ultimate title remained in the tribe. According to the statement of Mr. Miller, if the father dies, his land is divided between his widow and children, and if a woman, her land is divided equally between her sons and daughters. This is an important statement, because, assuming its correctness, it shows inheritance of children from both father and mother, a total departure from the principles of gentile inheritance. In 1878 I visited the Taos pueblo. I could not find among them the gens or clan,[1] and from lack of time did not inquire into their property regulations or rules of inheritance. The dozen large ovens I saw while there near the ends or in front of the two buildings, each of which was equal to the wants of more than one family, were adopted from the Spanish. They not unlikely had some connection with the old principle of communism.

---

[1] Mr. Bandelier has since ascertained that they are organized in gentes.

It will prove a very difficult undertaking to ascertain the old mode of life three hundred and fifty years ago in New Mexico, Mexico, and Central America, as it was then in full vitality, a natural outgrowth of Indian institutions. The experiment to recover this lost condition of Indian society has not been tried. The people have been environed with civilization during the latter portion of this period, and have been more or less affected by it from the beginning. Their further growth and development was arrested by the advent of European civilization, which blighted their more feeble culture. Since their discovery they have steadily declined in numbers, and they show no signs of recovery from the shock produced by their subjugation. Among the northern tribes, who were one Ethnical Period below the Pueblo Indians, their social organization and their mode of life have changed materially under similar influences since the period of discovery. The family has fallen more into the strictly monogamian form, each occupying a separate house; communism in living in large households has disappeared; the organization into gentes has in many cases fallen out or been rudely extinguished by external influences; and their religious usages have yielded. We must expect to find similar and even greater changes among the Village Indians of New Mexico The white race were upon them in Mexico and New Mexico a hundred years earlier than upon the Indian tribes of the United States. But, as if to stimulate investigation into their ancient mode of life, some of these tribes have continued through all these years to live in the same identical houses occupied by their forefathers in 1540 at Acoma, Jemez, and Taos. These pueblos were contemporary with the pueblo of Mexico captured by Cortez in 1520. The present inhabitants are likely to have retained some part of the old plan of life, or some traditionary knowledge of what it was. They must retain some of the usages and customs with respect to the ownership and inheritance of sections of these houses, and of the limitations upon the power of sale that they should not pass out of the kinship. The same also with respect to sections of the village garden. All the facts with respect to their ancient usages and mode of life should be ascertained, so far as it is now possible to do so from the present inhabitants of these pueblos. The information thus given will serve a useful purpose in explaining the pueblos in ruins in Yucatan and Central America, as well as on the San Juan, the Chaco, and the Gila.

At the time of their discovery the Pueblo Indians of New Mexico generally worshipped the sun as their principal divinity. Although under constraint they became nominally Roman Catholic, they still retain, in fact, their old religious beliefs. Mr. Miller has sent me some information upon this subject concerning the pueblos of Taos, Jemez, and Zia.

" Before the Spaniards forced their religion upon the people, the pueblo of Taos had the Sun for their God, and worshipped the Sun as such They had periodical assemblages of the authorities and the people in the estufas for offering prayers to the Sun, to supplicate him to repeat his diurnal visits, and to continue to make the maize, beans, and squashes grow for the sustenance of the people. 'The Sun and God,' said the governor (Mirabal) to me, 'are the same. We believe really in the Sun as our God, but we profess to believe in the God and Christ of the Catholic Church and of the Bible. When we die, we go to God in Heaven. I do not know whether Heaven is in the Sun, or the Sun is Heaven. The Spaniards required us to believe in their God, and we were compelled to adopt their God, their church, and their doctrines, willing or unwilling. We do not know that under the American Government we may exercise any religion we choose, and that the National Government and the church government are wholly disconnected. We have very great respect and reverence for the Sun. We fear that the Sun will punish us now, or at some future time, if we do evil. The modern pueblos have the Sun religion really; but they profess the Christian religion, of which they know nothing but what the Catholic religion teaches. They always believed that Montezuma would come again as the messiah of the pueblo. The Catholic religion has been so long outwardly practiced by the people that it could not now, they think, be easily laid aside, and the old Sun religion be established, because it is looked upon as established by the law of the land, and therefore necessarily practiced. Nevertheless, the Indians will always follow and practice, as they do, both religions. If,' said the governor, 'one Indian here at this pueblo were to declare that he intended to renounce and abandon the religion of his fathers (the worship of the Sun) and adopt the Christian religion as his only faith, and another Indian were to declare that he intended to repudiate the Christian religion and adopt and practice only the Sun religion, the former would be expelled the pueblo, and his property would be confiscated, but the other would be allowed to remain with all his rights'

"There are three old men in the pueblo whose duty it is to impart the traditions of the people to the rising generation. These traditions are communicated to the young men according to their ages and capacities to receive and appreciate them. The Taos Indians have a tradition that they came from the north; that they found other Indians at this place (Taos) living also in a pueblo; that these they ejected after much fighting, and took and have continued to occupy their place. How long ago this was they cannot say, but it must have been a long time ago. The Indians driven away lived here in a pueblo, as the Taos Indians now do."

Mr. Miller also communicates a conversation had with Juan José, a native of Zia, and José Miguel, a native of Pecos, but then (December, 1877) a resident of the pueblo of Jemez, which he wrote down at the time, as follows: "Before the Spaniards came, the religion of Jemez, Pecos and Zia, and the other pueblos, was the Montezuma religion. A principal feature of this religion was the celebration of Dances at the pueblo. In it, God was the sun. *Seh-un-yuh* was the land the Pueblo Indians came from, and to it they went when dead. This country (*Seh-un-yuh*) was at Great Salt Lake. They cannot say whether this lake was the place where the Mormons now live, but it was to the north. Under this great lake there was a big Indian Pueblo, and it is there yet.[1] The Indian dances were had only when prescribed by the cacique. The Pueblo Indians now have two religions, that of Montezuma, and the Roman Catholic. The Sun, Moon, and Stars were Gods, of which the greatest and most potent was the Sun; but greater than he was Montezuma. In time of drought, or actual or threatened calamity, the Pueblo Indians prayed to Montezuma, and also to the Sun, Moon, and Stars. The old religion (that of Montezuma) is believed in all the New Mexican pueblos. They practice the Catholic religion ostensibly; but in their consciences and in reality the old religion is that of the pueblos. The tenets of the old religion are preserved by tradition, which the old men communicate to the young in the estufas. At church worship the Pueblo Indians pray to God, and also to Montezuma

---

[1] The Iroquois have a similar tradition of the ancient existence of an Indian village under Otsego Lake in New York.

and the Sun; but at the dances they pray to Montezuma and the Sun only. During an actual or threatened calamity the dances are called by the cacique. They have two Gods; the God of the Pueblos, and the God of the Christians. Montezuma is the God of the Pueblo."

This account of the Sun worship of the Taos Indians, in which is intermingled that of Montezuma, and the further account of the worship of Montezuma at the pueblos of Zia and Jemez, with the recognition of the worship of the Sun, Moon, and Stars, are both interesting and suggestive. It is probable that Sun worship is the older of the two, while that of Montezuma, as a later growth, remained concurrent with the other in all the New Mexican pueblos without superseding it. In this supernatural person, known to them as Montezuma, who was once among them in bodily human form, and who left them with a promise that he would return again at a future day, may be recognized the *Hiawatha* of Longfellow's poem, the *Ha-yo-went'-ha* of the Iroquois. It is in each case a ramification of a widespread legend in the tribes of the American aborigines, of a personal human being, with supernatural powers, an instructor of the arts of life; an example of the highest virtues, beneficent, wise, and immortal.

"They have," remarks Mr. Miller, "one curious custom which has always been observed in the pueblo. It is for some one (sometimes several simultaneously) to seclude themselves entirely from the outer world, abstaining absolutely from all personal communication with others, and devoting themselves solely to prayer for the pueblo and its inhabitants. This seclusion lasts eighteen months, during which they are furnished daily, by a confidential messenger, with a little food, just enough to preserve life, and during which time they may not even inquire about their wives or children or be told anything of them though the messenger may know that some of them are sick or have died. The food the recluse is permitted to use is corn, beans, squashes, and buffalo and deer meat; that is, such food as was used before the coming of the Spaniards. This religious seclusion is in honor of the Sun. It is one of the rites of the ancient religion of the Pueblo, preserved and practiced now. One of the old men I talked with said that he had himself the previous year emerged from this hermitage; three others were now in, they having retired to exile in February, 1877, and will emerge in August, 1878, then to learn the news of the previous year and a half."

CHAPTER VII.

RUINS OF HOUSES OF THE SEDENTARY INDIANS OF THE SAN JUAN RIVER AND ITS TRIBUTARIES.

The finest structures of the Village Indians in New Mexico, and northward of its present boundary line, are found on the San Juan and its tributaries, unoccupied and in ruins. Even the regions in which they are principally situated are not now occupied by this class of Indians, but are roamed over by wild tribes of the Apaches and the Utes. The most conspicuous cluster of these ruined and deserted pueblos are in the cañon or valley of the Rio Chaco, which stream is an affluent of the San Juan, a tributary of the Colorado. Similar ruins of stone pueblos are also found in the valley of the Animas River, and also in the region of the Ute Mountain in Southwestern Colorado. Ruins of clusters of small single houses built of cobble-stone and adobe mortar, and of large pueblos of the same material, are to be seen in the La Plata Valley, and in the Montezuma Valley, west of the Mancos River. On the Mancos River are a large number of cliff houses of stone, and also round towers of stone, ot which the uses are not at present known. Cliff houses are also found on the Dolores River. Other ruins are found in the cañon of the Rio de Chelly.

The supposition is reasonable that the Village Indians north of Mexico had attained their highest culture and development where these stone structures are found. They are similar in style and plan to the present occupied pueblos in New Mexico, but superior in construction, as stone is superior to adobe or to cobble-stone and adobe mortar. They are also equal, if not superior, in size and in the extent of their accommodations, to any Indian pueblos ever constructed in North America. This fact gives additional interest to these ruins, which are here to be considered.

168

Two separate explorations and reports upon the Chaco ruins have been made. The first was by Lieut. J. H. Simpson, who examined them in 1849 and first brought them to notice, and the second was a re-examination by William H. Jackson in 1877. He was connected with Prof. F. V. Hayden's Geological and Geographical Survey of the Territories, and his report is in that of Professor Hayden, published in 1878, p. 411.

The cañon of the Chaco, which commences about one hundred and ten miles northwest from Santo Domingo, on the Rio Grande, is quite remarkable. It has enough of the characteristics of the cañon to justify the application of this peculiar term But it differs from the great cañons in the lowness of the bordering walls and in the great breadth of the space between. Neither Simpson nor Jackson describe the cañon or valley with as much particularity as could be desired, but Mr. Jackson has furnished a map, Fig. 29, showing the course of the stream with the walls of the cañon shaded in, and with the breaks or gullies through these walls reduced to a scale. This shows that the level plain between the encompassing walls ranges from half a mile to a mile in places. The walls of the cañon are composed of friable sandstone, and are usually vertical. Their height is not given with precision. The engraving also shows the outline forms and comparative size of the several structures, with specimens of three varieties of masonry used in the walls. No. 2 shows an alternation of courses of stone from four to six inches thick and from eight to twelve inches long, with intervening courses of several thin stones. The same alternation of courses reappears in the pueblos in ruins on the Animas River, about sixty miles north. The cañon commences very much like the McElmo Cañon in Southwestern Colorado, whose vertical walls are at first about three feet high, with a level space between from three hundred to five hundred feet in width; its walls rising slowly as you descend. Without a present running stream, and bordered with open prairie land, it makes a novel appearance to the eye. Lieutenant Simpson remarks that after leaving the pueblo Pintado, which is above the commencement of the cañon, "two miles over a slightly rolling country, our general course still being to the northwest, brought us to the commencement of the Cañon de Chaco, its width here being about two hundred yards. Friable sandstone rocks, massive above, stratified below, constitute its enclosing walls."[1]   And Mr. Jackson, who entered it from the same point, remarks that "two miles from the river we descended into the cañon of the Chaco. It is here only about fifty feet in depth, with vertical walls of yellowish gray sandstone."[2] At a point twelve miles down, at the Pueblo Una Vida, he remarks that "the cañon is here about five hundred yards wide, and is perfectly level from one side to the other."[3]   Farther down the walls of the cañon rise about a hundred feet, as appears in the restorations of the Pueblo Bonito and of the Pueblo of Hungo Pavie. Whether the cañon is accessible or not from the table-land above over against the several pueblos, by means of the arroyos which break through the walls and enter the cañon, does not appear from these reports; but it seems probable, Mr. Jackson says, that near the Pueblo Bonito he ascended to the top of the bluff by means of a stairway partly cut in the face of the rock.[4]

Lieutenant Simpson, in his report, has furnished ground plans of five of these structures with measurements. Mr. Jackson has furnished eleven ground plans with measurements, two of which are without the cañon. They agree substantially, but we shall follow Mr. Jackson, as his are the most complete. The following engravings, with two or three exceptions, are taken from his report. The remainder are from Lieutenant Simpson's report.

The great edifices on the Chaco are all constructed of the same materials, and upon the same general plan, but they differ in ground dimensions, in the number of rows of apartments, and, consequently, in the number of stories. They contained from one hundred to six hundred apartments each, and would severally accommodate from five hundred to four thousand persons, living in the fashion of Indians. Speaking of the Pueblo of Pintado, Lieutenant Simpson remarks as follows : "Forming one structure, and built of tabular pieces of hard, fine-grained, compact, gray sandstone (a material entirely unknown in the present architecture of New Mexico), to which the atmosphere has imparted a reddish tinge, the layers or beds being not thicker than three inches, and sometimes as thin as one-fourth of an inch, it discovers in the masonry a combination of science and art which can only

---

[1] Lieutenant Simpson's Report, p. 77.   [2] Hayden's Report, p. 436.   [3] Ib., p. 437.   [4] Ib., p. 448.

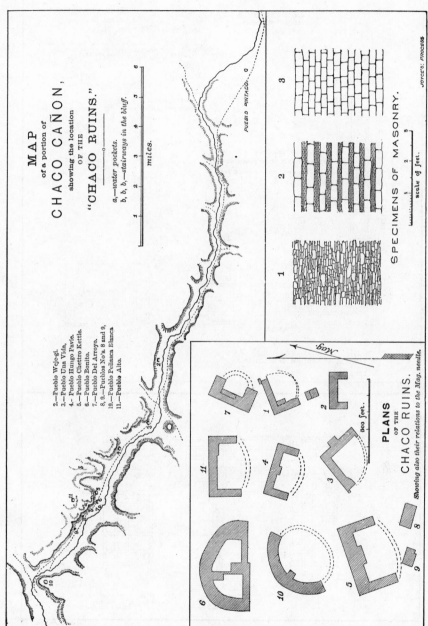

FIG. 29.—Chaco Cañon.

171

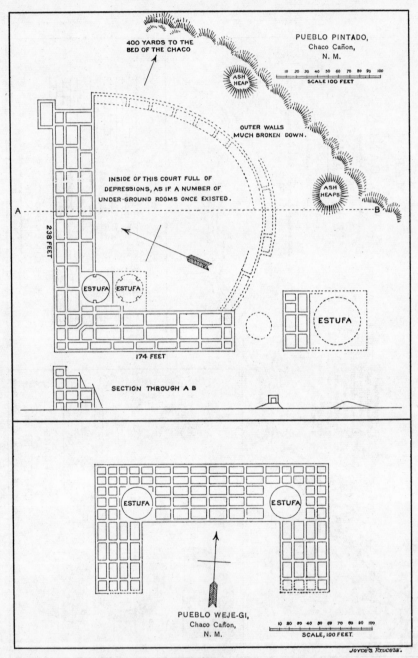

FIG. 30.—Ground plans of Pueblos Pintado and Wejegi.

be referred to a higher stage of civilization and refinement than is discoverable in the works of Mexicans or Pueblos of the present day. Indeed, so beautifully diminutive and true are the details of the structure as to cause it at a little distance to have all the appearance of a magnificent piece of mosaic work.

"In the outer face of the buildings there are no signs of mortar, the intervals between the beds being chinked with stones of the minutest thinness. The filling and backing are done in rubble masonry, the mortar presenting no indications of the presence of lime. The thickness of the main wall at base is within an inch or two of three feet; higher up, it is less, diminishing every story by retreating jogs on the inside, from bottom to top. Its elevation at its present highest point is between twenty-five and thirty feet, the series of floor beams indicating that there must have been originally three stories. The ground plan, including the court, in exterior development is about 403 feet. On the ground-floor, exclusive of the out-buildings, are fifty-four apartments, some of them as small as five feet square, and the largest about twelve by six feet. These rooms communicate with each other by very small doors, some of them as contracted as two and a half by two and a half feet; and in the case of the inner suite, the doors communicating with the interior court are as small as three and a half by two feet. The principal rooms, or those most in use, were, on account of their having large doors and windows, most probably those of the second story. The system of flooring seems to have been large transverse unhewn beams, six inches in diameter, laid transversely from wall to wall, and then a number of smaller ones, about three inches in diameter, laid longitudinally upon them. What was placed upon these does not appear, but most probably it was brush, bark, or slabs, covered with a layer of mud-mortar. The beams show no signs of the saw or axe; on the contrary, they appear to have been hacked off by means of some very imperfect instrument. On the west face of the structure, the windows, which are only in the second story, are three feet two inches by two feet two inches. On the north side they are only in the second and third stories, and are as small as fourteen by fourteen inches. At different points about the premises were three circular apartments sunk in the ground, the walls being of masonry. These apartments the Pueblo Indians called *estufas,* or places where the people held their political and religious meetings."[1]

The main building, Fig. 30, is two hundred and thirty-eight feet long, and the wing one hundred and seventy-four feet. It seems probable, from the symmetrical character of most of these structures, that the original plan contemplated an extension of the main building, the addition of another wing, to be followed by the connection of the wings with a wall, thus closing the court. These buildings were not all completed at once, but were extended and increased in the number of stories from generation to generation, as the people increased in numbers and prosperity. The plan upon which these houses were erected favored such extension. The great size of some of these structures can only be explained by the hypothesis of growth through long periods of time. The stone for building this pueblo was found quite near. Mr. Jackson remarks that " on the side of the bluff facing the valley is an outcrop of a yellowish-gray sandstone, showing in some places a seam of from twelve to eighteen inches in thickness, where the rock breaks into thin slate-like layers. It was from this stratum that most of the material in the walls was obtained."[2] He further remarks concerning the *estufas:* " In the northwest angle of the court are two circular rooms, or *estufas,* the best preserved one of which is built into the main building and forms a portion of it, while the other stands outside, but in juxtaposition, and is evidently a later and less perfect addition. They are each twenty-five feet in diameter. The inside walls are perfectly cylindrical, and in the case of the inner one are in good preservation for a height of about five feet. * * * There are no side apertures, so that light and access was probably obtained through the roof. These *estufas,* which figure so prominently in these ruins and in fact in all the ancient ruins extending southward from the basin of the Rio San Juan, are so identical in their structure, position, and evident uses with the similar ones in the pueblos now inhabited, that they indisputably connect one with the other, and show this region to have been covered at one time with a numerous population, of which the present inhabitants of the pueblos of Moki and of New Mexico are either the remnants or the descendants. * * * Beneath the ground plan [in Fig.

---

[1] Simpson's Report, p. 76.   [2] Jackson's Report, p. 433.

30] is a section through a restoration of the pueblo from north to south, showing the manner in which the stories were probably terraced from the interior of the court outward. There is no positive evidence in any of these ruins that they were thus built, but this arrangement naturally suggests itself as being the only way in which light and ease of access to the inner rooms could be readily obtained. It is also quite certain from the character of the standing walls that they were not terraced symmetrically but irregularly, after the manner of the present pueblos. There is every reason to believe that the first story was, in every case, reached from the outside by ladders, the succeeding stories being also approached from the outside, either by ladders or by stone stairways, after the manner of the Moqui pueblos. There is no positive evidence to sustain any conjecture upon this point, as in every ruin the upper stories are so entirely dismantled that no indications of any sort of stairway have ever been found. The ground-floor was divided into smaller apartments than the second floor, many of the rooms, as shown in the plan, being in the lower story divided into two or three. It would be impossible to say how high this story had been, as the floor is covered to a considerable extent with stones from the fallen walls. The second floor was ten feet between joists, and the third somewhat less, about seven feet, as near as we could judge from below. It is probable that there was a fourth story, but there is now very little evidence of it. Not a vestige of the *vigas* or other floor-timbers now remain. Some of the lintels over the doors or windows, composed of sticks of wood from one to two inches in thickness, laid close together, are now in fair preservation."[1]

Twelve miles down the cañon from the Pueblo Pintado, are the ruins of the Pueblo Wegé-gi, Fig. 30. The main building is two hundred and twenty-four feet, and the length of each wing is one hundred and twenty feet, measured on the outside, but which would include the depth of the main building. It is remarkably symmetrical. The rooms, Mr. Jackson says, are small, the largest being eight by fourteen feet, and the smallest eight feet square, and the *estufas* are each thirty feet in diameter. It is built like the last pueblo "of small tabular pieces of sandstone, arranged with beautiful effect of regularity and finish."

---

[1] Jackson's Report, p. 434.

The Pueblo of Una Vida, Fig. 31, seems to have been in process of construction, and designed, when completed, to have been one of the largest in the valley. The main building is two hundred and fifty feet in length, and the wing two hundred feet. It requires for its completion a considerable extension of the main building, and the addition of another wing. If this supposition is tenable, it serves to show that these great houses were of slow construction, by the process of addition and extension from time to time, with the increase of the people in numbers. Upon this theory of construction, the first row of the main building on the court side would first be completed one story high, and covered with a flat roof; after which, by adding one parallel wall with partition walls at intervals, as many more apartments would be obtained; and by a third and fourth parallel wall, with partitions, twice as many more. The second row was carried up two stories, the third three, and the fourth four; the successive stories receding from the court side in the form of great steps or terraces, one above the other. The wings would be commenced and completed in the same manner. Further than this, it seems evident, from the present condition of the structure, that the main building was to be considerably extended, with a second wing like the first to fill out the original design and produce a symmetrical edifice. If these inferences are warranted, the interesting conclusion is reached that these Indian architects commenced their great houses upon a definite plan, which was to be realized in its completeness after years and perhaps generations had passed away. Like the pueblo last named, it is built of tabular pieces of sandstone, and is two miles and a half lower down in the cañon.

The highest portions of the wall still standing in this pueblo are fifteen feet in height, twenty-five feet in Wegé-gi, and thirty feet in Hungo Pavie.

The Pueblo of Hungo Pavie or Crooked Nose, Fig. 31, is situated one mile further down in the cañon, upon the north side, and quite near the bordering walls. In exterior development, including the court, it is eight hundred and seventy-two feet, of which the back wall measures three hundred, and the side walls or wings one hundred and forty-four feet each. It is of medium size, but symmetrical, and larger than any single aboriginal structure in Central America in ground dimensions. There are seventy-three

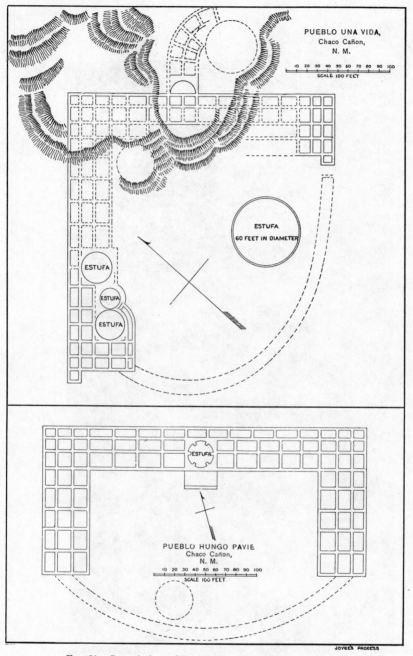

PUEBLO UNA VIDA,
Chaco Cañon,
N. M.

10 20 30 40 50 60 70 80 90 100
SCALE 100 FEET

ESTUFA
60 FEET IN DIAMETER

ESTUFA

ESTUFA

ESTUFA

PUEBLO HUNGO PAVIE
Chaco Cañon,
N. M.

10 20 30 40 50 60 70 80 90 100
SCALE 100 FEET

ESTUFA

JOYCES PROCESS

FIG. 31.—Ground plans of Pueblos Una Vida and Hungo Pavie.

Fig. 32.—Restoration of Pueblo Hungo Pavie.

178

apartments in the first story, some of which are unusually large, being about thirteen by eighteen feet, and with fifty-three rooms in the second story, and twenty-nine in the third, contain an aggregate of one hundred and fifty-five rooms. It would accommodate from eight hundred to one thousand Indians.

To complete the representation of the architectural design of these "great houses of stone," the annexed elevation is given, Fig. 32. It is a restoration of the Pueblo of Hungo Pavie, made by Mr. Kern, who accompanied General Simpson as draughtsman, and copied from his engraving. The walls of the cañon are seen in the background of engraving. We may recognize in this edifice, as it seems to the author, a very satisfactory reproduction of the so-called palaces of Montezuma, which, like this, were constructed on three sides of a court which opened on a street or causeway, and in the terraced form. From the light which this architecture throws upon that of the Aztecs, which was cotemporary, it appears extremely probable that these famous palaces, considered as exclusive residences of an Indian potentate, are purely fictitious; and that, on the contrary, they were neither more nor less than great communal or joint-tenement houses of the aboriginal American model, and with common Indians crowding all their apartments. From what is now known of the necessary constitution of society among the Village Indians, it scarcely admits of a doubt that the great house in which he lived was occupied on equal terms by many other families in common with his own, all the individuals of which were joint proprietors of the establishment which their own hands had constructed.

Two miles further down, and upon the north side of the cañon, near the bluff, are the ruins of the Pueblo of Chettro Kettle, or the Rain Pueblo, Fig. 33. The main building and the wings face the court, from which alone they are entered, and from which the several stories recede outward. Including the court, this great edifice has an exterior development of one thousand three hundred feet. The exterior wall of the main building measures four hundred and fifty-two feet in length, and the longest of the wings two hundred and twenty feet. These measurements are according to General Simpson.

From these measurements some impression may be formed of the extent of the accommodations such an edifice would afford, especially in Indian life, where a married pair and their children are found in a smaller space than one of these apartments supplied. The plan shows one hundred and seventy-five apartments in the ground story; one hundred and thirty-four in the second; one hundred and thirteen in the third; sixty in the fourth, and twenty-four in the fifth—making an aggregate of five hundred and six apartments. It is not probable that the several stories were carried up symmetrically, which would involve a diminution of some of the rooms in the upper stories. This pueblo is constructed of the same materials as those before named. "The circular *estufas*," Lieutenant Simpson remarks, "of which there are six in number, have a greater depth than any we have seen, and differ from them also in exhibiting more stories, one of them certainly showing two, and possibly three, the lowest one appearing to be almost covered up with *débris*."

This room, Fig. 34, is described by Lieutenant Simpson, but at the time of Mr. Jackson's visit he was unable to find it. "In the northwest corner of the ruins," Lieutenant Simpson remarks, "we found a room in an almost perfect state of preservation. * * * This room is fourteen by seven and a half feet in plan, and ten feet in elevation. It has an outside doorway, three and a half feet high by two and a quarter wide, and one at its west end, leading into the adjoining room, two feet wide, and at present, on account of rubbish, only two and a half feet high. The stone walls still have their plaster upon them in a tolerable state of preservation. In the south wall is a recess or niche, three feet two inches high by four feet five inches wide by four deep. Its position and size naturally suggested the idea that it might have been a fire-place, but if so, the smoke must have returned to the room, as there was no chimney outlet for it. In addition to this large recess, there were three smaller ones in the same wall. The ceiling showed two main beams, laid transversely; on these, longitudinally, were a number of smaller ones in juxtaposition, the ends being tied together by a species of wooden fibre, and the interstices chinked in with small stones; on these, again, transversely, in close contact, was a kind of lathing of the odor and appearance of cedar, all in a good state of preservation."[1] When

---

[1] Lieutenant Simpson's Report, p. 63.

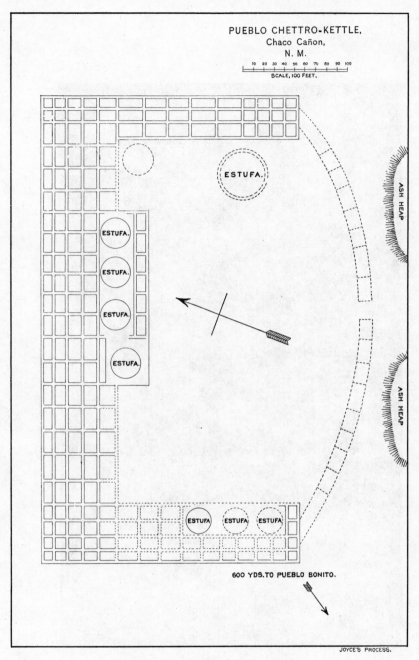

PUEBLO CHETTRO-KETTLE,
Chaco Cañon,
N. M.

SCALE, 100 FEET.

ESTUFA.

ESTUFA.

ESTUFA.

ESTUFA.

ESTUFA.

ASH HEAP

ASH HEAP

ESTUFA ESTUFA ESTUFA

600 YDS. TO PUEBLO BONITO.

JOYCE'S PROCESS.

Fig. 33.—Ground plan of Chettro Kettle.

181

Fig. 34.—Room in Pueblo Chettro Kettle.

182

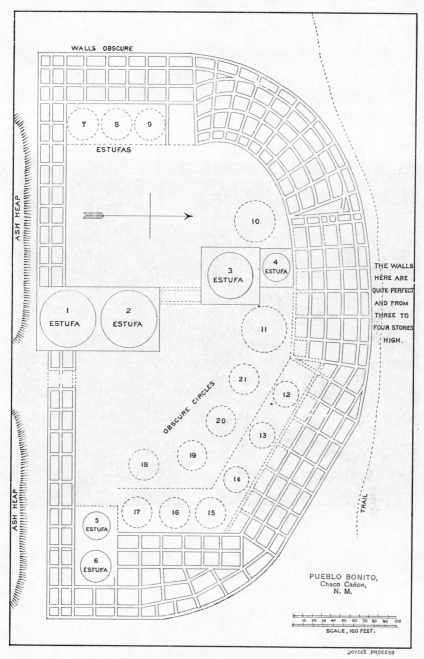

FIG. 35.—Ground plan of Pueblo Bonito.

183

FIG 36.—Room in Pueblo Bonito.

in its original condition, this fine pueblo must have made a very striking appearance.

Immediately under the walls of the cañon, and about a quarter of a mile below the last pueblo, are the ruins of the still greater Pueblo Bonito, Fig. 35. This edifice is, in some respects, the most interesting of the series as well as the best preserved in certain portions. Its exterior development, including the court, is one thousand three hundred feet. Its corners are rounded, and the east wing, now the most ruinous part of the structure, appears to have had row upon row of apartments added, until nearly one-third of the area of the court was covered. "Its present elevation," General Simpson observes, " shows that it had at least four stories of apartments. The number of rooms on the ground floor is one hundred and thirty-nine. In this enumeration, however, are not included the apartments which are not distinguishable in the eastern portion of the pueblo, and which would swell the number to about two hundred. There, then, having been at least four stories of rooms * * * there must be a reduction * * * of one range of rooms for every story after the first, which would increase the number to six hundred and forty-one."[1] No single edifice of equal accommodations, it may be here repeated, has ever been found in any part of North America. It would accommodate three thousand Indians

One of the best of its rooms is shown in the engraving, Fig. 36. It will compare, not unfavorably, with any of equal size to be found at Palenque or Uxmal, although, from the want of a vaulted ceiling, not equal in artistic design. The nice mechanical adjustment of the masonry and the finish of the ceiling are highly creditable to the taste and skill of the builders. " It is walled up," says Simpson, " with alternate beds of large and small stones, the regularity of the combination producing a very pleasant effect. The ceiling of this room is also more tasteful than any we have seen, the transverse beams being smaller and more numerous, and the longitudinal pieces, which rest upon them, only about an inch in diameter, and beautifully regular. These latter have somewhat the appearance of barked willow. The room has a doorway at each end, and one at the side, each of them leading

---

[1] Simpson's Report, p. 81

into adjacent apartments.   The light is let in by a window two feet by eight inches on the north side."[1]

Mr. Jackson's study of the ruins enabled him to produce a restoration, which is given in his report, and of whose plate Fig. 37 is a copy.   It is an interesting work, considered as a restoration, which can only claim to be an approximation.   It will be noticed that three passage-ways were left open into the court, although the ground plan shows but one.   In the Yucatan edifices, as the House of the Nuns at Uxmal, there is usually an arched gateway through the center of the building facing the court.   The court was also open at each of the four angles, which, however, might have been protected by palisades in time of danger.   The walls of the cañon are seen in the background of the engraving.

Of this pueblo, Mr. Jackson remarks that "three hundred yards below are the ruins of the Pueblo del Arroyo, Fig. 38, so named probably because it is on the verge of the deep arroyo which traverses the middle of the cañon." This was given only a passing glance by Simpson, but it well repays more careful inspection.   It is of the rectangular form, but with the open space or court facing a few degrees north of east.   The west wall is two hundred and sixty-eight feet long, and the two wings one hundred and twenty-five and one hundred and thirty-five feet, respectively; their ends connected by a narrow and low semi-circular wall.   The wings are the most massively-built and best-preserved portion of the whole building, that portion which lies between them and back of the court being much more ruinous and dissimilar in many respects.   The walls of the south wing, which are in the first story, very heavy and massive, are still standing to the height of the third story.   Many of the *vigas* are still in place, and are large and perfectly smooth and straight undressed logs of pine, averaging ten inches in thickness; none of the smaller beams or other wood-work now remains. There is one *estufa* thirty-seven feet in diameter in this wing.   In the north wing the walls are standing somewhat higher. but do not indicate more than three stories, though there was probably another.   The *vigas* of the second floor project through the wall for a distance of about five feet along its whole northern face, the same as in the Pueblo Hungo Pavie.   There are

---

[1] Simpson's Report, p. 81.

Fig. 37.—Restoration of Pueblo Bonito.

187

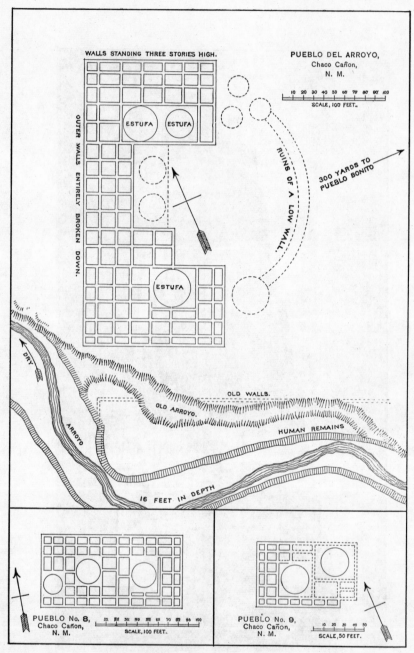

FIG. 38.—Ground plan of Pueblo Del Arroyo

two *estufas;* one near the east end of the wing, which is twenty-seven feet in diameter, was three stories in height. The floor-beams are removed, but the remains show this plainly. The interior is nearly filled up, but it was originally over twenty-five feet in depth. The ruins of the other *estufa* are insignificant compared with this, and it probably consisted of but one low room. Facing the center of the court are remains of what were three circular rooms. At the end of the wings, outside of the building, are faint outlines of other circular apartments or inclosures, shown by dotted lines on the plan. In the central portion of the ruin, between the two wings, some rooms have been preserved entire. I crawled down into one of these through a small hole in the covering, and found its walls to consist of delicate masonry, thinly plastered and whitewashed. The ceiling was formed in the usual manner, fine willow brush supporting the earthen floor above, instead of the lath-like sticks or thin boards that were used in the exceptional cases noted.

Two miles below the Pueblo del Arroyo are the ruins of the Pueblo of Peñasca Blanca, Fig. 39. "This is the largest pueblo in plan we have seen," Lieutenant Simpson remarks, "and differs from others in the arrangement of the stones composing its walls. The walls of the other pueblos were all of one uniform character in the several beds composing it; but in this there is a regular alternation of large and small stones, which are about one foot in length and one-half a foot in thickness, form but a single bed, and then, alternating with these, are three or four beds of very small stones, each about an inch in thickness. The general plan of the structure also differs from the others in approximating the form of the circle. The number of the rooms at present discoverable upon the first floor is one hundred and twelve; and the existing walls show that there have been at least three stories of apartments. The number of circular *estufas* we counted was seven."[1]

"In point of size," Mr. Jackson remarks, "the rooms of this ruin will average larger than in most of the others; the twenty-eight rooms, as they appear on the outer circumference, average twenty feet in length from wall to wall inside. The smallest, which are only ten feet wide, are at the two

---

[1] Simpson's Report, p. 64.

ends. The width of the rooms of each tier appears to have been constant throughout the length of the whole ruin. The dimensions given in these drawings are, in nearly every case, of those apartments which constitute the second story, as it is in those that there is the least obscuration of the walls.

"In most of the ruins the first floor is almost entirely filled up with *débris*, but when the ruins can be followed they show that this floor is generally divided into much smaller apartments, two or three occurring sometimes in place of each one above them. The eastern half of the ellipse, as above said, consists of a single continuous line of small apartments, with a uniform width of thirteen feet inside and an average length of twenty feet. By a curious coincidence the same number of rooms are in this row as in the outer tier of the main building. The walls of the central portion for a distance of about two hundred feet are in fair preservation, standing in places six to eight feet in height, the dividing walls showing apertures leading from one room to another. They are built of stones uniform in size, averaging six by nine by three and a half inches. Mortar was used between the stones instead of the small plates of stone. At both ends, for a distance of some two hundred feet from the point of juncture with the main building, the walls are entirely leveled, but enough remains to show the dimensions of each apartment. Twenty yards from the south end of the building are the ruins of a great circular room fifty feet in diameter, with some portions of its interior wall in such preservation that its character is readily discernible."[1]

Without the cañon, upon the mesa, and about half a mile back of the bluff, upon the north side, are the ruins of the Pueblo Alto, constructed of stone on three sides of a court, like those before described. The main building is three hundred feet long, and one wing is two hundred feet measured externally from the back end of the main building, the other wing is one hundred and seventy feet measured the same way. This wing is but two rooms deep, while the main building and the other wing are each three rooms deep. It has six estufas, with remains of a convex wall, connecting the two wings, and inclosing the court. These estufas, like those in the

---

[1] Hayden's Tenth Annual Report, 1878, p. 446.

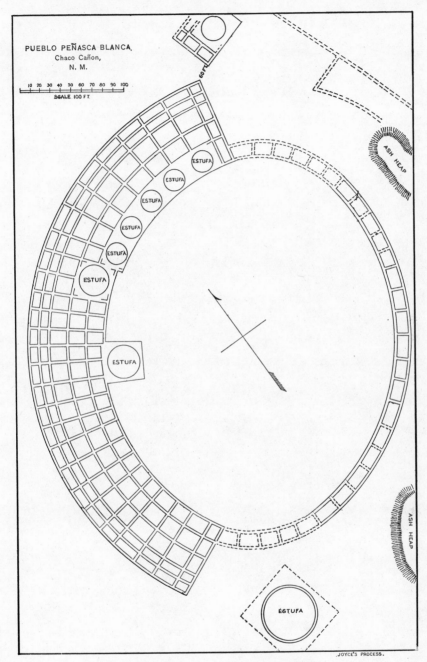

PUEBLO PEÑASCA BLANCA,
Chaco Cañon,
N. M.

10 20 30 40 50 60 70 80 90 100
SCALE 100 FT.

ESTUFA

ESTUFA

ESTUFA

ESTUFA

ESTUFA

ESTUFA

ESTUFA

ESTUFA

ASH HEAP

ASH HEAP

JOYCE'S PROCESS.

FIG. 39.—Ground plan of Pueblo Peñasca Blanca.

other pueblos, suggest the probability that they were places for holding the councils of the gentes and phratries.

This great ruin, with two others of smaller size, shown in Fig. 38 as No. 8 and No. 9, of which the first is one hundred and thirty-five feet long and one hundred feet deep, and the other seventy-eight by sixty-three feet, both of stone, complete the list of ruins in the cañon. The pueblo of Pintado, is, however, at the upper end, and without the cañon, and the Pueblo Alto, not yet described, is not in the cañon, but on the bluff. It is a remarkable display of ancient edifices; the most remarkable in New Mexico. With the bordering walls of the cañon, rising vertically, in places, one hundred feet high, it presented long vistas in either direction, with natural and inclosing walls. Shut in from all view of the table lands at the summit of these walls, this valley, at the time its great houses were occupied, must have presented a very striking picture of human life as it existed in the Middle Period of Barbarism. The greater part of the valley must have been covered with garden beds, from which the people derived their principal support, as the mesa lands without the cañon were too dry for cultivation. It no doubt presented an interesting picture of industrious and contented life, with a corresponding advancement in the arts of this period. There is still some uncertainty concerning the time when these pueblos were last occupied, and the fate of their inhabitants. There are a number of circumstances tending to show that they were the "Seven Cities of Cibola," against which the expedition of Coronado was directed in 1540–1542. There are seven pueblos in ruins in the cañon, without reckoning Nos. 8 and 9, the smallest in the valley. Some of the facts which point to these pueblos as the Towns of Cibola may here be noted.

In his Relation to the Viceroy, which is dated from the province of Cibola, August 3, 1540, Coronado describes his conquest and intimates his disappointment in the following language:

"It remaineth now to certify your Honor of the seven cities, and of the kingdoms and provinces whereof the Father Provincial made report unto your Lordship. And, to be brief, I can assure your Honor he said the truth in nothing that he reported, but all was quite contrary, saving only the names of the cities, and great houses of stone; for although they be not wrought with turqueses, nor with lime, nor bricks, yet they are very excellent good houses, of three, or four, or five lofts high, wherein are good lodgings and fair chambers, with ladders instead of stairs, and certain cellars under the ground, very good and paved, which are made for winter,—they are in manner like stoves; and the ladders which they have for their houses are in a manner moveable and portable, which are taken away and set down when they please; and they are made of two pieces of wood, with their steps, as ours be.   The seven cities are seven small towns, all made with these kind of houses that I speak of; and they stand all within four leagues together, and they are all called the Kingdom of Cibola, and every one of them have their particular name, and none of them is called Cibola, but all together they are called Cibola.   And this town, which I call a city, I have named Granada, as well because it is somewhat like unto it, as also in remembrance of your Lordship.   In this town where I now remain there may be some two hundred houses, all compassed with walls; and, I think, that, with the rest of the houses which are not so walled, they may be together five hundred.   There is another town near this, which is one of the seven, and it is somewhat bigger than this, and another of the same bigness that this is of, and the four are somewhat less; and I send them all painted unto your Lordship with the voyage.   And the parchment wherein the picture is was found here with other parchments.   The people of this town seem unto me of a reasonable stature, and witty, yet they seem not to be such as they should be, of that judgment and wit to build these houses in such sort as they are.   *   *   *   They travel eight days' journey unto certain plains lying towards the North Sea.   In this country there are certain skins, well dressed; and they dress them and paint them where they kill their oxen [buffalo]; for so they say themselves."[1]

On the fourth day after the capture of Cibola, Coronado further says: "They set in order all their goods and substance, their women and children, and fled to the hills, leaving their towns as it were abandoned, wherein remained very few of them."[2]

It will be observed that the phrases "great houses of stone," and "good houses of three, or four, or five lofts high," not only describe the

---

[1] Hakluyt, vol. iii, p. 377.   [2] Ib., vol. iii, p. 379.

pueblo on the Chaco in apt language, but there are no other pueblos in New Mexico, exclusively of stone, of which we have knowledge, except those of the Mokis, in the Cañon de Chelly, on the Animas River, and elsewhere in Southwestern Colorado. There is an apparent difficulty in the narrative, in the reference made to the number of houses; but it is evident, I think, that Coronado meant apartments or sections, treating each great house as a block of houses, and expressing a doubt of their "judgment and wit to build these houses in such sort as they are." If any doubt remained, it is entirely removed by the fact that all the pueblo houses in New Mexico, whether occupied or in ruins, are great edifices constructed like these on the communal principle, and that two hundred such houses grouped in one town were an utter impossibility.

Jaramillo, who wrote his Relation some time after the return of the expedition, remarks, "that all the water-courses that we fell in with, whether brook or river, as far as that of Cibola, and I believe for one or two days' journey beyond, flow in the direction of the South Sea [the Pacific]; farther on they take the direction of the North Sea [the Atlantic]."[1] This tends to show that Cibola was situated on a tributary of the Colorado, which gathers all the waters of New Mexico west of the Rio Grande and north of the Gila, and also that it was situated quite near the dividing ridge. It is but ten miles from the Cañon de Torrejon, on the Puerco, a tributary of the Rio Grande, to the commencement of the Rio de Chaco, an affluent of the San Juan, and but twenty-three miles to the Pueblo Pintado. In this respect the sites of the ruins on the Chaco are in close agreement with the description of the situations of the towns of Cibola. Castañeda, after speaking of the seven villages, and the character of the houses, remarks that "the valley is very narrow, between precipitous mountains" ["C'est une vallée très-étroite entre des montagues escarpées"],[2] which, in the light of Coronado's declaration, that "the country is all plain, and on no side mountains," may perhaps have reference to the encompassing walls of the cañon. This language, literally interpreted, does not describe this cañon, neither is there any valley in New Mexico, occupied by pueblos, which answers this description.

[1] Coll. H. Ternaux-Compans, vol. ix, p. 370.   [2] Castañeda Relation, Ternaux-Compans, ix, p. 164.

Upon the evidence contained in these several narratives, and with our present knowledge of New Mexico, the sites of the seven towns of Cibola cannot be determined with certainty. It is a question of probabilities; and those which seem the strongest in favor of the ruins on the Chaco are the following: Firstly, they are superior, architecturally, to any pueblos in New Mexico, now existing or in ruins, and agree in number and in proximity to each other, with the towns of Cibola as described Secondly, they are upon an affluent of the San Juan, and within "one or two days' journey" of the waters which flow into the Gulf of Mexico; in other words, they are near the summit of the watershed of the two oceans, where Jaramillo distinctly states Cibola was situated. Thirdly, they are within eight days of the buffalo ranges, the nearest of which are upon the northeastern confines of New Mexico. Cibola was said to be thus situated. Moreover, the name Cibola implies the buffalo country. We are also told by Friar Marcos that the Indians south of the Gila trafficked with the Cibolans for ox-hides, which he found them wearing. Zuñi, the only known place, showing a probability that it was one of the seven towns, is too far distant from the buffalo ranges to answer to this portion of the narrative. Lastly, the evidence, collectively, favors a far northern as well as far eastern position for Cibola. The people of Cibola knew nothing of either ocean. This could hardly have been true of the people of Zuñi with respect to the Pacific, or at least the Gulf of California. Coronado himself was in doubt as to which sea was nearest, and seems to have been conscious of the widening of the continent upon both sides of him. Assuming that the pueblos on the Chaco were inhabited in 1540, they were the finest structures then in New Mexico. Coronado captured all the villages on the Rio Grande, and probably sent a detachment to the Moki Pueblos, and remained two years in the country. It seems impossible, therefore, that he should have failed to find the pueblos on the Chaco; and they answer his description better than any other pueblos in New Mexico.

With respect to the manner of constructing these houses, it was probably done, as elsewhere remarked, from time to time, and from generation to generation. Like a feudal castle, each house was a growth by additions from small beginnings, made as exigencies required. When one of these houses, after attaining a sufficient size, became overcrowded with inhabitants, it is probable that a strong colony, like the swarm from the parent hive, moved out, and commenced a new house, above or below, in the same valley. This would be repeated, as the people prospered, until several pueblos grew up within an extent of twelve or fifteen miles, as in the valley of the Chaco. When the capabilities of the valley were becoming overtaxed for their joint subsistence, the colonists would seek more distant homes. At the period of the highest prosperity of these pueblos, the valley of the Chaco must have possessed remarkable advantages for subsistence The plain between the walls of the cañon was between half a mile and a mile in width near the several pueblos, but the amount of water now passing through it is small. In July, according to Lieutenant Simpson, the running stream was eight feet wide and a foot and a half deep at one of the pueblos; while Mr. Jackson found no running water and the valley entirely dry in the month of May, with the exception of pools of water in places and a reservoir of pure water in the rocks at the top of the bluff. The condition of the region is shown by these two statements. During the rainy season in the summer, which is also the season of the growing crops, there is an abundance of water; while in the dry season it is confined to springs, pools, and reservoirs. From the number of pueblos in the valley, indicating a population of several thousand, the gardens within it must have yielded a large amount of subsistence; the climate being favorable to its growth and ripening.

CHAPTER VIII.

RUINS OF HOUSES OF THE SEDENTARY INDIANS OF THE SAN JUAN RIVER AND ITS TRIBUTARIES—CONTINUED.

About sixty miles north of the pueblos on the Chaco, and in the valley of the Animas River, is a cluster of stone pueblos, very similar to the former. These I visited in 1878. The valley is broad at this point, and for some miles above and below to its mouth. At the time of our visit (July 22) the river was a broad stream, carrying a large volume of water. We followed down the river from the point of its rise in the dividing range, where it was a mere brook, nearly the whole distance through Silverton to Animas City. The constant accession of mountain streams, and the rapid descent of its bed, soon changed it into a noisy and dashing stream. About twenty miles above Animas City we were compelled to ascend to the top of the bordering mountains to avoid the narrow cañon below, which was impassable; and in descending from Animas City to visit these pueblos we crossed over to the La Plata Valley, and after passing through this valley we recrossed to the Animas Valley to avoid similar cañons also impassable. The supply of water for irrigation at the pueblo was abundant.

The pueblo of which the ground[1] plan is shown, Fig. 40, is one of four situated within the extent of one mile on the west side of the Animas River in New Mexico, about twelve miles above its mouth. Besides these four, there are five other smaller ruins of inferior structures within the same area. This pueblo was five or perhaps six stories high, consisting of a main building three hundred and sixty-eight feet long, and two wings two hundred and seventy feet long, measured along the external wall on the right and left sides, and one hundred and ninety-nine feet measured along the inside

---

[1] The engravings of Figs. 40, 41, and 41 a, were kindly loaned by Mr. F. W. Putnam of the Peabody Museum, Cambridge, Mass.

198

from the end back to the main building.   A fourth structure crosses from the end of one wing to the end of the other, thus inclosing an open court. It was of the width of one and perhaps two rows of apartments, and slightly

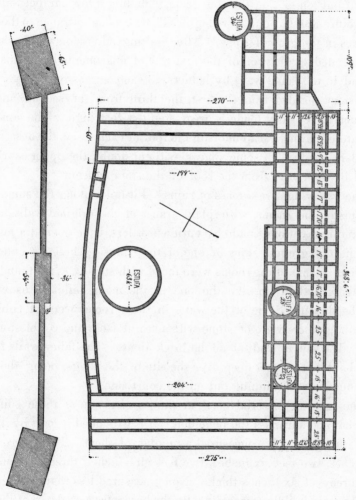

FIG. 40.—Ground plan of Pueblo on Animas River, N. M.

convex outward, which enlarged somewhat the size of the court.   The main building and the wings were built in the so-called terraced form; that is to say, the first row of apartments in the main building and in each wing on the court side were but one story high.   The second row back of these were carried up two stories high, the third row three stories, and so on to the number of five stories for the main building and four for each wing. The external wall rose forty or fifty feet where the structure was five stories high and but ten feet on the court side, including a low parapet wall, where the structure was but one story high. There was no entrance to these great structures in the ground story. After getting admission within the court, they ascended to the roof of the first row of apartments by means of ladders, and in the same way, by ladders, to each successive story. As the second story receded from the first, the third from the second, and so on, each successive story made a great step ten feet high. The apartments were entered through trap-doors in the roof of each story, the descent being by ladders inside. In some places, without doubt, the upper stories were entered by doorways from the roof of the story in front.

The two wings are a mass of ruins. Pit-holes along the summit show the forms of the rooms, with plain traces of the original walls here and there, and excavations, made by curious settlers, have opened a number of rooms in the ground story of one of the wings. These we entered and measured. Some of the rooms were faced with stone, i. e., we found a stone wall regularly laid up, like the one in the main building, as will elsewhere be shown. Some of the walls in these rooms were of cobblestone and adobe; others were of stone with natural faces and cobblestone intermixed. We saw no wall of adobe brick alone. The fallen walls formed a mass about twelve feet deep over the site of the wings, being the deepest on the outside and thinning out on the court side.

The mass of material used in the construction of these edifices was very great and surprises the beholder. It is explained in part by the thickness of the walls. We measured a number of them. They were two feet four inches, two feet six inches, two feet nine inches, three feet, and in rare cases three feet six inches thick. None measured less than two feet.

The main building was originally the best constructed part of the edifice, it may be supposed, because a part of it now remains standing. The walls of the first story, of some part of the second, and, in some places, of a part of the third story, forming the second row of apartments from the outside, are still standing, and rise about twenty-five feet from the ground. The measurements of the second row of apartments, as shown in the diagram, were from the standing walls, and were made in the second story.

The first or basement story is filled up with the rubbish of the fallen walls, ceilings, and floors, in the second row of apartments named. In some cases they are full above the line of the original ceilings; in others nearly up to them. The main ceiling beams were of yellow cedar from eight to twelve inches in diameter, usually three and four in number, and were placed across the narrow way of the room. Stubs of these beams still remain in the walls parallel with the court. Just above the line of these beams in the other two walls were the ends of a row of poles about four inches in diameter, which passed transversely across the cedar beams. Stubs of these poles, broken off short at the line of the walls, still remain in place. Upon these poles were originally thin pieces of split cedar limbs, and then the floor of adobe mortar, four or five inches thick. We thus get the position and height of the floor of the first and second stories, which were about nine feet six inches for the ground story, and nine feet for the second story.

The external wall of the main building has fallen the entire length of the structure. As these ruins are resorted to by the few settlers in the valley as a stone quarry to obtain stone for foundations to their houses and barns, and for stoning up their wells, the loose material is being gradually removed; and when the standing walls are more convenient to take they will be removed also. One farmer told me he thought that one quarter of the accessible material of this and the adjacent stone pueblo had already been removed. It is to be hoped that the number of these settlers inclined to Vandalism will not increase.

A part of the partition walls which connected the outside wall with the next parallel wall is still standing where the wall last named rises above the second story. They stand out for three or four feet like buttresses against the wall, and show that the masonry of the parallel and transverse walls was articulated, that the partition walls were continuous from front to rear, and that the walls of the several stories rested upon each other. All this is seen by a bare inspection of the walls as they now stand.

The masonry itself is the chief matter of interest in these structures.

Every room in the main building was faced with stone on the four sides, having an adobe floor and a wooden ceiling. Each room had, as far as walls now remain to show, two doorways through the walls parallel with the court, and four openings about twelve inches square, two on the side of each doorway, near the ceiling. These openings were for light and ventilation. In a limited sense it may be said that the stones were dressed, and also that they were laid in courses, but, in the high and strict meaning of these terms, neither is true. The stones used were small and of different sizes. Sometimes they were nearly square, from six to eight inches on a side; sometimes a foot long by six inches wide. The latter is the size of the stones used at Uxmal and Chichen Itza, according to Norman. In some cases longer and thicker stones were used without any attempt to square the ends. In some instances thin pieces of stone were employed with parallel faces. In all cases the stone was a sandstone, now of a reddish brown color. It is the prevailing stone in the bluffs of the Animas River, and of all the rivers parallel with it running into the San Juan, as far as personal observation enabled me to judge. It is a soft rather than a hard stone, usually of a buff color when first quarried, and some of it has decayed in the using. The wasted and weatherworn appearance of some of these stones would otherwise indicate a very great age for the structure. With stone of the size used a good face can be formed by simple fracture, and a joint sufficiently close may be made by a few strokes with a stone maul. If finer work was aimed at, it must have been accomplished by rubbing the stones to a face. But this work is sufficiently explained by the former processes. In the row of apartments and stories named, both faces of each wall were of stone, so that all of the apartments were of stone on the inside. They were fair walls, both in masonry and workmanship, and creditable to the builders. There was an attempt to lay up these walls in courses of uniform thickness, but each course differing from the one above and below it. The attempt was only partially successful. They did not hesitate to break in upon the regularity of the courses. Some of the standing walls are now sprung; but most of them are straight, and fairly vertical, the adobe mortar being sound and the bond unbroken.

The Indian had a string from time immemorial. With it he could strike a circle, and lay out the four sides of a quadrangular structure with tolerable correctness. It is not too much to assume that with a string and sinker attached the Village Indian had the plumb-line, and could prove his wall as well as we can. At all events, the eye still proves the general correctness of their work.

The adobe mortar of the Pueblo Indians is something more than mud mortar, although far below a mortar of lime and sand. Adobe is a kind of finely pulverized clay with a bond of considerable strength by mechanical cohesion. In Southern Colorado, in Arizona, and New Mexico, there are immense tracts covered with what is called adobe soil. It varies somewhat in the degree of its excellence. The kind of which they make their pottery has the largest per cent. of alumina, and its presence is indicated by the salt weed which grows in this particular soil. This kind also makes the best adobe mortar. The Indians use it freely in laying their walls, as freely as our masons use lime mortar; and although it never acquires the hardness of cement, it disintegrates slowly. The mortar in these walls is still sound, so that it requires some effort of strength to loosen a stone from the wall and remove it. But this adobe mortar is adapted only to the dry climate of Southern Colorado, Arizona, and New Mexico, where the precipitation is less than five inches per annum. The rains and frosts of a northern climate would speedily destroy it. To the presence of this adobe soil, found in such abundance in the regions named, and to the sandstone of the bluffs, where masses are often found in fragments, we must attribute the great progress made by these Indians in house-building.

The exclusive presence of this adobe mortar in all New Mexican structures of the aboriginal period shows that the tribes of New Mexico were then ignorant of a mortar of lime and sand. And here a digression may be allowed to consider whether a cement of this grade was known to the aborigines. Theoretically, the use of a mortar composed of quick-lime and sand, which gives a cement chemically united, would not be expected of the Indian tribes either in North or South America. There is no sufficient proof that they ever produced a cement of this high grade. It requires a kiln, artificially constructed, and a concentrated heat to burn limestone into lime, supposing they had learned that lime could be thus obtained, and some knowledge of the properties of quick-lime before they reached the idea of a true cement. The Spanish writers generally speak of walls of lime and stone, thus implying a mortar of lime and sand. Thus, Bernal Diaz speaks of the great temple in the Pueblo of Mexico as surrounded "with double enclosures built of stone and lime."[1]   Clavigero remarks that " the houses of lords and people of circumstances were built of stone and lime."[5]   Again, " the ignorant Mr. De Pauw denies that the Mexicans had either the knowledge or made use of lime; but it is evident from the testimony of all the historians of Mexico, by tribute rolls, and above all from the ancient buildings still remaining, that all these nations made the same use of lime as all the Europeans do."[3]   In like manner, Herrera, speaking of Zempoala, near Vera Cruz, remarks that the Spaniards, entering the town, found "the houses [were] built of lime and stone;"[4] and again, speaking of the houses in Yucatan, he remarks that "at the place where the encounter happened, there were three houses built of lime and stone."[5]   These several statements can hardly be said to prove the fact of the use of a mortar of lime and sand.   Mr. John L. Stephens, in speaking of the ruins at Palenque, is more explicit: "The building was constructed of stone, with a mortar of lime and sand, and the whole front was covered with stucco, and painted."[6] The back wall of the governor's house at Uxmal is nine feet thick through its length of two hundred and seventy feet   In this wall, by means of crowbars, " the Indians made a hole six and seven feet deep, but throughout the wall was solid and consisted of large stones imbedded in mortar, almost as hard as rock."[7]   At the ruins of Zayi, there was one row of ten apartments, two hundred and twenty feet long, called the Casas Cerrada, or closed house, because the core over which the triangular ceiling was constructed had not been removed when the house was abandoned, of which Stephens says, " We found ourselves in apartments finished with the walls and ceilings like the others, but filled up (except so far as they had

[1] The True History of the Conquest of Mexico, Keatinge's Translation, Salem ed., 1803, vol. i, p. 208.
[2] History of Mexico, Cullen's Trans., Phila. ed., 1817, vol. ii, p. 232.
[3] Ib., vol. ii, p. 237.
[4] History of America, Stevens' Trans., London ed., 1725, vol. ii, p. 266.
[5] Ib., p. 112.
[6] Central America, Chiapas and Yucatan, vol. ii, p. 310.
[7] Ib., vol. i, p. 178.

been emptied by the Indians) with solid masses of mortar and stones."[1] Norman, speaking of the ruins of the House of the Cacique at Chichen, remarks, "that the wall is made of large and uniformly square blocks of limestone set in mortar, which appears to be as durable as the stone itself."[2] Elsewhere, speaking of the ruins of Yucatan generally, he observes, "the stones are cut in *parallelopipeds* of about twelve inches in length and six in breadth, the interstices filled up of the same materials of which the terraces are composed."[3] That these tribes used mortar of some kind in their stone walls cannot be doubted, but these several statements do not prove the use of quick-lime, which is the main question Mr. Stephens' statement satisfied me until I saw the New Mexican pueblos. These show that a very efficient mortar can be had without the use of lime. The Indians of Mexico and the coast tribes near Vera Cruz plastered their houses externally with gypsum, which made them a brilliant white, and the stucco used upon the inner walls of houses in Chiapas and Yucatan was not unlikely made of gypsum. This mineral is abundant as well as easily treated. From it comes plaster of Paris, and from it may have come in some form the bond which held the mortar together, to the strength of which Mr. Stephens refers.

The neatness and general correctness of the masonry is now best seen in the doorways. In the standing walls of the second story, and of the first, where occasionally uncovered, there are to be seen two doorways in each room, as before stated, running in all cases across the building from the court side toward the external wall, and never in the direction of its length. These doorways measured some three feet two inches in height by two feet six inches in width, and others three feet four inches by two feet seven inches.

The stone used in these doorways are rather smaller than those in other parts of the wall, but prepared in the same manner.

I brought away two of these stones, taken from the standing walls of the main building, as samples of the character of the work with respect to size and dressing. Fig. 41 represents one of them, engraved from a photograph. It measures eight inches in its greatest length by six inches in its greatest width, and it is two and three-quarter inches in thickness. The

---

[1] Central American, Chiapas and Yucatan, vol. ii, p. 23. [2] Rambles in Yucatan, p. 120. [3] Ib., p. 127.

upper and lower faces of the stone are substantially, but not exactly, parallel. It also shows one angle, which is substantially, but not exactly, a right angle and it was so adjusted that the long edge was on the doorway and short one in the wall of a chamber or apartment, with the right angle at

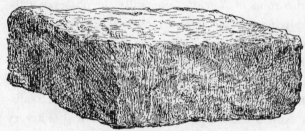

the corner between them. This stone was evidently prepared by fracture, probably with a stone maul, and the regularity of the breakage was doubtless partly due to skill and partly

FIG. 41.—Stone from doorway.

to accident. It shows no marks of the chisel or the drove, or of having been rubbed, and where the square is applied to the sides or angles the rudeness of the stone is perfectly apparent.

Fig. 41 a represents a sandstone cut by American skilled workmen in the form of a brick, and it is intended to show by comparison the great dif-

ference between the dressed stone of the civilized man and the ruder stone of the mason in the condition of barbarism. The comparison shows that no instruments of exactness were used in the stone work of the pueblo, and that exactness was not attempted. But the accuracy of a practiced eye and hand, such as their methods af-

FIG. 41 a.—A finished block of sandstone, for comparison with Fig. 41.

forded, was reached, and this was all they attempted. With stones as rude as that shown in the figure, a fair and even respectable stone wall may be laid. The art of architecture in stone is of slow and difficult growth. Stone prepared by fracture with a stone hammer precedes dressed stone, which requires metallic implements. In like manner mud mortar or adobe mortar precedes a mortar of lime and sand. The Village Indians of America were working their way experimentally, and step by step, in the art of house-building, as all mankind have been obliged to do, each race for itself; and the structures the Village Indians have raised in various parts of America, imperfect as they are by contrast, are highly creditable to their intelligence.

Stone lintels were not used for these doorways, as stones three feet long would have been required. No stones of half that length are to be seen in any of the walls. They had, however, the idea of a stone lintel, for they used them in this structure over the foot-square openings for light and air. We found a stone lintel over an opening eighteen inches wide in a cliff house on the Mancos River. This was so firmly imbedded that we found its removal impossible. They used for a lintel six round cedar cross-pieces, Fig. 42, each about four inches in diameter and now perfectly sound.

In some of these doorways we noticed a peculiar feature. On the side toward the external wall, one and sometimes two of these wooden lintels were placed, four and sometimes six inches lower than the remainder, so that on entering from the outside room into the second room, the top of the doorway rose higher as the room was entered. A necessity was experienced to save the head from bumps, and the wonder is that it did not occur

FIG. 42.—Section of Cedar Lintel.

to them to raise the doorways to the height of the body. As the doorways were always open, no doors being used, it may well be that larger openings would have created stronger currents of air through the building than they wished. The ends of these lintels were hacked off by stone implements of some kind.

The peculiar arrangement of the doorways tends to show that this great house was divided into sections by the partition walls extending from the court to the exterior wall; and that the rooms above were connected with those below by means of trap-doors and ladders. If this supposition be well founded, the five rooms on the ground floor, from the court back, communicated with each other by doorways. The four in the second story communicated with each other in the same manner, and with those below through trap-doors in the floors. The three rooms in the third story communicated with each other by doorways, and with those below as before. The same would be true of the two rooms of the fourth story. It seems probable that the connected rooms were occupied by a group of related families.

We afterwards found the same thing nearly exemplified in the present occupied Pueblo of Taos, in New Mexico. We found that the families lived in the second and upper stories, and used the rooms below them for storage and for granaries. Each family had two, four, and six rooms, and those who held the upper rooms held those below.

In the south wing before mentioned, several rooms on the ground floor are still perfect, with the ceilings in place upholding the rubbish above. The openings or trap-doorways of two of these rooms are still perfect, but the ladders are gone. The rooms had been opened, as elsewhere stated, by late explorers. One of these trap-doors measured sixteen by seventeen inches, and the other sixteen inches square. Each was formed in the floor by pieces of wood put together. The work was neatly done. These rooms were smaller than the rooms above. Some were as narrow as four feet six inches, others six feet, showing that one room had been divided into two. The basement rooms were probably occupied for storage exclusively, whence their division. They were dark, except as light entered through the trap-doorway from above.

The structure connecting the wings and bounding the court was evidently a single or double row of apartments. This is shown by the amount of fallen material, which is larger than a wall would require, and from pits or depressions which plainly marked the outline of apartments.

There are two circular *estufas* in the main building, one twenty-three feet and the other twenty-eight feet in diameter. A part of the wall of the first *estufa* is still standing. It is of stone, mostly of blocks about five inches square, and laid in courses, with considerable regularity. The work is equal to the best masonry in the edifice. In the open court, and near the outer structure, bounding it in front, is another *estufa* of great size, sixty-three and a half feet in diameter. These *estufas*, which are used as places of council, and for the performance of their religious rites, are still found at all the present occupied pueblos in New Mexico. There are six at Taos, three at each house, and they are partly sunk in the ground by an excavation. They are entered through a trap-doorway in the roof, the descent being by a ladder.

Outside the front wall closing the court, and about thirty feet distance therefrom, are the remains of a low wall crossing the entire front and extending beyond it. The end structures were about sixty-five feet long by forty feet wide, while at the center was a smaller structure, fifty-four feet long by eighteen wide. All its parts were connected. It was evidently erected for defensive purposes; but it is impossible to make out its character from the remains. One wing is several feet longer than the other, and the wall on the court side is about twenty feet longer than the opposite exterior wall, thus showing that they used no exact measurements.

There were no fire-places with chimneys in this structure. There are none in the ruins in Yucatan and Central America. It is a fair inference, therefore, that chimneys were entirely unknown to the aborigines at the time of their discovery. They have since that time been adopted into the old pueblo houses from American or Spanish sources. They are placed in one corner of the room. We saw recently at Taos two chimneys and two fire-places in one and the same room, one for cooking and the other for a fire to warm the room; proof conclusive that they were not to the chimney born. They were in an apartment of one of the principal chiefs.

In a number of rooms are recesses like niches left in the wall, about two feet six inches wide and high, and about eighteen inches deep. These furnished places to set household articles in, in the place of a mantel or shelf. We afterwards saw niches precisely similar at Taos, and thus used.

It remains to consider the number of rooms or apartments contained in this great edifice. It is plain that it was built in the terraced form, the second story set back from the first, the third from the second, and so on to the last, which was a single row of apartments, on the top somewhere, but not necessarily on the back side. Pueblos were not entirely uniform in this respect. The edifice at Taos recedes in front and rear and even upon the sides. This may have been built in the same way, but it can neither be proved nor disproved from the ruins. The number of apartments would not vary much whether the upper stories were symmetrically or irregularly formed. If symmetrical, the main building contained two hundred and sixty apartments, and each wing seventy, making the computation for the latter by area and from the number of depression still discernible, thus making an aggregate of four hundred rooms.

The house was a fortress, proving the insecurity in which the people lived. It was also a joint tenement house of the aboriginal American model, indicating a plan of life not well understood. It may indicate an ancient communism in living, practiced by large households formed on the principle of kin. In such a case the communism was limited to the household as a part of a kinship.

Those familiar with the remains of Indian Pueblos in ruins will recognize at once the resemblance between this pueblo and the stone pueblos in ruins on the Rio Chaco, in New Mexico, about sixty miles distant from these ruins, particularly the one called Hungo Pavie, so fully described by General J. H. Simpson. There is one particular in which the masonry agrees, viz., in the use of courses of thin stones, about half an inch in thickness, sometimes three together, and sometimes five and six. These courses are carried along the wall from one side to the other, but often broken in upon. The effect is quite pretty. These stones measure six inches in length by one-half an inch in thickness. General Simpson found the same courses of thin stones, and even thinner, in the Chaco ruins, and comments upon the pleasing effect they produced.

This edifice was a credit to the skill and industry of the men among the Village Indians; for the men, and not the women, were the architects and the masons, although the women undoubtedly assisted in doing the work. Women brought stone and adobe and cedar, and made adobe mortar, without a doubt, as they still do. One of the hopeful features in their advancement was the beginning of the reversal of the old usage which put all labor upon the women. It is now the rule among the Village Indians for the men to assume the heavy work, which was doubtless the case when this pueblo was constructed. They cultivated maize, beans, and squashes, in garden beds, and irrigated them with water drawn from the river by means of a canal, and passed in several smaller streams through their gardens. The men now engage in the work of cultivation. This is a sure sign of progress.

Off the south wing of the building, and without it, are the remains of an additional building, large enough for twenty or thirty rooms on the ground, some part of which were, doubtless, carried up two or more stories high; but it is a mass of indistinct ruins, about which little can be said except that some of the rooms were unusually large. This may have been the first building constructed, and the one occupied while the stone pueblo was being built.

This outline plan is submitted with some hesitation, because the sketch from which it is taken was made in haste, and with no expectation of using it. It is but an approximation. Near the pueblo last described, and about five hundred feet northeasterly therefrom, is another pueblo in two sections, Fig. 43, with a space about fifteen feet wide between them. They may have been, and probably were, connected and inhabited as one structure. Some of the walls are still standing,

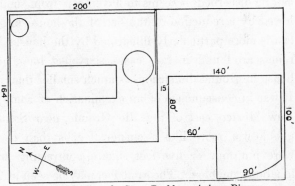

FIG. 43.—Outline of a Stone Pueblo on Animas River.

and a number of the rooms in the ground story are well preserved, the ceilings still remaining in place. Although the structure is chiefly of stone like the last, some of the walls are of cobblestone and adobe mortar. The largest section seems to have had an open court in the center in the form of a parallelogram. This feature increased the difficulty of understanding the original form of the house and the arrangement of the rooms. The walls of the first, of parts of the second, and occasionally of parts of the third story, are still standing in places. Many of the rooms are small, as the measurements of the following rooms in the second story of the smallest building of the two will show:

3 feet 4 inches by 6 feet 6 inches, 4 feet by 8 feet 4 inches, 4 feet 7 inches by 14 feet 2 inches, 6 feet 5 inches by 14 feet 9 inches, 7 feet 3 inches by 16 feet 9 inches, 6 feet 4 inches by 11 feet 7 inches, 7 feet 3 inches by 7 feet 5 inches, 8 feet 7 inches by 15 feet. Height of rooms, 8 feet. The rooms were faced with stone laid up in the main in courses. They were small, from four to eight inches square, and the walls from two to three feet in thickness. Adobe mortar was used abundantly in the inner part of the wall, but not showing on the face at the joints, the stones being laid together as closely as the natural surfaces of the stone would permit, and without mortar near the edge. This feature was also characteristic of the walls of the pueblo first described.

Mr. Bandelier made to me recently the important suggestion that as far as any progress or improvement in this architecture, in style or character, can be discerned, it seems to have been from smaller to larger rooms, followed by a reduction of the size of the house in ground dimensions. The last is more particularly illustrated by the houses in Yucatan, where single rooms are found, in rare cases, sixty feet long, but where the size of the house in ground dimensions is much smaller than of those in New Mexico. It was in consequence of an examination of some very old pueblo ruins in New Mexico, east of the Rio Grande, near Santo Domingo. There the pueblo was more like a cluster of cells than of rooms, as many of them were but four or five feet square, contrasting strongly with the present inhabited pueblos. The same fact may be seen at Taos. It was mentioned (p. 144) that the Taos Indians many years ago conquered and dispossessed the former occupants of a pueblo at this place, and that some remains of the old pueblo were still standing. In 1878 I visited one of the ground-rooms in the old structure still standing, and entirely alone. It was about five feet by six in ground-dimensions, and was then occupied by a solitary Taos Indian, a sort of hermit, as his place of residence. A bunk across one side furnished him both a bed and a seat, and the remaining room was scarcely sufficient to turn around in, but it gave him all the home he had, and, doubtless, all the room he needed Another room, a few feet distant, also a part of the old pueblo, was still standing. These rooms were of adobe, and were about six feet high. As the Indian gained in experience and knowledge in the use and construction of the joint-tenement houses, improvements would gradually manifest themselves. It is important to find and trace this progress, as we have every reason to believe that it is one system of architecture throughout North America at least, with a connection of all its forms.

Along the curving or westerly side of the first building, and along the northerly side, there are cedar beams projecting about four feet from the wall in the second story on the line of the ceiling. They are about four inches in diameter. Their object is not apparent.

In one of the basement rooms of the second building are a series of pictographs upon a plastered wall. Our limited time would not permit a sketch.

Midway between the pueblo, Fig. 40, and the one now being considered is a circular ruin three hundred and thirty feet in circuit, which seems to have consisted of two concentric rows of apartments around an inclosed estufa. It was built of cobblestone and adobe mortar. Pit-holes indicate the form and plan of the inclosing rooms, but the ruin is too indistinct to form a clear idea of its structure. A removal of the loose material would probably disclose the original ground plan.

A few hundred feet north are the ruins of four other structures of cobblestone and adobe quite near each other. They were, without doubt, pueblo houses, but they are now a mass of undistinguishable ruins, and, from present appearance, were probably ruins, when the stone pueblos were inhabited. The river here runs nearer the western border of the valley than the eastern, and quite near the pueblo last noticed, but from this point it bears toward the east side of the valley.

About a mile in a direction a little south of east and near the river are the ruins of two other large pueblos, of which the lower one is one thousand and forty feet in circuit, and the one above four hundred and fifty-two feet. Both are built of sandstone and cobblestone and adobe mortar. No part of the walls are standing above the rubbish; but they were apparently contemporary with the stone pueblos. The first stands upon the brink of the river, which is now cutting away its foundations, thus proving that it was insecurely located. The mass of fallen material is very great, showing an apparent depth of at least fifteen feet. Some of the basement rooms in each of these pueblos are probably still entire, judging from the great mass of material over them. Great pit-holes indicate the position of chambers and inclosing-walls. The largest of the two pueblos is 300 feet in depth. In one place, where some excavation has been done, the corner of a basement room is in sight. All these ruins ought to be re-examined, and so far excavated as to recover complete ground plans.

Near the mouth of the river are said to be still other ruins, and still others on the east side of the river, which we had no time to examine.

The valley of the Animas River is here broad and beautiful, about three miles wide. The river passes nearly through the center of the valley. The cliff, on the east side of the level plain, is bold and mountainous, rising from fifteen hundred to two thousand feet high, while on the west side the valley is bordered with the mesa formation in two benches, one rising back of the other, and both as level as a floor, with the highlands forming the divide between the Animas and La Plata Rivers in the distance.

From the number and size of the houses, there was probably a population of at least five thousand persons at this settlement, living by horticulture. It is not now known by what tribe of Indians these pueblos were inhabited or constructed.

These pueblos, newly constructed and in their best condition, must have presented a commanding appearance. From the materials used in their construction, from their palatial size and unique design, and from the cultivated gardens by which they were doubtless surrounded, they were calculated to impress the beholder very favorably with the degree of culture to which the people had attained. It is a singular fact that none of the occupied pueblos in New Mexico at the present time are equal in materials or in construction with those found in ruins. It tends to show a decadence of art among them since the period of European discovery.

Westward of the Animas, the La Plata, and the Mancos Rivers, which run southwesterly into the San Juan, is the Montezuma Valley, a broad and level plain, so named by General Heffernan, of Animas City. It is about fifty miles in length, and apparently ten miles wide at the ranch of Mr. Henry L. Mitchell, which is situated at the commencement of the

McElmo Cañon. It stretches southward thirty-six miles to the San Juan. In this valley, which has no flowing stream through it at present (and there is no certainty that it ever had), and which is without water, except in springs and pools, and has but a slight rainfall during the year, Mr. Mitchell was successfully cultivating, at the time of our visit, wheat, oats, maize, and the garden vegetables. The valley is uninhabited, except by the family of Mr. Mitchell, and a solitary man living four miles westward. Their nearest neighbors are on the Mancos River, twenty-five miles distant. The bluffs bordering the eastern side of the valley rise boldly about fifteen hundred feet, with table lands above, while on the west the valley is bordered with mountains. About t e n

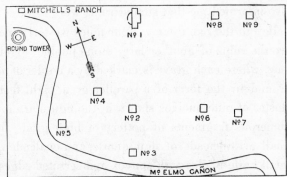

FIG. 44.—Pueblos at commencement of McElmo Cañon.

miles southwest of Mr. Mitchell's ranch the Ute Mountain rises out of the plain, and from this point appears as a solitary and detached mountain. The McElmo Cañon passes along its north and westerly sides, while the main valley passes southward along its eastern base. This high and noble mountain is situated in the southwest corner of Colorado, near the intersection of the boundary lines of Colorado, Utah, Arizona, and New Mexico. It is a conspicuous object from the La Plata Valley. The Montezuma Valley possesses features of remarkable natural beauty.

Near Mr. Mitchell's ranch, and within a space of less than a mile square, are the ruins of nine pueblo houses of moderate size. They are built of sandstone intermixed with cobblestone and adobe mortar. They are now in a very ruinous condition, without standing walls in any part of them above the rubbish. The largest of the number is marked No. 1 in the plan Fig. 44, of which the outline of the original structure is still discernible It is ninety-four feet in length and forty-seven feet in depth, and shows the remains of a stone wall in front inclosing a small court about fifteen feet wide. The mass of material over some parts of this structure is ten or twelve feet deep. There are, no doubt, rooms with a portion of the walls still standing covered with rubbish, the removal of which would reveal a considerable portion of the original ground-plan.

A short distance below the pueblos last named is another cluster of the same number of pueblos, and much in the same condition; and upon rising ground near the foot of the bluff, on the east side of the valley, there are, as Mr. Mitchell informed me, the ruins of several pueblos of stone. He also informed me that similar ruins were to be found here and there in the valley to the San Juan. Four miles westerly, near the ranch of Mr. Shirt, are the ruins of another large stone pueblo, together with an Indian cemetery, where each grave is marked by a border of flat stones set level with the ground in the form of a parallelogram eight feet by four feet. Near the cluster of nine pueblos shown in the figure are found strewn on the ground numerous fragments of pottery of high grade in the ornamentation, and small arrow-heads of flint, quartz, and chalcedony delicately formed, and small knife-blades with convex and serrated edges in considerable numbers.

This is an immense ruin with small portions of the walls still standing,

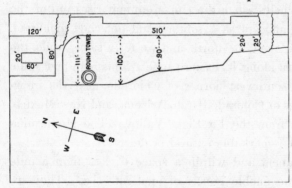

particularly of the round tower of stone of three concentric walls, incorporated in the structure, and a few chambers in the north end of the main building. The round tower is still standing nearly to the height of the first story. In its present condition it was

FIG. 45.—Outline plan of a stone pueblo near the base of Ute Mountain.

impossible to make a ground-plan showing the several chambers, or to determine with certainty which side was the front of the structure, assuming that it was constructed in the terraced form. It is situated upon a vertical bluff of yellowish sandstone rock about twenty feet high, and about four miles below Mr. Mitchell's ranch in the direction of the Ute Mountain and near its northeastern base. The bluff is broken through to the bottom in one place about twenty feet wide. Here there are some evidences that a spring of water was inclosed in a reservoir by means of masonry. The building is in two sections, separated by this break, of which the main one is five hundred and ten feet long, and the smallest one hundred and twenty feet, forming a nearly continuous front. They stand back ten or fifteen feet from the verge of the bluff, and are built of tabular pieces of sandstone and adobe mortar. Numerous pit-holes in each structure indicate the chambers and the line of the inclosing walls. The removal of the loose material would doubtless disclose the ground-plan, but it would involve immense labor. With the Ute Mountain rising majestically in the background, and the broad valley in front, the situation of the pueblo is remarkably fine.

The Round Tower is the most singular feature in this structure. While it resembles the ordinary *estufa*, common to all these structures, it differs from them in having three concentric walls. No doorways are visible in the portion still standing, consequently it must have been entered through the roof, in which respect it agrees with the ordinary *estufa* The inner chamber is about twenty feet in diameter, and the spaces between the encircling walls are about two feet each; the walls are about two feet in thickness, and were laid up mainly with stones about four inches square, and, for the most part, in courses. There is a similar round tower, having but two concentric walls, at the head of the McElmo Cañon, and near the ranch of Mr. Mitchell. It is shown in Fig. 44, and stands entirely isolated. The diameter of the tower is thirty-four feet, of which the inner chamber is twenty-three feet; the space between the two walls is about six feet, and the thickness of the walls about two feet six inches. It is laid up in the same manner as the one last named, with stones about the same size, and the walls still standing are about five feet in height. Partition walls divide the outer space, one of which measured twenty inches in thickness.

Several hundred feet from the pueblo last named, further down the valley, is another pueblo of large extent, and in a very ruined condition.

A mile or more below the ranch of Mr. Mitchell, in the bordering walls of the McElmo Cañon, are two cliff houses. The walls of the bluff are here about twenty feet high, with large cavities formed in them here and there.   These houses, each of which consists of but two or three small chambers, are built of stone, and stand but a few feet above the bottom of the cañon.   They are narrow, and not very high, as the cavity in the rock is not very deep.   Corrals for some kind of domestic animals are found by the side of these houses in the same hollows in the rock.   This is proved by a mass of excrement, about a foot in depth, still there, whether of the goat or sheep cannot be stated, but this fact shows that they were inhabited subsequent to the period of European discovery, although they may have been built and used before.   The cañon, at this point, is from three hundred to five hundred feet wide.

I wish to call attention again to the San Juan district, to its numerous ruins, and to its importance as an early seat of Village Indian life.   These ruins and those of a similar character in the valley of the Chaco, together with numerous remains of structures of sandstone, of cobblestone, and adobe in the San Juan Valley, in the Pine River Valley, in the La Plata Valley, in the Animas River Valley, in the Montezuma Valley, on the Hovenweep, and on the Rio Dolores, suggest the probability that the remarkable area within the drainage of the San Juan River and its tributaries has held a prominent place in the first and most ancient development of Village Indian life in America.   The evidence of Indian occupation and cultivation throughout the greater part of this area is sufficient to suggest the hypothesis that the Indian here first attained to the condition of the Middle Status of barbarism, and sent forth the migrating bands who carried this advanced culture to the Mississippi Valley, to Mexico, and Central America, and not unlikely to South America as well.

Indian migrations are gradual outflows from an overstocked area, followed by organization into independent tribes, and continuing through centuries of time, until the ethnic life of each tribe is expended, or a successful establishment is finally gained in a new and perhaps far distant land.   They planted gardens and constructed houses as they advanced from district to district, and removed as circumstances prompted a change of location.

Since the cultivation of maize and plants precedes or is synchronous with this stage of development, it leads to the supposition that maize must have been indigenous in this region, and that it was here first brought under cultivation. There are some facts that seem to favor this hypothesis.[1] At present I wish to call attention to such existing evidence as points to the San Juan district as the anterior home of a number of historic Indian tribes.

1. *The Mound-Builders.*—Although these tribes had disappeared at the epoch of European discovery, and cannot be classed with any known Indian stock, their condition as horticultural tribes, their knowledge of some of the native metals, and the high character of their stone implements and pottery place them in the class of Village Indians. The nearest region from which they could have been derived is New Mexico. There is no reason for referring them to the San Juan region more than to the nearer country of the Rio Grande, unless it should appear probable that the inhabitants of the latter valley were themselves migrants from the same region. But there are good reasons for deriving the Mound-Builders from the Village Indians in some part of New Mexico.

---

[1] Where maize was indigenous is unknown, except that it was somewhere upon the American continent. It is the only cereal America has given to the world. At the period of European discovery, it was found cultivated and a staple article of food in a large part of North America and in parts of South America. There were also found beans, squashes, and tobacco, with the addition in some areas of peppers, tomatoes, cocoa, and cotton. The problem of the place of the origin of maize is probably insoluble, but speculations are legitimate, and such are all that I have to offer.

The fecundity of plant-life in the Rocky Mountains is remarkable, particularly on the southern slopes, where they subside into the mesa, or table-land formation, north of the San Juan River. The continental divide is in the eastern margin of this region. The first suggestion I wish to make is that all cereals and cultivated plants must have originated in the great continental mountains of the two hemispheres, and have propagated themselves along the water courses of the mountain valleys down to the plains traversed by the great rivers formed by these mountain tributaries. All the cereals belong to the family of the Grasses (Gramineæ), and each of them, doubtless, is the last of a series of antecedent forms.

I saw rye, barley, and oats growing wild by self-propagation in the mountain valleys of Colorado the present season; also the wild pea, whose stunted seeds had the taste of the cultivated pea. Turnips, onions, tomatoes, and hops are found growing wild in the Pine River Valley, and the pie-plant or rhubarb is said to grow luxuriantly in the Elk Mountain valleys. I also saw wild flax and the gourd growing by self-propagation in the valley of the Animas. Currants, gooseberries, raspberries, and strawberries are found in the mountain valleys in numerous places, together with flowering plants of many species and varieties. Tiny forms of flowering plants are to be seen above patches of snow in places where the snow had recently melted. This fecundity of plant-life from ten to twelve thousand feet above sea level, and the relation of these mountain tributaries to the San Juan, which runs from east to west, not remotely from the base of these mountains, in such a manner as to invite and receive into its lap, so to express it, the vegetable wealth developed in these mountain chains, are facts that force themselves upon the attention of the observer.

The altitude of the San Juan Valley ranges from seven thousand feet at Pagosa Springs to five thousand nine hundred and seventy feet at the mouth of the Animas, and diminishing to four thousand four hundred and forty-six feet near the point where it empties into the Colorado (Hayden's Atlas of Colorado, Sheet 111). The altitude at Conejos is seven thousand eight hundred and eighty feet (Ib.,) which is about as great an elevation as admits of the successful cultivation of maize. I noticed in a field of maize growing at Conejos that the stalk grew only about three feet high, and the fact that the

2. *The Mexican Tribes.*—The seven principal tribes of Mexico, called collectively the Nahuatlacs, spoke dialects of the same language, and all alike had a tradition that their ancestors came from the north, and that the separate tribes came into Mexico at long intervals apart They arrived in the following order as to time: 1, Sochomilcos; 2, Chalcas; 3, Tepanecans; 4, Tescucans; 5, Tlatluicans; 6, Tlascalans; 7, Aztecs or Mexicans. They settled in different parts of Mexico The Cholulans, Tepeacas, and Huexatsincos spoke dialects of the Nahuatlac language, and were severally subdivisions of one or the other preceding tribes. They had the same tradition of a northern origin. These several tribes were among the most prominent in Mexico at the period of Spanish discovery. Some of the tribes of Yucatan and Central America also had similar traditions of an original migration of their ancestors from the north.

Acosta, who visited Mexico in 1585, and whose work was published at Seville in 1589, states the order of the migration of the Mexican tribes as above given, and further says that they "come from other far countries which lie toward the north, where now they have discovered a kingdom they call New Mexico. There are two provinces in this country, the one called *Aztlan*, which is to say, a place of Herons [Cranes], and the other Teculhuacan, which signifies a land of such whose grandfathers were divine. The Navatalcas [Nahuatlacs] point their beginning and first territory in the figure of a cave, and say they came forth of seven caves to come and people the land of Mexico."[1] The same tradition, substantially, is given by

ear grew out of it but six inches from the ground. Specimens of the ear we obtained showed that it was about five inches long, with the kernel small and flinty. The ear is in four colors, white, red, yellow, and black, each being one or the other of these colors. In a few cases two colors were intermixed in the same ear. It seemed probable that this was the primitive maize of the American aborigines, from which all other varieties have been developed. A few cobs which we found at a cliff house on the Mancos River corresponded with the Conejos ear in size, and were probably the same variety. Afterwards at Taos I found the same ear in white, red, yellow, and black; the staple maize now cultivated at this pueblo, but much larger. I brought away several fine ears saved for seed. One black ear measured twelve inches in length, with twelve rows of kernels, while the white variety, both at Conejos and Taos, had each fourteen rows.

Finally, a dry country, neither excessively hot nor moist, like the San Juan region, would seem to be most favorable for the development and self-propagation of maize as well as plants until man appeared for their domestication. These are but speculations, but if they should prompt further investigations concerning the place of nativity of this wonderful cereal, which has been such an important factor in the advancement of the Indian family, and which is also destined to prove such a support to our own, these suggestions will not have been made in vain.

[1] The Natural and Moral History of the East and West Indies, London ed., 1604, Grimstone's Trans., pp. 497, 504.

Herrera,[1] and also by Clavigero.[2] If by the word Aztlan was intended "place of Cranes", and on the supposition that these tribes migrated from the San Juan region, the reasons for the designation are justified. The Sandhill Crane (*Grus Canadensis*) is one of the largest and most conspicuous of American birds, and is still found from the British Possessions to New Mexico, and winters in the latter. I saw a pair of these great birds in 1878, in the valley of the Animas River. Dr. Coues remarks that "thousands of Sandhill Cranes repair each year to the Colorado River Valley, flock succeeding flock along the course of the great stream from their arrival in September until their departure the following spring. Taller than the Wood Ibises or the largest Herons with which they are associated, the stately birds stand in the foreground of the scenery of the valley. * * * Such ponderous bodies moving with slowly-beating wings give a great idea of momentum from mere weight, a force of motion without swiftness; for they plod along heavily, seeming to need every inch of their ample wings to sustain themselves."[3] It is an Indian trait to mark localities by some conspicuous feature or fact, and the selection of the Sandhill Crane to indicate their home country would have accorded with Indian usages.

Again, Herrera, who presents the current traditions, observes, that "these peoples painted their original in the manner of a cave, and said they came out of seven caves to people the country of Mexico. * * * After the six above mentioned races departed from their country, and settled in New Spain, where they were much increased, the seventh race being the Mexican nation, a warlike and polite people, who adoring their god *Vitsilpuztli*, he commanded them to leave their own country, promising them they should rule over other races in a plentiful country, and much wealth."[4]

It is worthy of remark that the cave dwellings or cliff houses are in the San Juan district, the most of them being on the Mancos River, and on the western portion of the San Juan. These traditions may in fact refer to these cave dwellings as the original homes of their ancestors, and at the same time without precluding the supposition that they also constructed

[1] General History of America, London ed., 1725, Stevens's Trans., III, 188.
[2] History of Mexico, Cullen's Trans., 1, 119.
[3] Birds of the Northwest, 1874, p. 534.
[4] History of America, iii, p. 188, 190.

and inhabited some of the pueblo structures now in ruins in other parts of the same area. All the early accounts concur in representing the Aztecs or Mexicans, when they first arrived in Mexico, as subsisting by the cultivation of maize and plants, as constructing houses of stone, and with a religious system which recognized personal gods. These statements are probably true. They had attained to the status of Village Indians. This again renders New Mexico their probable original home as the only area in the north where ruins of structures of tribes so far advanced have been found.

The San Juan district is remarkably situated in its geographical relations. This river, rising in the crests of the high mountains forming the water-shed or divide between the Atlantic and Pacific, flows southward until it enters the table-land formation, through which it flows in a southwesterly and then northwesterly direction, making a long, sweeping curve in New Mexico and Arizona, after which it runs westerly to its confluence with the Colorado. It receives from the north the following tributaries, rising like itself in the high mountains, the Piedra, Pine River (Los Pinos), the Animas, the La Plata, the Mancos, the McElmo, now dry, and the Hovenweep and Montezuma creeks, now nearly dry. Its southern tributaries are the Navajo, Chaco, and De Chelly.

With such evidences of ancient occupation, here and elsewhere in the San Juan country, we are led to the conclusion that the Village Indians increased and multiplied in this area, and that at some early period there was here a remarkable display of this form of Indian life, and of house architecture in the nature of fortresses, which must have made itself felt in distant parts of the continent. On the hypothesis that the valley of the Columbia was the seed-land of the Ganowanian family, where they depended chiefly upon a fish subsistence, we have in the San Juan country a second center and initial point of migrations founded upon farinaceous subsistence. That the struggle of the Village Indians to resist the ever continuous streams of migration flowing southward along the mountain chains has been a hard one through many centuries of time, is proved by the many ruins of abandoned or conquered pueblos which still mark their settlements in so many places. At the present moment there is not a Village Indian in the San Juan district. It is entirely deserted of this class of inhabitants.

That the original ancestors of the principal historic tribes of Mexico once inhabited the San Juan country is extremely probable. That the ancestors of the principal tribes of Yucatan and Central America owe their remote origin to the same region is equally probable. And that the Mound Builders came originally from the same country, is, with our present knowledge, at least a reasonable conclusion.

Indian migrations have occurred under the influence, almost exclusively, of physical causes, operating in a uniform manner. These migrations, involving the entire period of the existence here of the inhabitants of both American continents, will be found to have a common and connected history A study of all the facts may yet lead to an elucidation and explanation of these migrations with some degree of certainty. The hypothesis that the valley of the Columbia River was the seed-land of the Ganowanian family holds the best chance of solving the great problem of the origin and distribution of the Indian tribes.

CHAPTER IX.

HOUSES OF THE MOUND-BUILDERS.

The general view of the house-life and houses of the Indian tribes thus far presented will tend to strengthen the hypothesis about to be stated concerning the earth-works of the Mound-Builders. Apart from the explanation that the long-houses of the Northern Tribes and the joint-tenement house of the Sedentary Indians are capable of affording, they are wholly inexplicable. The Mound-Builders worked native copper, cultivated maize and plants, manufactured pottery and stone implements of higher grade than the tribes of the Lower Status of barbarism; and they raised earthworks of great magnitude, superior to any works of the former tribes. They fairly belong to the class of Sedentary Village Indians, though not in all respects of an equal grade of culture and development. Their embankments, which inclosed a rectangular space, were in all probability, the foundations upon which they erected their houses. It is proposed to consider these embankments under this hypothesis.

Under the name of Mound-Builders certain unknown tribes of the American aborigines are recognized, who formerly inhabited as their chief area the valley of the Ohio and its tributary streams. Traces of their occupation have been found in other places, from the Gulf of Mexico to Lakes Erie and Superior, and from the Alleghanies to the Mississippi, and in some localities west of this river.

Without entering upon a discussion of these works, this chapter will be confined to four principal questions:

I. The house-life of the American aborigines, in the usages of which the Mound-Builders were necessarily involved.

II. The probable center from which the Mound-Builders emigrated into these areas.

224

III. The uses for which their principal earth-works were designed, with a conjectural restoration of one of their pueblos; and,

IV. The probable numbers of the people.

The Mound-Builders have disappeared, or, at least, have fallen out of human knowledge, leaving these works and their fabrics as the only evidence of their existence. Consequently the proposed questions, excepting the first, are incapable of specific answers; but they are not beyond the reach of approximate solutions. The mystery in which these tribes are enshrouded, and the unique character of their earth-works, will lead to deceptive inferences, unless facts and principles are carefully considered and rigorously applied, and such deductions only are made as they will fairly warrant. It is easy to magnify the significance of these remains and to form extravagant conclusions concerning them; but neither will advance the truth. They represent a status of human advancement forming a connecting link in the progressive development of man. If, then, the nature of their arts, and more especially the character of their institutions, can be determined with reasonable certainty, the true position of the Mound-Builders can be assigned to them in the scale of human progress, and what was possible and what impossible on their part can be known.

THE HOUSE-LIFE OF THE AMERICAN ABORIGINES, IN THE USAGES OF WHICH THE MOUND-BUILDERS WERE NECESSARILY INVOLVED.

It will be assumed that the tribes who constructed the earth-works of the Ohio Valley were American Indians. No other supposition is tenable. The implements and utensils found in the mounds indicate very plainly that they had attained to the Middle Status of barbarism. They do not fully answer the tests of this condition, since they neither cultivated by irrigation, so far as is known, nor constructed houses of adobe bricks or of stone; but, in addition to the earth-works to be considered, they mined native copper and wrought it into implements and utensils—acts performed by none of the tribes in the Lower Status of barbarism; and they depended chiefly upon horticulture for subsistence. They had also carried the art of pottery to the ornamental stage, and manufactured textile fabrics of cotton or flax, remains of which have been found wrapped around copper chisels. These facts, with others that will appear, justify their recognition as in the same status with the Village Indians of New and Old Mexico and Central America. They occupied areas free from lakes as a rule, and, therefore, the poorest for a fish subsistence. This shows of itself that their chief reliance was upon horticulture. The principal places where their villages were situated were unoccupied areas at the epoch of European discovery, because unadapted to tribes in the Lower Status of barbarism, who depended upon fish and game as well as upon maize and plants.

A knowledge of the general character of the houses of the American aborigines will enable us to infer what must have been the general character of those of the Mound-Builders. This, again, was influenced by the condition of the family. Among the Indian tribes, in whatever stage of advancement, the family was found in the pairing form, with separation at the option of either party. It was founded upon marriage between single pairs, but it fell below the monogamian family of civilized society. In their condition it was too weak an organization to face alone the struggle of life, and it sought shelter in large households, formed on the basis of kin, with communism in living as an incident of their plan of life. While exceptional cases of single families living by themselves existed among all the tribes, it did not break the general rule of large households, and the practice in them of communism in living. These usages entered into and determined the character of their house architecture. In all parts of North and South America, at the period of European discovery, were found communal or joint-tenement houses, from those large enough to accommodate five, ten, and twenty families, to those large enough for fifty, a hundred, and in some cases two hundred or more, families. These houses differed among themselves in their plan and structure as well as size; but a common principle ran through them which was revealed by their adaptation to communistic uses. They reflect their condition and their plan of life with such singular distinctness as to afford practical hints concerning the houses of the Mound-Builders.

THE PROBABLE CENTER FROM WHICH THE MOUND-BUILDERS EMIGRATED INTO THESE AREAS.

It is well known that the highest type of Village Indian life was found in Yucatan, Chiapas, and Guatemala, and that the standard declines with the advance of the type northward into Mexico and New Mexico, thus tending to show that it was best adapted to a warm climate; but it does not follow that we must look to these distant regions for the original home of the Mound-Builders.   The nearest point from which they could have been derived was New Mexico, and that is rendered the probable point from physical considerations, and still more from their greater nearness in condition to the Village Indians of New Mexico, below whom they must be ranked.   The migrations of the American Indian tribes were gradual movements under the operation of physical causes, occupying long periods of time and with slow progress.   There is no reason for supposing, in any number of cases, that they were deliberate migrations with a definite destination.   With maize, beans, and squashes (the staples of an established horticulture), the Village Indians were independent of fish and game as primary means of subsistence, and with the former they possessed superior resources for migrating over the wide expanses of open prairies between New Mexico and the Mississippi.   The movement of the tribes who constructed the earth-works in question can be explained as a natural spread of Village Indians from the valley of the Rio Grande, or the San Juan, to the shores of the Gulf of Mexico, and thence northward to the valley of the Ohio, which was both easy and feasible.   Its successful extension for any considerable distance north of the gulf was rendered improbable, by reason of the increasing severity of the climate.   There are some reasons for supposing that climate delayed the movement for centuries, and finally defeated the attempt to transplant permanently even the New Mexican type of village life into a northern temperature so much lower during the greater part of the year.

A number of archæologists, who have considered the question of the probable anterior home of the Mound-Builders, are inclined to derive them from Central America. The ground for this opinion seems to be the fact that horticulture must have originated in a semi-tropical region, where this type of village life was first developed, and, therefore, that all the forms of this life were derived from thence. It would be a mistake, as it seems to the writer, to adopt the track of horticulture as that of Indian migration. In its first spread horticulture would be more apt to return upon the line of the latter than wait to be carried, by actual migrations, with the people. Moreover it is unnecessary to invoke such an argument, for the reason that New Mexico had been for ages the seat of horticultural and Village Indians, and was necessarily occupied by them long before the country east of the Mississippi. Every presumption is in favor of their derivation from New Mexico as their immediate anterior home, where they were accustomed to snow and to a moderate degree of cold.[1]

THE USES FOR WHICH THEIR PRINCIPAL EARTHWORKS WERE DESIGNED, WITH A CONJECTURAL RESTORATION OF ONE OF THEIR PUEBLOS.

A brief reference to the character and extent of these works is necessary as a means of understanding their uses. The authors of the volume "The Ancient Monuments of the Mississippi Valley" remark, in their preface, that "the ancient inclosures and groups of works personally examined and surveyed are upwards of one hundred. * * * About two hundred mounds of all forms and sizes, and occupying every variety of position, have also been excavated."[2] Out of ninety-five earthworks, exclusive of mounds, figured and described in this valuable memoir, and which probably mark the sites of Indian villages, forty-seven are of the same type and may unhesitatingly be assigned to the Mound-Builders; fourteen are groups of emblematical earthworks, mostly in Wisconsin, and may also be assigned to them; but the remaining thirty-four are very inferior as well as different in character. They are not above the works of the Indians in the

---

[1] At a recent meeting of the National Academy of Science at Washington, where this subject was presented, Prof. O. C. Marsh remarked, in confirmation of this suggestion, that "in a series of comparisons of Indian skulls, he had been struck with the similarity between those of the Pueblo Indians of New Mexico and of the Mound-Builders. As the shape of the Mound-Builder's skull is very peculiar, the coincidence is a very striking one."

[2] Smithsonian Cont. to Knowledge, Preface, XXXIV.

Lower Status of barbarism, and, therefore, do not probably belong to the Village Indians who constructed the works in the Scioto Valley. If to those first named are added the emblematical earth-works figured and described by Lapham,[1] and a few other works not known to Squier and Davis, and since described by other persons, there are something more than one hundred works, large and small, indicating the sites of Indian villages, of which perhaps three quarters were occupied at the same time.[2] The conical mounds raised over Indian graves, which are numerous, are not included.

"A large, perhaps the larger portion of these works," observe the same authors, "are regular in outline, the square and circle predominating. * * * The regular works are almost invariably erected on level river terraces. * * * The square and the circle often occur in combination, frequently connecting with each other. * * * Most of the circular works are small, varying from two hundred and fifty to three hundred feet in diameter, while others are a mile or more in circuit."[3] These embankments are, for the most part, slight, varying from two feet to six, eight, ten, and twelve feet in height, with a broad base, caused by the washing down of the banks in the course of centuries. These facts are shown by numerous cross-sections furnished with the ground-plans by the authors. But the circular embankments are usually about half as high as the rectangular.

Some idea of the size of Indian villages, and of their nearness to each other, is necessary to form an impression of their plan of life and mode of settlement. The illustrations should be drawn from the Village Indians, to which class the Mound-Builders undoubtedly belonged. Not knowing the use of wells, they established their settlements on the margins of rivers and small streams, which afforded alluvial land for cultivation, and often within a few miles of each other. In the valley of the Rio Chaco, in New Mexico, there were several pueblos within an extent of twelve miles, each consisting of a single joint-tenement house, constructed usually upon three sides of a court; and westward of the Chaco Valley were, and still are, the seven Moki pueblos, within an extent of twenty-five miles. At the present time, in the valley of the Rio Grande, a single pueblo house, accommodating

---

[1] Smithsonian Cont. to Knowledge, Vol. V.

[2] When a calamity befalls an Indian settlement it is usually abandoned.

[3] Smithsonian Cont. to Knowledge, I, pp. 6 and 8.

five hundred persons, makes an Indian village.   Two or three such houses, as at Taos and Santo Domingo, form a large pueblo ; and a group of several such houses, as at Zuñi, a pueblo of the largest size, which once contained perhaps five thousand persons, now reduced to fifteen hundred.   There are no reasons for supposing that any pueblo in Yucatan or Central America contained as high a number as ten thousand inhabitants at the period of the Spanish conquest, although these countries were extremely favorable for an increase of Indian population.   Their villages were numerous and small. Castañeda, who accompanied the expedition of Coronado to New Mexico in 1540–1542, estimated the population of the seventy villages visited by detachments and situated between the Colorado River, Zuñi, and the Arkansas at twenty thousand men, which would give a total population in this wide area of a hundred thousand Indians.[1]   There were seven villages each of Cibola, Tusayan, Quivira, and Hemes, and twelve of Tiguex; it would give an average of about fourteen hundred and fifty persons to each village.   In all probability these are fair samples as to the number of inhabitants of the villages of the Mound-Builders, with exceptional cases, as the village on the site of Marietta, in Ohio, where there may have been five thousand, if an impression may be formed from the extent of the earth-works occupied in the manner hereafter suggested.   Where several villages were found near each other on the same stream, as in New Mexico, the people usually spoke the same dialect, which tends to show that those in each group were colonists from one original village.

The earth-works of the Mound-Builders must be regarded as the sites of their villages.   The question then recurs, for what purpose did they raise these embankments at an expenditure of so much labor?   They must have lived somewhere, in, upon, or around them.   No answer has been given to this question, and no serious attempt has been made to explain their uses. They have been called "defensive enclosures"; but it is not supposable that they lived in houses within the embankments, for this would turn the places into slaughter-pens in case of an attack.   Some of them have been called "sacred enclosures", but this goes for nothing apart from some knowledge of their uses.   They were constructed for a practical, intelligent purpose,

---

[1] Coll. Ternaux-Compans, vol. ix, pp. 181–183.

and that purpose must be sought in the needs and mode of life of the Mound-Builders as Village Indians; and it should be expressed in the works themselves. If a sensible use for these embankments can be found, its acceptance will relieve us from the delusive inferences which are certain to be drawn from them so long as they are allowed to remain in the category of the mysteries.

It is proposed to submit a conjectural explanation of the objects and uses of the principal embankments, and to advocate its acceptance on the ground of inherent probability. It will be founded on the assumption that the Mound-Builders were horticultural Village Indians who had immigrated from beyond the Mississippi; that as such they had been accustomed to live in houses of adobe bricks, like those found in New Mexico; that they had become habituated to living upon their roof terraces as elevated platforms, and in large households; and that their houses were in the nature of fortresses, in consequence of the insecurity in which they lived. Further than this, that before they emigrated to the valley of the Ohio they were accustomed to snow, and to a moderate degree of winter cold; wore skin garments, and possibly woven mantles of cotton, as the Cibolans of New Mexico did at the time of Coronado's expedition.[1] The food of the New Mexicans, at this time, consisted of maize, beans, and squashes, and a limited amount of game, which was doubtless the food of the Mound-Builders. Captain Juan Jaramillo, who accompanied the same expedition, remarks in his relation that the Cibolans "had hardly provisions enough for themselves; what they had consisted of maize, beans, and squashes (*maiz, des haricots, et des courges*). * * * The Indians clothe themselves with deer skins, very well prepared. They have also buffalo-skins tanned, in which they wrap themselves."[2] Although several centuries earlier in time, the Mound-Builders, with habits of life similar to those of the Cibolans, in 1540, would

---

[1] "The snow and cold are wont to be great," Coronado remarks in his relation, "for so say the inhabitants of the country; and it is very likely so to be, both in respect of the manner of the country and of the fashion of their houses, and their furs and other things, which the people have to defend them from cold. * * * They have no cotton-wool growing, because the country is cold, yet they wear mantles thereof, as your honor may see by the show thereof; and true it is that there was found in their houses certain yarn made of cotton-wool. * * * In this country there are certain skins, well dressed, and they dress them and paint them when they kill their oxen [buffaloes], for so they say themselves."—Hakluyt's Coll. of Voyages, Lond. ed., 1600, iii, 377.

[2] Coll. Ternaux-Compans, ix, 369.

understand, besides horticulture, the use of adobe bricks, and the art of constructing long joint-tenement houses, closed up in the first story for defensive reasons, and built in the terraced form two, three, and four stories high, the ascent to the roof of the first story being made by ladders.

If, then, a tribe of Village Indians, with such habits and experience, emigrated centuries ago in search of new homes, and in course of time they, or their descendants, reached the Scioto Valley, in Ohio, they would find it impossible to construct houses of adobe bricks able to resist the rains and frosts of that climate, even if they found adobe soil. Some modification of their house architecture would be forced upon them through climatic reasons. They might have used stone, if possessed of sufficient skill to quarry it and construct walls of stone; but they did not produce such houses. Or they might have fallen back upon a house of inferior grade, located upon the level ground, such as the timber-framed houses of the Minnitarees and Mandans, in which case there would have been no necessity for the embankments in question. Or, *they might have raised these embankments of earth, inclosing rectangles or squares, and constructed long houses upon them,* which, it is submitted, is precisely what they did. Such houses would agree in general character and in plan, and in the uses to which they were adapted, with those of the aborigines found in all parts of America

The elevated platform of earth as a house-site is an element in Indian architecture which reappears in a conspicuous manner in the solid pyramidal platforms upon which the great stone structures in Yucatan and Central America were erected, and which sprang from the defensive and the communal principles in living. This latter principle required large houses for the accommodation of a number of families in the Lower Status of barbarism, and large enough in some cases, when the people were in the Middle Status, to accommodate an entire tribe. When adobe bricks were used the house was usually a single structure, three or four rooms deep and three or four stories high, constructed in a block, and in the nature of a fortress. The ground story was little used, except for storage, and they lived, practically, upon the roof terraces. When the use of stone came in, the structure often consisted of a main building four or five hundred feet long, and two wings two and three hundred feet in length, inclosing three sides of an open court, the fourth side being protected by a low stone wall. Such were the pueblos now in ruins upon the Rio Chaco in New Mexico.

In the highest form of this architecture in Yucatan and Chiapas, the pyramidal elevation appears faced with dry stone walls. The buildings upon its summit were often in the form of a quadrangle, with an open court in the center; but the buildings were generally disconnected at the four angles, as in the House of the Nuns at Uxmal. All of these forms are parts of one system of indigenous architecture; and the several parts are susceptible of articulation in a series representing a progressive development of a common thought, that of joint residence, with the practice of communism in living in large groups in the same house, or in one group consisting of the entire household.

Let us, then, inquire whether the principal embankments of the Mound-Builders were adapted, as raised platforms of earth, for the sites of long houses constructed on the communistic principle, and in the general style of the houses of the American aborigines.

In the valley of the Scioto, in Ohio, and within an extent of twelve miles, were found the remains of seven villages of the Mound-Builders, four upon the east and three upon the west side of the river. They are among the best of their works, and furnish fair examples of the whole. One of the number, the High Bank Pueblo, is shown in ground-plan in the engraving, Fig. 46. It is the only one in which the inclosure is octagonal instead of square. The remains of each of the seven consist principally of embankments like railway grades several feet high and correspondingly broad at the base, inclosing a square or slightly irregular area, the embankment on each of the four sides being about a thousand feet long, with an opening or gateway in the middle and at the four angles of the square. Attached to or quite near to five of the seven are large circular inclosures, each formed by a similar though lower embankment of earth and inclosing a space somewhat larger than the squares. The respective heights of the embankments, forming four of the rectangles, are given at four, six, ten, and twelve feet; and of three of the circular embankments, at five and six feet, respectively.

The embankments inclosing the squares were probably the sites of their houses; since, as the highest, and because they are straight, they were best adapted to the purpose.   The situations of these pueblos at short distances from each other on the same stream accords with the usages of the Village Indians of New and Old Mexico and Central America in locating their villages   These pueblos were probably occupied by Mound-Builders of the same tribe, and were not unlikely under a common government, consisting of a council of chiefs.   It is probable, also, that they were constructed, one after the other, by colonists from an original village.

In the engraving, Fig. 46, the form and relations of the embankments are shown, with cross-sections indicating their elevation and present ground-dimensions.   It was taken from the work of Squier and Davis.[1]   These authors remark that "the principal work consists of an octagon and circle, the former measuring nine hundred and fifty feet, the latter ten hundred and fifty feet in diameter.   *   *   *   The walls of the octagon are very bold, and, where they have been least subject to cultivation, are now between eleven and twelve feet in height by about fifty feet base.   The wall of the circle is much less, nowhere measuring over four or five feet in altitude.   In all these respects, as in the absence of a ditch and the presence of the two small circles, this work resembles the Hopeton Works."[2]   Of the latter, which is nine miles above on the Scioto, they remark that "the walls of the rectangular work are composed of a clayey loam twelve feet high by fifty feet base   *   *   *   They resemble the heavy grading of a railway, and are broad enough on the top to admit of the passage of a coach."[3]

It will be noticed that the octagonal work shown in the engraving consists of seven distinct embankments.   Six of these are about four hundred and fifty feet long, and the remaining one, which once consisted of two equal sections, as shown by the mound to face an original opening in the center, now forms one continuous embankment facing one side of the inclosed area.   If these embankments were reformed, with the materials washed down and now spread over a base of fifty feet, with sloping sides and a level summit, they would form new embankments thirty-seven feet wide at base, ten feet high, and with a summit platform twenty-two feet wide.   If a surface coating of clay were used, the sides could be made

---

[1] Smith Con., vol. i, pl. xvi.   [2] Ib., p. 50.   [3] Ib., p. 51.

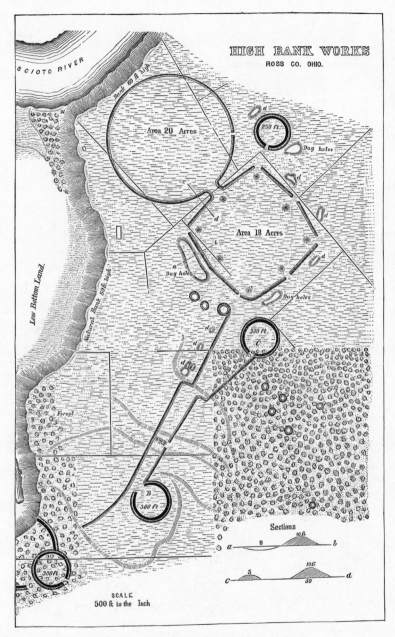

FIG. 46.—Ground plan of High Bank Pueblo.

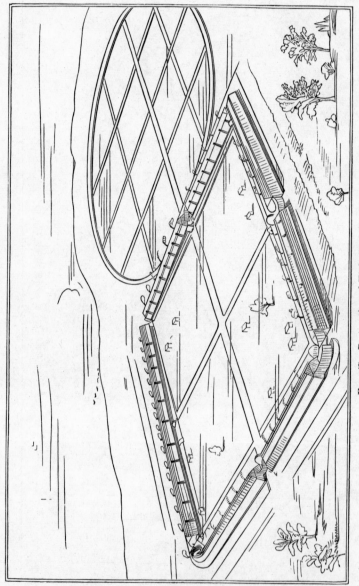

Fig. 47.—Restoration of High Bank Pueblo.

236

steeper and the summit platform broader. On embankments thus reformed out of their original materials respectable as well as sufficient sites would be provided for long joint-tenement houses, comparted into chambers like stalls opening upon a central passage way through the structure from end to end, as in the long-houses of the Iroquois. Such embankments were strikingly adapted to houses of the aboriginal American model, the characteristic feature of which was sufficient length to afford a number of apartments. This feature became more marked in the houses of the Village Indians, among whom houses three hundred, four hundred, and even five hundred feet in length have been found, as elsewhere stated.

These embankments answered as a substitute for the first story of the house constructed of adobe bricks, which was usually from ten to twelve feet high, and closed up solid on the ground, externally. The gateways entering the square were protected, it may be supposed, with palisades of round timber set in the ground, each row of stakes commencing at the opposite ends of the embankments and contracting after passing each other to a narrow opening on the inside, which might be permanently closed. Indian tribes in a lower condition than the Mound-Builders were familiar with palisades. The inclosed square was thus completely protected by the long-houses standing upon these embankments and the gateways guarding the several entrances. The pueblo, externally, would present continuous ramparts of earth ten feet high, around an inclosed area, surmounted with timber-framed houses with walls sloping like the embankments, and coated with earth mixed with clay and gravel, rising ten or twelve feet above their summits; the two forming a sloping wall of earth twenty feet high. It seems extremely probable, for the reasons stated, that they raised these embankments as foundations, and planted their long-houses upon them, thus uniting the defensive principle with that of communism in living. Such houses would harmonize with the general plan of life of the American aborigines, and with the general type of their house architecture.

It is not necessary to know the exact form or internal plan of these houses in order to establish this hypothesis. It is sufficient to show that these embankments as restored were not only adapted, but admirably adapted, to joint-tenement houses of the aboriginal American type.

The restoration, Fig. 47, was drawn by my friend James G. Cutler, esq., of Rochester, architect, in accordance with the foregoing suggestions. It shows not only the feasibility of occupying these embankments with long houses, but also that each pueblo was designed by the Mound-Builders to be a fortress, able to resist assault with the appliances of Indian warfare. From the defensive character of the great houses of the Village Indian in general, this feature might have been expected to appear in the houses of the Mound-Builders.

In this restoration the houses are nearly triangular and of simple construction. Indians much ruder than they are supposed to have been, as the Minnitarees and Mandans, walled their houses with slabs of wood standing on a slope, and roofed them at a lower angle, covering both the sloping external walls and the roof with a "concrete of tough clay and gravel," a foot or more thick. Long triangular houses of the width of the summit of these embankments, with their doorways opening upon the square, and with the interior comparted in the form of stalls upon each side of a central passage way, would realize, with the inclosed court, some of the features and nearly all the advantages of the New Mexican pueblo houses. Occupying to the edge of the embankments, these of the Mound-Builders could not be successfully assailed from without either by Indian weapons or by fire; and within, their apartments would be as secure and capacious as those of the Village Indians in general at the period of their discovery. The inclosed court, which is of unusual size, is one of the remarkable features of the plan. It afforded a protected place for the villagers and a place of recreation for their children, as well as room for their drying-scaffolds, of which Mr. Cutler has introduced a number of the Minnitaree and Mandan model, and for gardens if they chose to use a part of the area for that purpose. They would also require room for a large accumulation of fuel for winter use. The only assailable points are the gateways, of which the embankments show seven. These undoubtedly were protected by rows of round timber set in the ground, and passing each other in such a manner as to leave a narrow opening, with a mound back of each, upon which archers could stand and shoot their arrows over the heads of those between them

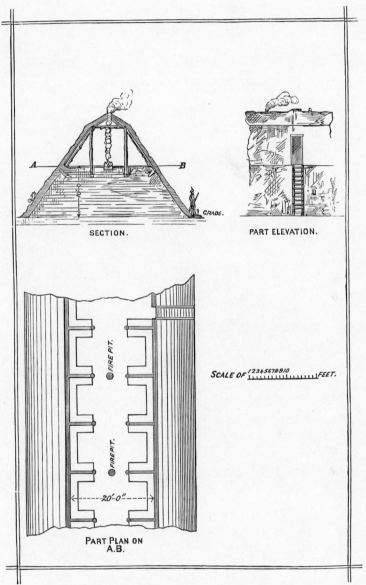

SECTION.

PART ELEVATION.

FIRE PIT.

FIREPIT.

SCALE OF 12345678910 FEET.

20'-0"

PART PLAN ON
A.B.

FIG. 48.—Ground plan and sections of house, High Bank Pueblo.

and the gateway in front.   Such at least is the object which the presence of the mound in each case suggests.

In the engraving, Fig. 48, there is a ground plan of a section of one of the long-houses resting upon the restored embankment.   It shows eight apartments upon opposite sides of the central passage, each nine feet wide by six feet deep, and surrounded by raised bunks used both for seats and beds.   The passage is eight feet wide and runs through the house from end to end, with fire-pits in the center for each four apartments.   In interior plan it is an exact transcript of the long-house of the Iroquois, and therefore adapted to the joint habitation of a large number of related families, and to the practice of communism.

Another section shows the embankment below the line A–B, which, as stated, is ten feet high upon a base thirty-seven feet wide, and with a summit platform twenty-two feet wide, which forms the floor of the house. Above this is a cross-section of the structure.   Round posts six inches in diameter are set in the ground upon the lines of the central passage, defining also the several stalls.   These posts, which rise eight feet above the level of the floor and are forked at the top, support string-pieces which run the length of the house.   Against these, planks of split timber are placed so as to form a sloping external wall, and these are covered with clay and gravel a foot or more thick.   A simpler method would be the use of poles set close together and sunk in the ground, afterwards coated in the same manner.   Cross-pieces of round timber rest upon the stringers over each pair of posts.   The roof over the central passage is formed independently of poles bracing against each other at the center from opposite sides.   This is also covered with concrete or mud mortar.   Openings through the roof are left over the fire-pits for the exit of the smoke.   The principle of construction adopted is that employed in the dirt lodges of the Minnitarees and Mandans of the Upper Missouri.[1]   As thus restored, this pueblo of the Mound-Builders is not superior in the mechanism of the houses to those of the tribes named.

An elevation of a portion of one of the houses, on the court side, is also furnished, showing the embankment with a ladder resting upon it used

---

[1] There are some reasons for supposing that the Minnitarees are descendants of the Mound-Builders.

as steps, and which could be taken up at night; also one of the doors by which the house was entered.

It is not necessary, as before suggested, that the actual form and structure of the houses of the Mound-Builders should be shown to establish the hypothesis that these embankments were the veritable sites of their houses. If it is made evident that the summit platforms of these embankments, when reformed from their own materials, would afford practicable sites for houses, which when constructed would have been comfortable dwellings adapted to the climate and to Indian life in the Middle Status of barbarism, this is all that can be required. The restoration of this pueblo establishes the affirmative of this proposition, with the superadded confirmation of that defensive character which marks all the house architecture of the Village Indians in New and Old Mexico and Central America.

With their undoubted advancement beyond the Iroquois and Minnitarees, the Mound-Builders may have constructed better houses upon these platform elevations than the plans indicate. No remains of adobes have been found in connection with these embankments, and nothing to indicate that walls of such brick had ever been raised upon them. The disintegrated mass would have shown itself in the form of the embankment after the lapse of many centuries. On the contrary, they were found in the precise form they would have assumed, under atmospheric influences, after structures of the kind described had perished, and the embankments had been abandoned for centuries.

These embankments, therefore, require triangular houses of the kind described, and long-houses, as well, covering their entire length. But the interior plan might have been different; for example, the passage way might have been along the exterior wall, and the stalls or apartments on the court side, and but half as many in number; and, instead of one continuous house in the interior, four hundred and fifty feet in length, it might have been divided into several, separated from each other by cross partitions. The plan of life, however, which we are justified in ascribing to them, from known usages of Indian tribes in a similar condition of advancement, would lead us to expect large households formed on the basis of kin, with the practice of communism in living in each household, whether large or small.

There is a direct connection in principle between the platform elevations inclosing a large square on which the High Bank Pueblo was constructed, and the pyramidal platforms in Yucatan, smaller in diameter but
higher in elevation, upon which were erected the most artistic houses constructed by the American aborigines. In the latter cases the central area
rises to the common level of the embankments upon which the houses were
constructed. The former has the security gained by a house-site above
the level of the surrounding ground; and it represents about all the
advance made by the Village Indians in the art of war above the tribes in
a lower condition of barbarism. They placed their houses and homes in a
position unassailable by the methods of Indian warfare.

There is some diversity, as would be expected, in the size of the
squares inclosed by these embankments. They range from four hundred
and fifty to seventeen hundred feet, the majority measuring between eight
hundred and fifty and a thousand feet. Gateways are usually found at the
four angles and at the center of each side. A comparison of the dimensions of twenty of these squares, figured in the "Ancient Monuments of
the Mississippi Valley," gives for the average nine hundred and thirty-seven
feet. The aggregate length of the embankments shown in Fig. 46 is three
thousand six hundred feet, which, at an average of ten feet for each apartment, would give three hundred and sixty upon each side of the passage
way, or seven hundred and twenty in all. From this number should be
deducted such as were used for storage, for doorways, and for public uses.
Allowing two apartments for each family of five persons, the High Bank
Pueblo would have accommodated from fifteen hundred to two thousand
persons, living in the fashion of Indians, which is about the number of an
average pueblo of the Village Indians. This result may be strengthened
by comparing houses of existing Indian tribes. The Seneca-Iroquois village of Tiotohatton, two centuries ago, was estimated at a hundred and
twenty houses. Taking the number at one hundred, with an average
length of fifty feet, and it would give a lineal length of house-room of five
thousand feet. It was the largest of the Seneca, and the largest of the
Iroquois villages, and contained about two thousand inhabitants. A similar result is obtained by another comparison. The aggregate length of the

apartments in the pueblo of Chetro Kettle, in New Mexico, now in ruins, including those in the several stories, is four thousand seven hundred feet. It contained probably about the same number of inhabitants.

The foregoing explanation of the uses of these embankments rests upon the defensive principle in the house architecture of the Village Indians, and upon a state of the family requiring joint-tenement houses communistic in character. To both of these requirements this conjectural restoration of one of the pueblos of the Mound-Builders responds in a remarkable manner. In the diversified forms of the houses of the Village Indians, in all parts of America, the defensive principle is a constant feature. Among the Mound-Builders a rampart of earth ten feet high around a village would afford no protection; but surmounted with long-houses, the walls of which rose continuous with the embankments, the strength of these walls, though of timber coated with earth, would render a rampart thus surmounted and doubled in height a formidable barrier against Indian assault. The second principle, that of communism in living in joint-tenement houses, which is impressed not less clearly upon the houses of the Village Indians in general than upon the supposed houses of the Mound-Builders, harmonized completely with the first. From the two together sprang the house architecture of the American aborigines, with its diversities of form, and they seem sufficient for its interpretation. The Mound-Builders in their new area east of the Mississippi, finding it impossible to construct joint-tenement houses of adobe bricks to which they had been accustomed, substituted solid embankments of earth in the place of the first story closed up on the ground, and erected triangular houses upon them covered with earth. When circumstances compelled a change of plan, the second is not a violent departure from the first. There is a natural connection between them. Finally, it is deemed quite sufficient to sustain the interpretation given, that these embankments were eminently adapted to the uses indicated; and that the pueblo as restored, and with its inclosed court, would have afforded to its inhabitants pleasant, protected, and attractive homes.

With respect to the large circular inclosures, adjacent to and communicating with the squares, it is not necessary that we should know their object. The one attached to the High Bank Pueblo contains twenty acres of land, and doubtless subserved some useful purpose in their plan of life. The first suggestion which presents itself is, that as a substitute for a fence it surrounded the garden of the village in which they cultivated their maize, beans, squashes, and tobacco. At the Minnitaree village a similar inclosure may now be seen by the side of the village surrounding their cultivated land, consisting partly of hedge and partly of stakes, the open prairie stretching out beyond. We cannot know all the necessities that attended their mode of life; although houses, gardens, food, and raiment were among those which must have existed.

There is another class of circular embankments, about two hundred and fifty feet in diameter, connected with each other in some cases by long and low parallel embankments, as may be seen in Fig. 46. Undoubtedly they were for some useful purpose, which may or may not be divined correctly, but a knowledge of which is not necessary to our hypothesis respecting the principal embankments. It may be suggested as probable that the Mound-Builders were organized in gentes, phratries, and tribes. If this were the case, the phratries would need separate places for holding their councils and for performing their religious observances. These ring embankments suggest the circular estufas found in connection with the New Mexican pueblos, two, four, and sometimes five at one pueblo. The circles were adapted to open-air councils, after the fashion of the American Indian tribes. As there are two of these connected with each other, and two not connected, it is not improbable that the Mound-Builders at this village were organized in two and perhaps four phratries, and that they performed their religious ceremonies and public business in these open estufas.[1]

Practice of Cremation.—Among other works are the conical mounds, which are numerous, found in or near circular embankments. They vary in height from five to ten and twenty feet; with one, the Grave Creek Mound, seventy feet high. They are classified by Squier and Davis, who

---

[1] The solid rectangular platforms found at Marietta, Ohio, and at several places in the Gulf region, are analogous to those in Yucatan. They are an advance upon the ring inclosures, and were probably designed for religious uses.

That the Mound-Builders were at one time accustomed to adobe brick is proven by their presence at Seltzertown, in the State of Mississippi, forming a part of the wall of a mound. (See Foster's Pre-Historic Races of the U. S., p. 112.)

surveyed and examined them, into "Mounds of Sacrifice," "Mounds of Sepulture," and "Mounds of Observation." The first kind only, in which the so-called "altars" are found, will be noticed.

At the center of each of the mounds of this class, and on the ground-level, there was found a bed of clay, artificially formed into a shallow basin, and then hardened by fire. These basins have been termed "altars" by Squier and Davis in their work on the "Ancient Monuments of the Missis-

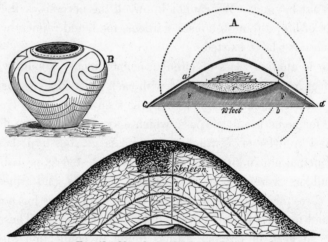

FIG. 49.—Mound, Artificial Clay Basin.

sippi Valley." Mr. Squier remarks in a résumé of this work, published separately, that "some are round, others elliptical, and others square or parallelograms.   *   *   *   The usual dimensions are from five to eight feet."[1]

At Mound City, on the Scioto River, there is a group of twenty-six mounds in one inclosure, an engraving of one of which, taken from Mr. Squier's paper, is shown in Fig. 49. It is seven feet high by fifty-five feet base, and contained the artificial clay basin in question. F F is the basin, which is round, and measures from c to d nine feet, and from a to e five feet. The height from b to e is twenty inches, and the dip of the curve, a to e, is nine inches. "The body of the altar," Mr. Squier remarks, "is burned throughout, though in a greater degree within the basin, where it

---

[1] Observations, etc., Trans. Am. Eth. Soc., ii, 158.

was so hard as to resist the blow of a heavy hatchet, the instrument rebounding as if struck upon a rock. The basin, or hollow of the altar, was filled up even full with dry ashes, intermingled with which were some fragments of pottery. * * * One of the vases, taken in fragments from the mound, has been very nearly restored. The sketch B presents its outlines and the character of its ornaments. Its height is six, and its greatest diameter eight inches * * * Above the deposit of ashes, and covering the entire basin, was a layer of silvery or opaque mica in sheets overlapping each other; and immediately over the center of the basin was heaped a quantity of human bones, probably the amount of a single skeleton, in fragments. The position of these is indicated by O in the section. The layer of mica and calcined bones, it should be remarked to prevent misapprehension, was peculiar to this individual mound, and not found in any other of the class."[1] Calcined bones, however, were found in three out of some twenty mounds of this class examined.[2]

The question now recurs, what was the use of the basin of clay, and what the object of the mound itself? The terms "altars" and "mounds of sacrifice," employed in describing them, imply that human sacrifices were offered on these "altars," "upon which glowed the sacrificial fires."[3] There is no propriety, I respectfully submit, in the use of either of these terms, or in the conclusions they would force us to adopt.

Human sacrifices were unknown in the Lower Status of barbarism; but they were introduced in the Middle Status, when the first organized priesthood, distinguished by their apparel, appears. In parts of Mexico, and, it is claimed, in parts of Central America, these atrocious rites were performed; but they were unknown in New Mexico, and, without better evidence than these miscalled altars afford, they cannot be fastened upon the Mound-Builders. Moreover, these clay beds were not adapted to the barbarous work. Wherever human sacrifices are known to have occurred among the American aborigines, the place was an elevated mound platform, in the nature of a temple, as the Teocalli of Mexico, and the raised altar or sacrificial stone stood before the idol in whose worship the rites were performed. There is neither a temple nor an idol; but a hollow bed of clay

---

[1] Observations, etc., Trans. Am. Eth. Soc., ii, p. 161.　[2] Anc. Mon., etc., pp. 157, 159.　[3] Ib., p. 155.

covered by a mound raised in honor over the ashes of a deceased chief, for assuredly such a mound would not have been raised over the ashes of a victim. Indians never exchanged prisoners of war. Adoption or burning at the stake was the alternative of capture; but no mound was ever raised over the burned remains. Human sacrifices seem to have originated in an attempt to utilize the predetermined death of prisoners of war in the service of the gods, until slavery finally offered a profitable substitute, in the Upper Status of barbarism.

Another use suggests itself for this artificial basin more in accordance with Indian usages and customs, namely, that cremation of the body of a deceased chief was performed upon it, after which the mound in question was raised over his ashes in accordance with Indian custom.

Cremation was practiced by the Village Indians only among the American aborigines. It was not general even among them, burial in the ground being the common usage; but it was more or less general in the case of chiefs. The mode of cremation varied in different areas, but the full particulars are not given in any instance. In Nicarauga the body of a deceased chief of the highest grade was wrapped in clothes and suspended by ropes before a fire until the body was baked to dryness; then, after keeping it a year, it was taken to the market-place, where they burned it, believing that the smoke went "to the place where the dead man's soul was."[1] From this or some similar conceit the practice of cremation probably originated.

THE PROBABLE NUMBERS OF THE MOUND-BUILDERS.

There are no reasons for supposing, from the number of their villages, that the Mound-Builders were a numerous people. My friend, Prof. Charles Whittlesey, in a discussion of the rate of increase of the human race, estimates them at 500,000.[2] With thanks for the moderateness of the estimate, one-third of that number would have been more satisfactory. Dense populations, an expression sometimes applied to the Mound-Builders, have never

---

[1] Herrera's Hist. America, ii, 133.   [2] Trans. Am. Ass. for the Adv. of Science, 1873, p. 320.

existed without either flocks and herds, or field agriculture with the use of the plow. In some favored areas, where the facilities for irrigation were unusual, a considerable population has been developed upon horticulture; but no traces of irrigating canals have been found in connection with the works of the Mound-Builders. Furthermore, it was unnecessary in their areas. Transplanted from a comparatively mild to a cold climate, they must have found the struggle for existence intensified. Like the Cibolans in '540, it was doubtless at all times equally true of them, that "they had barely provisions enough for themselves." And yet there is no cereal equal to maize in the rich reward it returns even for poor cultivation. It grows in the hill, can be eaten green as well as ripe, and is hardy and prolific. At the same time, while it can be made the basis of human subsistence, it is not sufficient of itself for the maintenance of vigorous, healthful life. Vegetables and game were requisite to complete the supply of food. The difficulties in the way of production set a limit to their numbers. These also explain the small number of their settlements in the large areas over which they spread. Although they found native copper on the south shore of Lake Superior, and beat it into chisels and a species of pointed spade, the number of copper tools found is small, much too small to lead to the supposition that it sensibly influenced their cultivation. A pick pointed with a stone chisel, a spade of wood, and a triangular piece of flint set in a wooden handle and used as a knife, were as perfect implements as they were able to command. Horticulture practiced thus rudely was necessarily of limited productiveness.

The idea has been advanced that "the condition of society among the Mound-Builders was not that of freemen, or, in other words, that the state possessed absolute power over the lives and fortunes of its subjects."[1] It is a sufficient answer to this remarkable passage that a people unable to dig a well or build a dry stone wall must have been unable to establish political society, which was necessary to the existence of a state.

From the absence of all traditionary knowledge of the Mound-Builders among the tribes found east of the Mississippi, an inference arises that the

---

[1] Foster's Pre-historic Races, etc., p. 386.

period of their occupation was ancient. Their withdrawal was probably gradual, and completed before the advent of the ancestors of the present tribes, or simultaneous with their arrival. It seems more likely that their retirement from the country was voluntary than that they were expelled by an influx of wild tribes. If their expulsion had been the result of a protracted warfare, all remembrance of so remarkable an event would scarcely have been lost among the tribes by whom they were displaced. A warm climate was necessary for the successful maintenance of the highest form of Village Indian life. In the struggle for existence in this cold climate Indian arts and ingenuity must have been taxed quite as heavily to provide clothing as food. It is therefore not improbable that the attempt to transplant the New Mexican type of village life into the valley of the Ohio proved a failure, and that after great efforts, continued through centuries of time, it was finally abandoned by their withdrawal, first into the gulf region through which they entered, and, lastly, from the country altogether.

The Tlascalans practiced cremation, but it was generally limited to the chiefs.[1] It was the same among the Aztecs. "Others were burnt and the ashes buried in the temples, but they were all interred with whatever things of value they possessed.[2] The Mayas of Yucatan came nearer the Romans in the practice, for they preserved the ashes in earthen vessels. "The dead were much lamented," remarks Herrera, "in silence by day and with dismal shrieks by night * * * filling their mouths with ground wheat [maize] that they might not want food in the other world. * * * The bodies of their lords were burnt and their ashes put into large vessels, over which temples were built. Some made wooden statues of their parents, and leaving an hollow in the necks of them, put in their ashes and kept them among their idols with great veneration."[3] In New Mexico cremation is occasionally practiced at the present time.

That the Mound-Builders should have had this custom, in view of its prevalence among the Village Indians, would afford no cause of surprise. I think we may, not without reason, recognize in this artificial basin of clay a cremation bed, upon which the body was placed in a sitting posture, covered with fuel, and then burned—in some cases partially, and in others

---

[1] Herrera's Hist. America, ii, 302.   [2] Ib., iii, 220.   [3] Ib., iv, 175.

until every vestige of the body had been burned to ashes—after which, or even before the burning, a mound was raised over them as a mark of honor and respect. These mounds have yielded a large number of copper and stone implements, pipes, fragments of water jars, and other articles usually entombed with the remains of the dead. It seems to have been their method of cremation; and it must be admitted to be quite as respectable as any known form of this strange practice of a large portion of the human race.

CHAPTER X.

HOUSES OF THE AZTECS OR ANCIENT MEXICANS.

The first accounts of the pueblo of Mexico created a powerful sensation in Europe. In the West India Islands the Spanish discoverers found small Indian tribes under the government of chiefs; but on the continent, in the Valley of Mexico, they found a confederacy of three Indian tribes under a more advanced but similar government. In the midst of the valley was a large pueblo, the largest in America, surrounded with water, approached by causeways; in fine, a water-girt fortress impregnable to Indian assault. This pueblo presented to the Spanish adventurers the extraordinary spectacle of an Indian society lying two ethnical periods back of European society, but with a government and plan of life at once intelligent, orderly, and complete. There was aroused an insatiable curiosity for additional particulars, which has continued for three centuries, and which has called into existence a larger number of works than were ever before written upon any people of the same number and of the same importance.

The Spanish adventurers who captured the pueblo of Mexico saw a king in Montezuma, lords in Aztec chiefs, and a palace in the large joint-tenement house occupied, Indian fashion, by Montezuma and his fellow-householders. It was, perhaps, an unavoidable self-deception at the time, because they knew nothing of the Aztec social system. Unfortunately it inaugurated American aboriginal history upon a misconception of Indian life which has remained substantially unquestioned until recently. The first eye-witnesses gave the keynote to this history by introducing Montezuma as a king, occupying a palace of great extent crowded with retainers, and situated in the midst of a grand and populous city, over which, and much beside, he was reputed master. But king and kingdom were in time found too common to express all the glory and splendor the imagination was

252

beginning to conceive of Aztec society; and emperor and empire gradually superseded the more humble conception of the conquerors.[1]

A psychological fact, which deserves a moment's notice, is revealed by these works, written as they were with a desire for the truth and without intending to deceive   These writers ought to have known that every Indian tribe in America was an organized society, with definite institutions, usages, and customs, which, when ascertained, would have perfectly explained its government, the social relations of the people, and their plan of life   Indian society could be explained as completely and understood as perfectly as the civilized society of Europe or America by finding its exact organization   This, strange to say, was never attempted, or at least never accomplished, by any one of these numerous and voluminous writers.   To every author, from Cortes and Bernal Diaz to Brasseur de Bourbourg and Hubert H Bancroft, Indian society was an unfathomable mystery, and their works have left it a mystery still.   Ignorant of its structure and principles, and unable to comprehend its peculiarities, they invoked the imagination to supply whatever was necessary to fill out the picture.   When the reason, from want of facts, is unable to understand and therefore unable to explain the structure of a given society, imagination walks bravely in and fearlessly rears its glittering fabric to the skies.   Thus, in this case, we have a grand historical romance, strung upon

---

[1] In the Despatches of Cortes the term King "El rey" is not used in speaking of Montezuma, but señor and cacique.

The Valley of Mexico, including the adjacent mountain slopes and excluding the area covered by water, was about equal to the State of Rhode Island, which contains thirteen hundred square miles; an insignificant area for a single American Indian tribe.   But the confederacy had subdued a number of tribes southward and southeastward from the valley as far as Guatemala, and placed them under tribute.   Under their plan of government it was impossible to incorporate these tribes in the Aztec confederacy; the barrier of language furnished an insuperable objection; and they were left to govern themselves through their own chiefs, and according to their own usages and customs.   As they were neither under Aztec government nor Aztec usages, there is no occasion to speak of them as a part of the Aztec confederacy, or even as an appendage of its government.   The power of this confederacy did not extend a hundred miles beyond the Pueblo of Mexico on the west, northwest, north, northeast, or east sides, in each of which directions they were confronted by independent and hostile tribes.

The population of the three confederate tribes was confined to the valley, and did not probably exceed two hundred and fifty thousand souls, including the Moquiltes, Xochomileos, and Chaleans, if it equaled that number, which would give nearly twice the present population of New York to the square mile, and a greater population to the square mile than Rhode Island now contains.   The Spanish estimates of Indian populations were gross exaggerations.   Those who claim a greater population for the Valley of Mexico than that indicated will be bound to show how a barbarous people, without flocks and herds and without field agriculture, could have sustained in equal areas a larger number of inhabitants than a civilized people armed with these advantages.

the conquest of Mexico as upon a thread; the acts of the Spaniards, the pueblo of Mexico, and its capture, are historical, while the descriptions of Indian society and government are imaginary and delusive. These picturesque tales have been read with wonder and admiration, as they successively appeared, for three hundred and fifty years; though shown to be romances, they will continue to be read as Robinson Crusoe is read, not because they are true, but because they are pleasing. The psychological revelation is the eager, undefinable interest aroused by any picture of ancient society. It is felt by every stranger when he first walks the streets of Pompeii, and, standing within the walls of its roofless houses, strives to picture to himself the life and the society which flourished there eighteen hundred years ago. In Mexico the Spaniards found an organized society several thousand years further back of their own than Pompeian society, in its arts, institutions, and state of advancement. It was this revelation of a phase of the ancient life of mankind which possessed and still possesses such power to kindle the imagination and inspire enthusiasm. It caught the imagination and overcame the critical judgment of Prescott, our most charming writer; it ravaged the sprightly brain of Brasseur de Bourbourg, and it carried up in a whirlwind our author at the Golden Gate.

The commendation these works have received from critical journals reveals with painful distinctness the fact that we have no science of American ethnology. Such a science, resting as it must upon verified facts, and dealing with the institutions, arts and inventions, usages and customs, languages, religious beliefs, and plan of government of the Indian tribes, would, were it fairly established, command as well as deserve the respect of the American people. With the exception of an amateur here and there, American scholars have not been willing to devote themselves to so vast a work. It may be truly said at this moment that the structure and principles of Indian society are but partially known, and that the American Indian himself is still an enigma among us. The question is still before us as a nation whether we will undertake the work of furnishing to the world a scientific exposition of Indian society, or leave it as it now appears, crude, unmeaning, unintelligible, a chaos of contradictions and puerile absurdities. With a field of unequaled richness and of vast extent, with the same Red Race in all the stages of advancement indicated by three great ethnical periods, namely the Status of savagery, the Lower Status of barbarism, and the Middle Status of barbarism,[1] more persons ought to be found willing to work upon this material for the credit of American scholarship. It will be necessary for them to do as Herodotus did in Asia and Africa, to visit the native tribes at their villages and encampments, and study their institutions as living organisms, their condition, and their plan of life. When this has been done from the region of the Arctic Sea to Patagonia, Indian society will become intelligible, because its structure and principles will be understood. It exhibits three distinct phases, each with a culture peculiar to itself, lying back of civilization, and back of the Upper Status of barbarism, having very little in common with European society of three hundred years ago, and very little in common with American society of to-day. Its institutions, inventions, and customs find no analogues in those of civilized nations, and cannot be explained in terms adapted to such a society. Our later investigators are doing their work more and more on the plan of direct visitation, and I make no doubt a science of American ethnology will yet come into existence among us and rise high in public estimation from the important results it will rapidly achieve. Precisely what is now needed is the ascertainment and scientific treatment of this material.

After so general a condemnation of Spanish and American writers, so far as they represent Aztec society and government, some facts and some reasons ought to be presented to justify the charge. Recognizing the obligation, I propose to question the credibility of so much of the second volume of "The Native Races" and of so much of other Spanish histories as relate to two subjects—the character of the house in which Montezuma resided, which is styled a palace; and the account of the celebrated dinner of Montezuma, which is represented as the daily banquet of an imperial potentate. Neither subject, considered in itself, is of much importance; but if the accounts in these two particulars are found to be fictitious and delusive, a breach will be made in a vital section of the fabric of Aztec romance, now the most deadly encumbrance upon American ethnology.

---

[1] See *ante*, page 43, note, for a definition of proposed ethnical or culture periods, and Ancient Society, chapter 1, "Ethnical Periods."

It may be premised that there is a strong probability, from what is known of Indian life and society, that the house in which Montezuma lived was a joint-tenement house of the aboriginal American model, owned by a large number of related families, and occupied by them in common as joint proprietors; that the dinner in question was the usual single daily meal of a communal household, prepared in a common cook-house from common stores, and divided, Indian fashion, from the kettle; and that all the Spaniards found in Mexico was a simple confederacy of three Indian tribes, the counterpart of which was found in all parts of America.

It may be premised further that the Spanish adventures who thronged to the New World after its discovery found the same race of Red Indians in the West India Islands, in Central and South America, in Florida, and in Mexico.[1]   In their mode of life and means of subsistence, in their weapons, arts, usages, and customs, in their institutions, and in their mental and physical characteristics, they were the same people in different stages of advancement.   No distinction of race was observed, and none in fact existed.   They were broken up into numerous independent tribes, each under the government of a council of chiefs.   Among the more advanced tribes, confederacies existed, which represented the highest stage their governmental institutions had attained.   In some of them, as in the Aztec confederacy, they had a principal war-chief, elected for life or during good behavior, who was the general commander of the military bands.   His powers were those of a general, and necessarily arbitrary when in the field. Behind this war-chief—noticed, it is true, by Spanish writers, but without explaining or even ascertaining its functions—was the council of chiefs, " the great council without whose authority," Acosta remarks, Montezuma " might not do anything of importance."[2]   The civil and military powers of the government were in a certain sense co-ordinated between the council of chiefs and the military commander.   The government of the Aztec confederacy was essentially democratic, because its organization and institu-

---

[1] "But among all the other inhabitants of America there is such a striking similitude in the form of their bodies, and the qualities of their minds, that notwithstanding the diversities occasioned by the influence of climate, or unequal progress in improvement, we must pronounce them to be descended from one source."—*Robertson's History of America*, Law's ed., p. 69.

[2] The Natural and Moral History of the East and West Indies, Lond. ed., 1604, Grimstone's Trans., p. 485.

tions were so. If a more special designation is needed, it will be sufficient to describe it as a military democracy.

The Spaniards who overran Mexico and Peru gave a very different interpretation of these two organizations. Having found, as they supposed, two absolute monarchies with feudal characteristics, the history of American Indian institutions was cast in this mold. The chief attention of Europeans in the sixteenth century was directed to these two governments, to which the affairs of the numerous remaining tribes and confederacies were made subordinate. Subsequent history has run in the same grooves for more than three centuries, striving diligently to confirm that of which confirmation was impossible. The generalization was perhaps proper enough, that if the institutions of the Aztecs and Peruvians, such well-advanced Indian tribes, culminated in monarchy, those of the Indian tribes generally were essentially monarchical, and therefore those of Mexico and Peru should represent the institutions of the Red Race.

It may be premised, finally, that the histories of Spanish America may be trusted in whatever relates to the acts of the Spaniards, and to the acts and personal characteristics of the Indians; in whatever relates to their weapons, implements, and utensils, fabrics, food, and raiment, and things of a similar character. But in whatever relates to Indian society and government, their social relations and plan of life, they are nearly worthless, because they learned nothing and knew nothing of either. We are at full liberty to reject them in these respects, and commence anew; using any facts they may contain which harmonize with what is known of Indian society. It was a calamity to the entire Red Race that the achievements of the Village Indians of Mexico and Central America, in the development of their institutions, should have suffered a shipwreck so nearly total. The only remedy for the evil done them is to recover, if possible, a knowledge of their institutions, which alone can place them in their proper position in the history of mankind.

In order to understand so simple an event in Indian life as Montezuma's dinner, it is necessary to know certain usages and customs, and even certain institutions of the Indian tribes generally, which had a direct bearing upon the dinner of every Indian in America at the epoch of the Spanish conquest. Although it may seem strange to the reader, it requires a knowledge of several classes of facts to comprehend this dinner, such as: 1. The organization in gentes, phratries, and tribes. 2. The ownership of lands in common. 3. The law of hospitality. 4. The practice of communism in living. 5. The communal character of their houses. 6. Their custom of having but one prepared meal each day, a dinner. 7 Their separation at meals, the men eating first, and the women and children afterwards. These several topics have been considered in previous chapters.

Not a vestige of the ancient pueblo of Mexico (Tenochtitlan) remains to assist us to a knowledge of its architecture. Its structures, which were useless to a people of European habits, were speedily destroyed to make room for a city adapted to the wants of a civilized race. We must seek for its characteristics in contemporary Indian houses which still remain in ruins, and in such of the early descriptions as have come down to us, and then leave the subject with but little accurate knowledge. Its situation, partly on dry land and partly in the waters of a shallow artificial pond formed by causeways and dikes, led to the formation of streets and squares, which were unusual in Indian pueblos, and gave to it a remarkable appearance. "There were three sorts of broad and spacious streets," Herrera remarks; "one sort all water with bridges, another all earth, and a third of earth and water, there being a space to walk along on land and the rest for canoes to pass, so that most of the streets had walks on the sides and water in the middle."[1] Many of the houses were large, far beyond the supposable wants of a single Indian family. They were constructed of adobe brick and of stone, and plastered over in both cases with gypsum, which made them a brilliant white; and some were constructed of a red porous stone. In cutting and dressing this stone flint implements were used.[2] The fact that the houses were plastered externally leads us to infer that they had not learned to dress stone and lay them in courses. It is not certainly established that they had learned the use of a mortar of lime and sand. In the final attack and capture, it is said that Cortes, in the course of seventeen days, destroyed and leveled three-quarters of the pueblo, which demonstrates the flimsy character of the masonry. Some of the houses were constructed on

---

[1] History of America, ii, 361. [2] Clavigero, ii, 238.

three sides of a court, like those on the Rio Chaco in New Mexico, others probably surrounded an open court or quadrangle, like the House of the Nuns at Uxmal; but this is not clearly shown. The best houses were usually two stories high, an upper and lower floor being mentioned. The second story receded from the first, probably in the terraced form. Clavigero remarks that "the houses of the lords and people of circumstance were built of stone and lime. They consisted of two floors, having halls, large court-yards, and the chambers fitly disposed; the roofs were flat and terraced; the walls were so well whitened, polished, and shining that they appeared to the Spaniards when at a distance to have been silver. The pavement or floor was plaster, perfectly level, plain, and smooth. * * * The large houses of the capital had in general two entrances, the principal one to the street, the other to the canal. They had no wooden doors to their houses."[1] The house was entered through doorways from the street, or from the court, on the ground-floor. Not a house in Mexico is mentioned by any of the early writers as occupied by a single family. They were evidently joint-tenement houses of the aboriginal American model, each occupied by a number of families ranging from five and ten to one hundred, and perhaps in some cases two hundred families in a house.

Before considering the house architecture of the Aztecs, it remains to notice, briefly, the general character of the houses of the Village Indians within the areas of Spanish visitation. They were joint-tenement houses, usually, of the American model, adapted to communism in living, like those previously described, and will aid us to understand the houses of the pueblo of Mexico.

Herrera, speaking of the natives of Cuba, remarks that "they had caciques and towns of two hundred houses, with several families in each of them, as was usual in Hispaniola."[2] The Cubans were below the Sedentary Indians. In Yucatan, the houses of the Mayas, and of the tribes of Guatemala, Chiapas, and Honduras, remain in ruins to speak for themselves, and will form the subject of the ensuing chapter. On the march to Mexico, Cortez and his men, "being come down into the plain, took up their quarters in a country house that had many apartments."[3] "At Iztapalapa he was

---

[1] History of Mexico, ii, 232.   [2] Ib., ii, 15.   [3] Ib., ii, 320.

entertained in a house that had large courts, upper and lower floors, and very delightful gardens. The walls were of stone, the timber-work well wrought; there were many and spacious rooms, hung with cotton hangings, extraordinary rich in their way."[1] His accommodations in the pueblo of Mexico will elsewhere be noticed. After the capture of the pueblo, Alvaredo was sent southward with two hundred foot and forty horse to the province of Tututlepec, on the Pacific. "When he arrived, the lord of Tututlepec offered to quarter the Spaniards in his palace, which was very magnificent."[2] In 1525 Cortez made his celebrated march to Guatemala with one hundred and fifty horse, the same number of foot, and three hundred Indians. "Being well received in the city of Apoxpalan, Cortez and all the Spaniards, with their horses, were quartered in one house, the Mexicans being dispersed into others, and all of them plentifully supplied with provisions during their stay."[3] The first "palace" described by Herrera was discovered by Balboa somewhere in the present Costa Rica, and *Comagre* has gone into history as its proprietor. "This palace was more remarkable and better built than any that had been yet seen on the islands, or the little that was then known of the continent, being one hundred and fifty paces in length and eighty in breadth, founded on very large posts, inclosed by a stone wall, with timber intermixed at the top, and hollow spaces, so beautifully wrought that the Spaniards were amazed at the sight of it, and could not express the manner and curiosity of it. There were in it several chambers and apartments, and one that was like a buttery and full of such provisions as the country afforded, as bread, venison, swine's flesh, &c. There was another large room like a cellar, full of earthern vessels, containing several sorts of white and red liquors, made of Indian wheat,"[4] etc. The noticeable fact in this description is the two chambers, containing provisions and stores for the household, which was undoubtedly the case with all of those named. Zempoala, near Vera Cruz, is described as "a very large town, with stately buildings of good timber work, and every house had a garden with water, so that it looked like a terrestrial paradise. * * * The scouts, advancing on horseback, came to the great square and courts where the prime houses were, which having been lately new plastered over, were

---

[1] History of America, ii, 325.　　[2] Ib., iii, 273.　　[3] Ib., iii, 273.　　[4] Ib., ii, 297.

very light, the Indians being extraordinary expert at that work"[1] Herrera further states that the houses were built of "lime and stone."

These pueblos were generally small, consisting of three or four large joint-tenement houses, with other houses smaller in size, the different grades of houses representing the relative thrift and prosperity of the several groups by whom they were owned and occupied. It is doubtful whether there was a single pueblo in North America, with the exception of Tlascala, Cholula, Tezcuco, and Mexico, which contained ten thousand inhabitants. There is no occasion to apply the term "city" to any of them. None of the Spanish descriptions enable us to realize the exact form and structure of these houses, or their relations to each other in forming a pueblo. But for the pueblos, occupied or in ruins, in New Mexico, and the more remarkable pueblos in ruins in Yucatan and Central America, we would know very little concerning the house architecture of the Sedentary Village Indians. It is evident from the citations made that the largest of these joint-tenement houses would accommodate from five hundred to a thousand or more people, living in the fashion of Indians; and that the courts were probably quadrangles, formed by constructing the building on three sides of an inclosed space, as in the New Mexican pueblos, or upon the four sides, as in the House of the Nuns, at Uxmal.

The writers on the conquest have failed to describe the Aztec house in such a manner that it can be fairly comprehended. They have also failed to explain the mode of life within it. But it can safely be said that most of these houses were large, far beyond any supposable wants of a single Indian family; that they were constructed, when on dry land, of adobe brick, and when in the water, of stone imbedded in some kind of mortar, and plastered over in both cases with gypsum, which made them a brilliant white. Some also were constructed of a red porous stone. Some of these houses were built on three sides of a court, like those on the Chaco, but the court opened on a street or causeway. Others not unlikely surrounded an open court or quadrangle, which must have been entered through a gateway; but this is not clearly shown. The large houses were probably two stories high; an upper and a lower floor are mentioned in some cases, but rarely a third.

---

[1] History of America, ii, 211.

Communism in living in large households, the communism being confined to the household, was probably the rule of life among the ancient Mexicans at the time of the Conquest.[1]

Two of the houses in Mexico were more particularly noted by the soldiers of Cortes than others—that in which they were quartered, and that in which Montezuma lived.   Neither can be said to have been described. I shall confine myself to these two structures.

Cortes made his first entry into Mexico in November, 1519, with four hundred and fifty Spaniards, according to Bernal Diaz,[2] accompanied by a thousand Tlascalan allies.   They were lodged in a vacant palace of Montezuma's late father, Diaz naively remarks, observing that "the whole of this palace was very light, airy, clean, and pleasant, the entry being through a great court."[3]   Cortes, after describing his reception, informs us that Montezuma "returned along the street in the order already described, until he reached a very large and splendid palace in which we were to be quartered. He then took me by the hand and led me into a spacious saloon, in front of which was a court through which we had entered."[4]   So much for the statements of two eye-witnesses.   Herrera gathered some additional particulars.   He states that "they came to a very large court, which was the wardrobe of the idols, and had been the house of Axayacatzin, Montezuma's father.   *   *   *   Being lodged in so large a house, that, though it seems incredible, contained so many capacious rooms, with bedchambers, that one hundred and fifty Spaniards could all lie single.   It was also worth observing that though the house was so big, every part of it to the last corner was very clean, neat, matted, and hung with hangings of cotton and feather work of several colors, and had beds and mats with pavilions over them. No man of whatsoever quality having any other sort of bed, no other being

---

[1] My learned friend, Mr. Ad. F. Bandelier, of Highland, Ill., has arrived at the same conclusion, substantially, as stated in the conclusion of his recent "Memoir on the Social Organization and Mode of Government of the Ancient Mexicans," 12th Annual Report of the Peabody Museum of American Archæology and Ethnology.   Cambridge, 1880, p. 699.

"Taking all this together, and adding to it the results of our investigations into the military organization of the ancient Mexicans, as well as of their communal mode of holding and enjoying the soil, we feel authorized to conclude *that the social organization and mode of government of the ancient Mexicans was a military democracy, originally based upon communism in living.*"

[2] Diaz Conquest of Mex., ed. 1803, Keatinge's Trans., i, 181, 189.   Herrera says, 300, ii. 327.

[3] Diaz, I, 191.

[4] Dispatches of Cortes, Folsom's Trans., p. 86.

used."[1] In the tidiness of these rooms we gain some evidence of the character of Aztec women.

Joint-tenement houses, and the mode of life they indicate, were at this time unknown in Europe. They belonged to a more ancient condition of society. It is not surprising, therefore, that the Spaniards, astonished at their magnitude, should have styled them palaces, and having been received with a great array by Montezuma, as the general commander of the Aztec forces, should have regarded him as a king, since monarchical government was the form with which they were chiefly acquainted. Suffice, it then, to say that one of the great houses of the Aztecs was large enough to accommodate Cortes and his fourteen hundred and fifty men including Indian allies as they had previously been accommodated in one Cholulan house and elsewhere, on the way to Mexico. From New Mexico to the Isthmus of Panama there was scarcely a principal village in which an equal number could not have found accommodations in a single house. When it is found to be unnecessary to call it a palace in order to account for its size, we are led to the conclusion that an ordinary Aztec house was emptied of its inhabitants to make room for their unwelcome visitors. After their reception, Aztec hospitality supplied them with provisions. Mr. Bandelier has, in the article above referred to, explained this house in a very satisfactory manner as "the tecpan, or official house of the tribe." He says: "The house where the Spaniards were quartered was the 'tecpan,' or official house of the tribe, vacated by the official household for that purpose." In sallying forth to greet the new-comers at the dike, "Wrathy chief (Montezuma) acted simply as the representative of the tribal hospitality, extending unusual courtesies to unusual, mysterious, and therefore dreaded guests. Leaving these in possession of the 'tecpan,' he retired to another of the large communal buildings surrounding the central square, where the official business was, meanwhile, transacted His return to the Spanish quarters, even if compulsory, had less in it to strike the natives than is commonly believed. It was a re-installation in old quarters, and therefore the 'Tlatocan (Council of Chiefs) itself felt no hesitancy in meeting there again, until the real nature of the dangerous visitors was ascertained, when the council gradually withdrew from the snare, leaving the unfortunate 'chief of men' in Spanish hands."[2]

---

[1] History of America, ii, 330.　　　[2] 12 Annual Report of Peabody Museum, p. 680.

We are next to consider the second so-called palace, that in which Montezuma lived, and the dinner of Montezuma which these soldiers witnessed, and which has gone into history as a part of the evidence that a monarchy of the feudal type existed in Mexico.   They had but little time to make their observations, for this imaginary kingdom perished almost immediately, and the people, in the main, dispersed.   The so-called palace of Montezuma is not described by Diaz, for the reason, probably, that there was nothing to distinguish it from a number of similar structures in the pueblo.   Neither is it described by Cortes or the Anonymous Conqueror; Cortes merely remarking generally that " within the city his palaces were so wonderful that it is hardly possible to describe their beauty and extent; I can only say that in Spain there is nothing equal to them."[1]   Gothic cathedrals were then standing in Spain, the Alhambra in Grenada, and, without doubt, public and private buildings of dressed stone laid in courses. While the comparison was mendacious, we can understand the desire of the conqueror to magnify his exploits.   Herrera, who came later and had additional resources, remarks that the palace in which Montezuma resided " had twenty gates, all of them to the square or market-place, and the principal streets, and three spacious courts, and in one of them a very large fountain. * * * There were many halls one hundred feet in length, and rooms of twenty-five and thirty, and one hundred baths.   The timber-work was small, without nails, but very fine and strong, which the Spaniards much admired. The walls were of marble, jasper, porphyry, a black sort of stone with red veins like blood, white stone, and another sort that is transparent.   The roofs were of wood, well wrought and carved.   * * *   The rooms were painted and matted, and many of them had rich hangings of cotton and coney wool, or of feather-work.   The beds were not answerable to the grandeur of the house and furniture, being poor and wretched, consisting of blankets upon mats or on hay.   * * *   Few men lie in this palace, but there were one thousand women in it, and some say three thousand, which is reckoned most likely.   * * *   Montezuma took to himself the ladies that were the daughters of great men, being many in number."[2]

The external walls of the houses were covered with plaster.   From the

---

[1] Despatches, p. 121.   [2] History of America, ii, 345.

description it seems probable that in the interior of the large rooms the natural faces of the stone in the walls were seen here and there, some of the red porous stone, some of marble, and some resembling porphyry, for it is not supposable that they could cut this stone with flint implements. Large stones used on the inner faces of the walls might have been left uncovered, and thus have presented the mottled appearance mentioned. The Aztecs had no structures comparable with those of Yucatan. Their architecture resembles that of New Mexico wherever its features distinctly appear upon evidence that can be trusted. The best rooms found in the latter region are of thin pieces of sandstone prepared by fracture and laid up with a uniform face. Herrera had no occasion to speak of the use of marble and porphyry in the walls of this house in such a vague manner and upon more vague information. The reference to the thousand or more women as forming the harem of Montezuma is a gross libel.

Mr. Hubert H. Bancroft, the last of the long line of writers who have treated the affairs of the Aztecs, has put the finishing touch to this picture in the following language: "The principal palace of the king of Mexico was an irregular pile of low buildings enormous in extent, constructed of huge blocks of *tetzontli*, a kind of porous stone common to that country, cemented with mortar. The arrangement of the buildings was such that they enclosed three great plazas or public squares, in one of which a beautiful fountain incessantly played. Twenty great doors opened on the squares and on the streets, and over these was sculptured in stone the coat-of-arms of the king of Mexico, an eagle griping in his talons a jaguar. In the interior were many halls, and one in particular is said by a writer who accompanied Cortes, known as the Anonymous Conqueror, to have been of sufficient extent to contain three thousand men. * * * In addition to these were more than one hundred smaller rooms, and the same number of marble baths. * * * The walls and floors of halls and apartments were many of them faced with polished slabs of marble, jasper, obsidian, and white *tecali;* lofty columns of the same fine stones supported marble balconies and porticos, every inch and corner of which was filled with wondrous ornamental carving, or held a grinning, grotesquely sculptured head. The beams and casings were of cedar, cypress, and other valuable woods profusely carved and put together without nails.   *   *   *   Superb mats of most exquisite finish were spread upon the marble floors; the tapestry that draped the walls and the curtains that hung before the windows were made of a fabric most wonderful for its delicate texture, elegant designs, and brilliant colors; through the halls and corridors a thousand golden censers, in which burned precious spices and perfumes, diffused a subtle odor."[1]

Upon this rhapsody it will be sufficient to remark that halls were entirely unknown in Indian architecture.   Neither a hall, as that term is used by us, has ever been seen in an Indian house, nor has one been found in the ruins of any Indian structure.   An external corridor has occasionally been found in ruins of houses in Central America.   The great doors open on the squares and streets; aztec window-curtains of delicate texture, marble baths and porticos, and floors of polished slabs of marble, as figments of a troubled imagination, recall the glowing description of the great kingdom of the Sandwich Islands—with its king, its cabinet ministers, its parliament, its army and navy, which Mark Twain has fitly characterized as "an attempt to navigate a sardine dish with Great Eastern machinery"; and it suggested also the Indian chief humorously mentioned by Irving as generously "decked out in cocked hat and military coat, in contrast with his breech clout and leathern leggins, being grand officer at top and ragged Indian at bottom."[2]   Whatever may be said by credulous and enthusiastic authors to decorate this Indian pueblo, its houses and its breech-cloth people, cannot conceal the "ragged Indian" therein by dressing him in a European costume.

On the seventh day after the entry into Mexico, Montezuma was induced by intimidation to leave the house in which he lived and take up his quarters with Cortes, where he was held a prisoner until his death, which occurred a few weeks later.   Whatever was seen of his mode of life in his usual place of residence was practically limited to the five days between the coming of the Spaniards and his capture.   Our knowledge of the facts is in the main derived from what these soldiers reported upon slight and imperfect means of observation.   Bernal Diaz and Cortes have left us an extraordinary description, not of his residence, but of his daily

[1] Native Races of the Pacific States, ii, 160.   [2] Bonneville, p. 34.

life, and more particularly of the dinner, which will now be considered. It is worth the attempt to take up the pictures of these and succeeding authors, and see whether the real truth of the matter cannot be elicited from their own statements. There was undoubtedly a basis of facts underneath them, because without such a basis the superstructure could not have been created.

It may with reason be supposed that the Spaniards found Montezuma, with his gentile kindred, in a large joint-tenement house, containing perhaps fifty or a hundred families united in a communal household   The dinner they witnessed was the single daily meal of this household, prepared in a common cook-house from common stores, and divided at the kettle. The dinner of each person was placed in an earthern bowl, with which in his hand an Indian needed neither chair nor table, and, moreover, had neither the one nor the other. The men ate first, and by themselves, Indian fashion; and the women, of whom only a few were seen, afterwards and by themselves. On this hypothesis the dinner in question is susceptible of a satisfactory explanation.

It has been shown that each Aztec community of persons owned lands in common, from which they derived their support. Their mode of tillage and of distribution of the products, whatever it may have been, would have returned to each family or household, large or small, its rightful share. Communism in living in large households composed of related families springs naturally from such a soil. It may be considered a law of their condition, and, plainly enough, the most economical mode of life they could adopt until the idea of property had been sufficiently developed in their minds to lead to the division of lands among individuals with ownership in fee, and power of alienation. Their social system, which tended to unite kindred families in a common household, their ownership of lands in common, and their ownership, as a group, of a joint-tenement house, which would necessarily follow, would not admit a right in persons to sell, and thus to introduce strangers into the ownership of such lands or such houses. Lands and houses were owned and held under a common system which entered into their plan of life. The idea of property was forming in their minds, but it was still in that immature state which pertains to the Middle

Status of barbarism. They had no money, but traded by barter of commodities; very little personal property, and scarcely anything of value to Europeans. They were still a breech-cloth people, wearing this rag of barbarism as the unmistakable evidence of their condition; and the family was in the syndyasmian or pairing form, with separation at any moment at the option of either party. It was the weakness of the family, its inability to face alone the struggle of life, which led to the construction of joint-tenement houses throughout North and South America by the Indian tribes; and it was the gentile organization which led them to fill these houses, on the principle of kin, with related families.

In a pueblo as large as that of Mexico, which was the largest found in America, and may possibly have contained thirty thousand inhabitants, there must have been a number of large communal houses of different sizes, from those that were called palaces, because of their size, to those filled by a few families. Degrees of prosperity are shown in barbarous as well as in civilized life in the quarters of the people. Herrera states that the houses of the poorer sort of people were " small, low, and mean," but that, " as small as the houses were, they commonly contained two, four, and six families."[1] Wherever a household is found in Indian life, be the married pairs composing it few or many, that household practiced communism in living. In the largest of these houses it would not follow necessarily that all its inmates lived from common stores, because they might form several household groups in the same house; but in the large household of which Montezuma was a member, it is plain that it was fed from common stores prepared in a common cook-house, and divided from the kettle in earthen bowls, each containing the dinner of a single person. Montezuma was supposed to be absolute master of Mexico, and what they saw at this dinner was interpreted with exclusive reference to him as the central figure. The result is remarkably grotesque. It was their own self-deception, without any assistance from the Aztecs. The accounts given by Diaz and Cortes, and which subsequent writers have built upon with glowing enthusiasm and free additions, is simply the gossip of a camp of soldiers suddenly cast into an earlier form of society, which the Village Indians of

---

[1] History of America, ii, 360.

America, of all mankind, then best represented. That they could understand it was not to have been expected. Accustomed to monarchy and to
privileged classes, the principal Aztec war-chief seemed to them quite naturally a king, and sachems and chiefs followed in their vision as princes
and lords. But that they should have remained in history as such for three
centuries is an amusing commentary upon the value of historical writings
in general.

The dinner of Montezuma, witnessed within the five days named by
the Spanish soldiers, comes down to us with a slender proportion of reliable
facts. The accounts of Bernal Diaz and of Cortes form the basis of all
subsequent descriptions.[1] Montezuma was the central figure around whom
all the others are made to move. A number of men, as Diaz states, were
to be seen in the house and in the courts, going to and fro, a part of whom
were thought to be chiefs in attendance upon Montezuma, and the remainder were supposed to be guards. Better proof of the use of guards is
needed than the suggestion of Diaz. It implies a knowledge of military
discipline unknown by Indian tribes. It was noticed that Indians went
barefooted into the presence of Montezuma, which was interpreted as an
act of servility and deference, although bare feet must have been the rule
rather than the exception in Tenochtitlan. Diaz further informs us that
"his cooks had upwards of thirty different ways of dressing meats, and
they had earthen vessels so contrived as to keep them always hot. For the
table of Montezuma himself above three hundred dishes were dressed, and
for his guards above a thousand. Before dinner Montezuma would go out
and inspect the preparations, and his officers would point out to him which
were the best, and explain of what birds and flesh they were composed;
and of these he would eat. * * * Montezuma was seated on a low
throne or chair at a table proportionate to the height of his seat. The
table was covered with white cloth and napkins, and four beautiful women
presented him with water for his hands in vessels which they called xicales,
with other vessels under them like plates to catch the water; they also
presented him with towels. Then two other women brought him small
cakes of bread, and when the king began to eat, a large screen of wood-

---

[1] The Anonymous Conqueror does not notice it.

gilt was placed before him, so that people should not during that time see him. The women having retired to a little distance, four ancient lords stood by the throne, to whom Montezuma from time to time spoke or addressed questions, and as a matter of particular favor gave to each of them a plate of that which he was eating. * * * This was served on earthenware of Cholula, red and black. * * * I observed a number of jars, about fifty, brought in filled with foaming chocolate, of which he took some which the women presented to him. During the time Montezuma was at dinner, two very beautiful women were busily employed making small cakes, with eggs and other things mixed therein. These were delicately white, and when made they presented them to him on plates covered with napkins. Also another kind of bread was brought to him in long loaves, and plates of cakes resembling wafers. After he had dined they presented to him three little canes, highly ornamented, containing liquid amber mixed with an herb they call tobacco; and when he had sufficiently viewed the singers, dancers, and buffoons, he took a little of the smoke of one of these canes and then laid himself down to sleep; and thus his principal meal concluded. After this was over, all his guards and domestics sat down to dinner, and as near as I can judge, above a thousand plates of these eatables that I have mentioned were laid before them, with vessels of foaming chocolate, and fruit in immense quantity. For his women and various inferior servants, his establishment was a prodigious expense, and we were astonished, amid such a profusion, at the vast regularity that prevailed."[1] Diaz wrote his history more than thirty years after the conquest (he says he was writing it in 1568),[2] which may serve to excuse him for implying the use of veritable chairs and a table where neither existed, and for describing the remainder as sitting down to dinner. Tezozomoc, who is followed by Herrera, says the table of Montezuma consisted of two skins. How they were fastened together and supported does not appear.

The statements in the Despatches of Cortes, as they now appear, are an improvement upon Diaz, the pitch being on a higher key. He remarks that Montezuma "was served in the following manner: Every day, as soon

---

[1] History of the Conquest of Mexico, i, 198–202.   [2] Ib., ii, 423.

as it was light, six hundred nobles and men of rank were in attendance at the palace, who either sat or walked about in the halls and galleries, and passed their time in conversation, but without entering the apartment where his person was. The servants and attendants of these nobles remained in the court-yards, of which there were two or three of great extent, and in the adjoining street, which was also very spacious. They all remained in attendance from morning till night; and when his meals were served, the nobles were likewise served with equal profusion, and their servants and secretaries also had their allowance. Daily his larder and wine-cellar were open to all who wished to eat or drink. The meals were served by three or four hundred youths, who brought in an infinite number of dishes; indeed, whenever he dined or supped the table was loaded with every kind of flesh, fish, fruits and vegetables that the country produced. As the climate is cold, they put a chafing-dish with live coals under every plate and dish, to keep them warm. The meals were served in a large hall in which Montezuma was accustomed to eat, and the dishes quite filled the room, which was covered with mats and kept very clean. He sat on a small cushion, curiously wrought of leather. During the meal there were present, at a little distance from him, five or six elderly caciques, to whom he presented some of the food. And there was constantly in attendance one of the servants, who arranged and handed the dishes, and who received from others whatever was wanted for the supply of the table. Both at the beginning and end of every meal, they furnished water for the hands; and the napkins used on these occasions were never used a second time, and this was the case also with the plates and dishes, which were not brought again, but new ones in place of them; it was the same with the chafing-dishes."[1]

Since cursive writing was unknown among the Aztecs, the presence of these secretaries is an amusing feature in the account. The wine-cellar also is remarkable for two reasons; firstly, because the level of the streets and courts was but four feet above the level of the water, which made cellars impossible; and, secondly, because the Aztecs had no knowledge of wine. An acid beer (pulque), made by fermenting the juice of the maguey, was a common beverage of the Aztecs; but it is hardly supposable that even this

---

[1] Despatches of Cortes, Folsom's Trans., p. 123.

was used at dinner.   It will be noticed that according to this account the dinner was served to all at the same time, Montezuma and several chiefs eating at one end of the room, but no mention is made of the manner in which the remainder ate.   The six hundred men (or less) who remained about the house and courts during the day, we may well suppose, were, with their families, joint residents and joint proprietors with Montezuma of the establishment.   Two or three structures are mingled in these descriptions, which were probably entirely distinct in their uses.

Herrera gathered up the subsequent growth of the story, which undoubtedly made a great sensation in Europe as a part of the picture of life in the New World; and embellished it from sheer delight in a marvelous tale.   The few facts stated by Bernal Diaz, expressing the interpretation of the Spanish soldiers, were fruitful seeds planted three hundred years ago, which the imaginations of enthusiastic authors have developed into a glowing and picturesque narrative.   The principal part of Herrera's account runs as follows: "Montezuma did always eat alone, and so great a quantity of meat was served up to his table, such great variety, and so richly dressed, that there was sufficient for all the prime men of his household. His table was a cushion, or two pieces of colored leather; instead of a chair, a little low stool, made of one piece, the seat hollowed out, carved and painted in the best manner that could be; the table-cloth, napkins, and towels of very fine cotton as white as snow, and never served any more than once, being the fees of the proper officers.   The meat was brought in by four hundred pages, all gentlemen, sons of lords, and set down together in a hall; the king went thither, and with a rod, or his hand, pointed to what he liked, and then the sewer set it upon the chafing-dishes that it might not be cold; and this he never failed to do, unless the steward at any time very much recommended to him some particular dishes.   Before he sat down, twenty of the most beautiful women came and brought him water to wash his hands, and when seated the sewer did shut a wooded rail that divided the room, lest the nobility that went to see him dine should encumber the table, and he alone set on and took off the dishes, for the pages neither came near nor spoke a word.   Strict silence was observed, none daring to speak unless it was some jester, or the person of whom he asked a question. The sewer was always upon his knees and barefooted, attending him without lifting up his eyes. No man with shoes on was to come into the room upon pain of death. The sewer also gave him drink in a cup of several shapes, sometimes of gold, and sometimes of silver, sometimes of gourd, and sometimes of the shells of fishes.[1] Six ancient lords attended at a distance, to whom he gave some dishes of what he liked best, which they did eat there with much respect. He had always music of flutes, reeds, horns, shells, kettle-drums, and other instruments, nothing agreeable to the ears of the Spaniards. * * * There were always at dinner dwarfs, crooked and other deformed persons, to provoke laughter, and they did eat of what was left at the further end of the hall, with the jesters and buffoons. What remained was given to three thousand Indians, that were constantly upon guard in the courts and squares, and therefore there were always three thousand dishes of meat and as many cups of liquor; the larder and cellar were never shut, by reason of their continual carrying in and out. In the kitchen they dressed all sorts of meat that were sold in the market, being a prodigious quantity, besides what was brought in by hunters, tenants, and tributaries. The dishes and all utensils were all of good earthenware, and served the king but once. He had abundance of vessels of gold and silver, yet made no use of them, because they should not serve twice."[2]

Further on, and out of its place, Herrera gives us what seems to have been a call of the scattered household to dinner "When it was dinnertime," he remarks, "eight or ten men whistled very loud, beating the kettle-drums hard, as it were to warn those that were to dance after dinner; then the dancers came, who, to entertain their great sovereign, were all to be men of quality, clad as richly as they could, with costly mantles, white, red, green, yellow, and some of several colors."[3]

The four women of Diaz who brought water to Montezuma have now increased to twenty; but, as the Spanish writers claimed a wide latitude in the matter of numbers, fivefold is not, perhaps, unreasonable, especially as

---

[1] Solis, thinking a cocoanut shell altogether too plain, embellishes the shell with jewels: "He had cups of gold, and salvers of the same; and sometimes he drank out of cocoas and natural shells very richly set with jewels."—History of the Conquest of Mexico, Lond., ed. 1738, Townshend's Trans., I, 417.

[2] History of America, ii, 336.   [3] Ib., 443.

it did not occur to Herrera that Diaz may, at the outset, have quadrupled the actual number. The "three or four hundred youths" who brought in the dinner, according to Cortes, settle down under Herrera to "four hundred pages, all gentlemen, sons of lords"; and here we must recognize the discrimination of the historian in that he found the highest number stated by Cortes fully adequate to the occasion. Two other things may be noticed: shoes have disappeared from all Indian feet in the face of a terrific penalty, and three thousand hungry Indians stand in peaceful quietude, while their dinner grows cold upon the floor, as Montezuma eats alone in solitary grandeur. No American Indian could be made to comprehend this picture. It lacks the realism of Indian life, and embodies an amount of puerility of which the Indian nature is not susceptible. Europeans and Americans may rise to the height of the occasion because their mental range is wider, and their imaginations have fed more deeply upon nursery tales. Diaz had contented himself with saying that Montezuma "had two hundred of his nobility on guard in apartments adjoining his own,"[1] in whom may be recognized his fellow householders; but Cortes generously increased the number to "six hundred nobles and men of rank," who appeared at daylight and remained in attendance during the day. Neither number, however, was quite sufficient to meet the conceptions of the historiographer of Spain, and accordingly three thousand, all guards, were adopted by Herrera as a suitable number to give éclat to Montezuma's dinner. If any man conversant with Indian character could show by what instrumentality five hundred Indians could be kept together twelve hours in attendance upon any human being from a sense of duty, he would add something to our knowledge of the Red Race; and could he prove further that they had actually waited, in the presence of as many earthen bowls, smoking with their several dinners, while their war-chief in the same room was making his repast alone, the verifier would thereby endow the Indian character with an element of forbearance he has never since been known to display. The block of wood hollowed out for a stool or seat may be accepted, for it savors of the simplicity of Indian art. That the Aztecs had napkins of coarse texture, woven by hand, is probable; as also that they were white, because cotton is white.

---

[1] History of the Conquest of Mexico, I, 198.

Imagination might easily expand a napkin into a table-cloth, provided a table existed to spread it upon; but in this case, without duly considering the relation between the two, the table-cloth has been created, but the table refuses to appear. The napkin business, therefore, seems to have been slightly overdone. Finally, the call of the scattered household to dinner by kettle-drums and whistling savors too strongly of Indian ways and usages to be diverted into a summons to the dancers, as Herrera suggests. This Aztec dinner-call, on a scale commensurate with a large communal household, would have been lost to history but for the special use discerned in it to decorate a tale. It recognizes the loitering habits of an Aztec household, and perhaps the irregularity of the dinner-hour.

Passing over the descriptions of Sahagun, Clavigero, and Prescott, who have kindled into enthusiasm over this dinner of Montezuma, Mr. Hubert H. Bancroft shall be allowed to furnish us with the very latest version. "Every day," he remarks, "from sunrise until sunset the ante-chambers of Montezuma's palace in Mexico were occupied by six hundred noblemen and gentlemen, who passed their time lounging about and discussing the gossip of the day in low tones, for it was considered disrespectful to speak loudly or make any noise within the palace limits. They were provided with apartments in the palace, and took their meals from what remained of the superabundance of the royal table, as did after them their own servants, of whom each person of quality was entitled to from one to thirty according to his rank. These retainers, numbering two or three thousand, filled several outer courts during the day. The king took his meals alone in one of the largest halls of the palace. * * * He was seated upon a low leather cushion, upon which were thrown various soft skins, and his table was of a similar description, except that it was larger and rather higher, and was covered with white cotton cloths of the finest texture. The dinner-service was of the finest ware of Cholula, and many of the goblets were of gold and silver, or fashioned with beautiful shells. He is said to have possessed a complete service of solid gold, but as it was considered below a king's dignity to use anything at table twice, Montezuma, with all his extravagance, was obliged to keep this costly dinner-set in the temple. The bill of fare comprised everything edible of fish, flesh, and fowl that could be procured in the empire or imported beyond it.   Relays of couriers were employed in bringing delicacies from afar.   *   *   *   There were cunning cooks among the Aztecs, and at these extravagant meals there was almost as much variety in the cookery as in the matter cooked.   Sahagun gives a most formidable list of roast, stewed, and broiled dishes, of meat, fish, and poultry, seasoned with many kinds of herbs, of which, however, that most frequently mentioned is chile.   He further describes many kinds of bread, all bearing a more or less close resemblance to the Mexican tortilla,   *   *   *   then tamales of all kinds, and many other curious messes, such as frog spawn and stewed ants, cooked with chile.   *   *   *   Each dish was kept warm on a chafing-dish placed under it.   Writers do not agree as to the exact quantity of food served up at each meal, but it must have been immense, since the lowest number of dishes given is three hundred and the highest three thousand   They were brought into the hall by four hundred pages of noble birth, who placed their burdens upon the matted floor and retired noiselessly.   The king then pointed out such viands as he wished to partake of, or left the selection to his steward, who doubtless took pains to study the likes and dislikes of the royal palate.   The steward was a functionary of the highest rank and importance; he alone was privileged to place the designated delicacies before the king upon the table; he appears to have done duty both as royal carver and cup-bearer;[1] and, according to Torquemada, to have done it barefooted and on his knees.   Everything being in readiness, a number of the most beautiful of the king's women entered, bearing water in round vessels called Xicales, for the king to wash his hands in, and towels that he might dry them, other vessels being placed upon the ground to catch the drippings.   Two other women at the same time brought him some small loaves of a very delicate kind of bread, made of the finest maize flour, beaten up with eggs.   This done, a wooden screen, carved and gilt, was placed before him that no one might see him while eating.   There were always present five or six aged lords, who stood near the royal chair barefooted and with bowed heads.   To these, as a special mark of favor, the king occasionally sent a choice morsel from his own plate.   During the meal the monarch

---

[1] The "cup-bearer" agrees reasonably well with the "window-curtains."

amused himself by watching the performances of his jugglers and tumblers, whose marvellous feats of strength and dexterity I shall describe in another place; at other times there was dancing, accompanied by singing and music. * * * The more solid food was followed by pastry, sweetmeats, and a magnificent dessert of fruit. The only beverage drank was chocolate, of which about fifty jars were provided; it was taken with a spoon, finely wrought of gold or shell, from a goblet of the same material Having finished his dinner, the king again washed his hands in water brought to him, as before, by the women After this, several painted and gilt pipes were brought, from which he inhaled, through his mouth or nose, as best suited him, the smoke of a mixture of liquid amber and an herb called tobacco. This siesta over, he devoted himself to business, and proceeded to give audience to foreign ambassadors or deputations from cities in the empire, and to such of his lords and ministers as had business to transact with him."[1]

In this account, although founded upon those of Diaz and Cortes, and showing nothing essentially new, we have the final growth of the story to the present time, but without any assurance that the limits of its possible expansion have been reached. The purification of our aboriginal history, by casting out the mass of trash with which it is so heavily freighted, is forced upon us to save American intelligence from deserved disgrace. Whatever may be said of the American aborigines in general, or of the Aztecs in particular, they were endowed with common sense in the matter of their daily food, which cost them labor, forethought, and care to provide. The picture of Indian life here presented is simply impossible. Village Indians in the Middle Status of barbarism were below the age of tables and chairs for dinner service; neither had they learned to arrange a dinner to be eaten socially at a common table, or even to share their dinner with their wives and children. Their joint-tenement houses, their common stores, their communism in living, and the separation of the sexes at their meals, are genuine Indian customs and usages which explain this dinner. It was misconceived by the Spaniards quite naturally, and with the grotesque results herein

---

[1] Native Races of the Pacific States, ii, 174–178.

presented; but there is no excuse for continuing this misconception in the presence of known facts accessible to all.

There is no doubt whatever that Montezuma was treated with great consideration by all classes of persons. Indians respect and venerate their chiefs. As their principal war-chief, Montezuma held the highest official position among them. He is represented as amiable, generous, and manly, although unnerved by the sudden appearance and the novel and deadly arms of the Spaniards. He had charge of the reception and entertainment of Cortes and his men, who requited him savagely for his hospitality and kindness. But when his home-life is considered, he fared no better than his fellow-householders, sharing with them their common dinner. These accounts, when divested of their misconceptions, render it probable that Montezuma was living with his gentle kinsmen in a house they owned in common; and that what the Spaniards saw was a dinner in common by this household, which, with the women and children, may have numbered from five hundred to a thousand persons. When the scattered members of the household had been summoned, the single daily meal was brought in by a number of persons from the common cook-house in earthen bowls and dishes, and set down upon the floor of an apartment used as a place for dinner in the fashion of Indians. Indians as they were, they doubtless took up these bowls one by one, each containing the dinner of one person divided at the kettle. They ate standing, or it may be sitting upon the floor, or upon the ground in the open court. Indians as they were, the men ate first and by themselves, and the women and children afterwards. After dinner was over, they were diverted, probably, with music and dancing, and made themselves merry, as well-fed Indians are apt to do. That the same dinner, conducted in a similar manner, occurred at all the houses in the pueblo, large and small, once a day, there can scarcely be a doubt

The dinner of Montezuma which has gone into history, and been read for three centuries with wonder and admiration, is an excellent illustration of the slender material out of which American aboriginal history has been made. It shows, moreover, as a warning, what results flow from great misconceptions through the constructive faculty of authors.

A confederacy of three Indian tribes, speaking dialects of the same language, was precisely what the Spaniards found in Mexico, and this was all they found. They had no occasion in their accounts to advance a step beyond this simple fact. A satisfactory explanation of this confederacy can be found in similar Indian confederacies. It was a growth from the common institutions of the Indian family. Underneath these delusive pictures a council of chiefs is revealed, which was the natural and legitimate instrument of government under Indian institutions. No other form of government was possible among them. They had, beside, which was an equally legitimate part of this system, an elective and deposable war-chief (Teuchtli), the power to elect and to depose being held by a fixed constituency ever present, and ready to act when occasion required. The Aztec organization stood plainly before the Spaniards as a confederacy of Indian tribes. Nothing but the grossest perversion of obvious facts could have enabled Spanish writers to fabricate the Aztec monarchy out of a democratic organization.

Without ascertaining the unit of their social system, if organized in gentes, as they probably were, and without gaining any knowledge of the organization that did exist, they boldly invented for the Aztecs a monarchy, with high feudal characteristics, out of the reception of Cortes by their principal war-chief, and such other flimsy materials as Montezuma's dinner. This misconception has stood, through American indolence, quite as long as it deserves to stand.

Since the foregoing was written, the investigations of Mr. Bandelier "On the Social Organization and Mode of Government of the Ancient Mexicans" have been published. With the new light thus thrown upon the subject, this chapter should have been re-written. He shows that the Aztecs were composed of twenty gentes or clans. "The existence of *twenty* autonomous consanguine groups is thus revealed, and we find them again at the time of the conquest, while their last vestiges were perpetuated until after 1690, when Fray Augustin de Vetancurt mentions four chief quarters with their original Indian names, comprising and subdivided into *twenty* 'barrios.' Now the Spanish word '*barrio*' is equivalent to the Mexican term '*calpulli*.' Both indicate the kin, localized and settled with the view to permanence."[1] This organization, as was to have been expected, lies at the

---

[1] Twelfth Annual Report of the Peabody Museum of Archæology and Ethnology, Cambridge, 1880, p. 591.

foundation of their social system.   He names the following as among the rights, duties, and obligations of the kinship:

I. *The kin claimed the right to name its members.*

II. *It was the duty of the kin to educate or train its members to every branch of public life.*

III. *The kin had the right to regulate and to control marriage.*

IV. *It was one of the attributes of the kin to enjoy common burial.*

V. *The right of the kin to 'separate worship' appears not only established within the kin's territory, but it is also recognized even at the central medicine-lodge of the tribe.*

VI. *The kin was obligated to protect and defend the persons and property of its members, and to resent and punish any injury done to them, as if it were a crime committed against the kin itself.*

VII. *The kin had the right to elect its officers, as well as the right to remove or depose them for misbehavior.*[1]

He also regards the four "brotherhoods" who occupied the four quarters of the pueblo as probably phratries.[2]   He also shows that the government was under the control of a council, *Tlatocan*, composed of a body of chiefs.[3]

One of the most interesting results of this investigation is the discovery of a class of persons unattached to any gens, "outcasts from the bond of kinship."[4]   Such a class grows up in every gentile society, when as far advanced as the Aztecs were.   It finds its analogue in the Roman Plebeians. This remarkable essay will abundantly repay a careful study.

When we have learned to speak of the American Indians in language adapted to Indian life and Indian institutions, they will become comprehensible.   So long as we apply to their social organizations and domestic institutions terms adapted to the organizations and to the institutions of civilized society, we caricature the Indians and deceive ourselves.   There was neither a political society, nor a state, nor any civilization in America when it was discovered; and, excluding the Eskimos, but one race of Indians, the Red Race.

---

[1] Twelfth Ann. Rept. Peabody Museum, pp. 615–638.   [2] Ib., p. 584.   [3] Ib., p. 646, *et seq.*   [4] Ib., p. 608, *et seq.*

CHAPTER XI.

RUINS OF HOUSES OF THE SEDENTARY INDIANS OF YUCATAN AND CENTRAL AMERICA.

At the epoch of their discovery, Yucatan, Chiapas, and Guatemala were probably more thickly peopled than any other portion of North America of equal area; and their inhabitants were more advanced than the remaining aborigines. Their pueblos were planted along the rivers and streams, often quite near each other, and presented the same picture of occupation and of village life which might have been seen at the same time in the valley of the Rio Grande, of the Rio Chaco, and probably of the San Juan, and, at a still earlier period, of the Scioto. They consisted of a single great house, or of a cluster of houses near each other, forming one pueblo or village. In some cases, four or more structures were grouped together upon the same elevated platform; and where there were several of these platforms, each surmounted with one or more edifices, one of them was devoted to religious, and a portion of another to social and public uses. But there is no reason for supposing, from any ruins yet found, or from what is known of the people historically, that any one pueblo contained, at most, ten thousand inhabitants. No one tribe, or confederacy of tribes, had risen to supremacy within either of these areas by the consolidation of surrounding tribes. They were found, on the contrary, in the same state of subdivision and independence which invariably accompanies the gentile organization. Confederacies in all probability existed among such contiguous pueblos as spoke the same dialect, as the Cibolans were probably confederated, and as the Aztecs, Tezcucans, and Tlacopans are known to have been. Such confederacies, however, could not have reached beyond a common language of the tribes confederated.

The great houses of stone of the Village Indians within the areas named, and particularly in Yucatan and Central America, have done more than all other considerations to give to them their present position in the estimation of mankind. They are the highest constructive works of the Indian tribes. It may also be again suggested that, from the beginning, a false interpretation has been put upon this architecture, from a failure to understand its object and uses, or the condition and plan of domestic life of the people who occupied these structures. The design and object for which these edifices were constructed still await an intelligent explanation.

The highest type of architecture which then existed among the aborigines in any part of America was found in the regions named; particularly in Yucatan, Chiapas, and Honduras   Speaking of Yucatan, Herrera remarks that "the language is everywhere the same," the Maya being the language of its principal tribes, but "the whole country," he continues, "is divided into eighteen districts."[1]   If this reference is to a classification by tribes, it shows that the Mayas had fallen, by the process of segmentation, into this number of independent groups; the pueblos in each district being united under one government for mutual defense. It seems probable, however, that the group was smaller than a tribe. It is difficult in some cases to determine, from Herrera's language, whether he refers to native or Spanish divisions. In like manner, speaking of Chiapas, he remarks, that "this province is divided into four nations of different languages, which are the Chiapanecans, the *Toques*, the *Zelsales*, and the *Quelenes*, all of which differ in some particulars * * *   There are in it twenty-five towns, the chief of them called *Tecpatlan*" (*i. e.*, among the Toques). * * * The nation of *Zelsales* has thirteen towns, * * * the *Quelenes* have twenty-five towns."[2]   Sixty-three pueblos in three of the four tribes who occupied the small territory of Chiapas is a very large number, except on the supposition that each pueblo consisted usually of a single great house, like those in New Mexico, which is probable; but even then it seems excessive. It tends, however, to show the mode of occupation and settlement of the Village Indians in general. They planted their pueblos on the watercourses, where such existed, each tribe or subdivision of a tribe gathering

---

[1] History of America, l. c., iv, 161.

[2] Ib., iv, 189.

in a cluster of houses, four or five in number, or in a single house; and, as may be inferred from the descriptions of Las Casas, so near together on the same rivulet that had not the native forest obstructed the view they would have been in sight of each other for miles along its banks. The scattered ruins of these pueblos in Yucatan at the present time, often consisting of a single large structure, confirms this view.

The tropical region of Yucatan and Central America, then as now, was undoubtedly covered with forests, except the limited clearings around the pueblos, and, apart from these pueblos, substantially uninhabited. Field agriculture was of course unknown, as they had neither domestic animals nor plows; but the Indians cultivated maize, beans, squashes, pepper, cotton, cacao, and tobacco in garden beds, and exercised some care over certain native fruits; cultivation tending to localize them in villages. Herrera remarks of the Village Indians of Honduras that "they sow thrice a year, and they were wont to grub up great woods with hatchets made of flint."[1] Without metallic implements to subdue the forest, or even with copper axes, such as were found among the Aztecs, a very small portion only of the country would have been brought under cultivation, and that confined mainly to the margins of the streams.

Las Casas, bishop of Chiapas, who was in Yucatan and Chiapas about 1539, after remarking of the people of the former country that they were "better civilized in morals and in what belongs to the good order of societies than the rest of the Indians," proceeds as follows: "The pretence of subjecting the Indians to the government of Spain is only made to carry on the design of subjecting them to the dominion of private men, who make them all their slaves."[2] And, again, he quotes from a letter of the bishop of St. Martha to the King of Spain, to this effect: "To redress the grievances of this province, it ought to be delivered from the tyranny of those who ravage it, and committed to the care of persons of integrity, who will treat the inhabitants with more kindness and humanity; for if it be left to the mercy of the governors, who commit all sorts of outrages with impunity, the province will be destroyed in a very short time."[3]

---

[1] History of America, iv., 133.
[2] An Account of the First Voyages, etc., in America, Lond. ed., Trans., p. 52.
[3] Ib., p. 61.

There are two material questions which require priority of consideration: First, whether or not the houses now in ruins in Yucatan and Central America were occupied at the time of the Spanish conquest; and, second, whether or not the present Indians of the country are the descendants of the people who constructed them. There is no basis whatever for the negative of either proposition; but it is assumed by those who regard the so-called *palace* at Palenque and the Governor's House at Uxmal as the ancient residences of Indian potentates that great cities which once surrounded them have perished, and, further, that these ruins have an antiquity reaching far back of the Spanish conquest.

Mr. Stephens adopts the conclusion "that at the time of the conquest, and afterwards, the Indians were living in and occupied these very cities."[1] He also regarded the present Indians of the country as the descendants of those in possession at the time of the conquest. He might have added that as the Maya was the language of the aborigines of Yucatan at the epoch of the discovery, and is now the language of the greater part of the natives who have not lost their original speech, there was no ground for either supposition. Herrera remarks of the inhabitants of Yucatan, that the "people were then found living together very politely in towns, kept very clean; * * * and the reason of their living so close together was because of the wars which exposed them to the danger of being taken, sold, and sacrificed; but the wars of the Spaniards made them disperse."[2] This last statement is very significant. Mr. Stephens, whose works and whose observations are in the main so valuable, is responsible to no small extent for the delusive inferences which have been drawn from the architecture of Yucatan, Honduras, and Chiapas. If he had repressed his imagination and confined himself to what he found, namely, certain Indian pueblos built of dressed stone, and in good architecture, which are sufficiently remarkable just as they are, in ruins, and had omitted altogether such terms as "*palaces*" and *great cities*, his readers would have escaped the deceptive conclusions with respect to the actual condition of society among the aborigines which his terminology and mode of treatment were certain to suggest.

It is sufficiently ascertained that within a few years after the conquest

---

[1] Incidents of Travel in Yucatan, ii, 348, 375.   [2] History of America, iv, 168.

of Mexico, Yucatan and Central America were overrun by military adventurers whose rapacity and violence drove the harmless and timid Village Indians from their pueblos into the forests; thus destroying in a few years a higher culture than the Spaniards were able to substitute in its place. Nothing can be plainer, I think, than this additional fact, that all there ever was of Palenque, Uxmal, Copan, and other Indian pueblos in these areas, building for building and stone for stone, is there now in ruins.

There are reasons for believing, from the more advanced condition of their house architecture, that Yucatan was inhabited by Village Indians from an earlier, and for a much longer, period than the valley of Mexico. The traditions of the Yzaes of Chichenisa, possibly Chichen Itza, and of the Cocomes of Mayapan, related by Herrera,[1] claim a more ancient occupation of Yucatan than the Aztec traditions claim for the occupation of the valley of Mexico. The type of village life among the American aborigines was adapted to a warm climate, and presented in this area its highest exemplification.

The notices of the great houses in Yucatan are brief and general in the Spanish histories. Speaking of its eighteen districts, Herrera remarks that "in all of them were so many, and such stately stone buildings, that it was amazing, and the greatest wonder is, that having no use of any metal, they were able to raise such structures, which seem to have been temples, for their houses were always of timber and thatched."[1] This last statement is not only at variance with a previous one quoted above, but is another of the numerous misconceptions which impair so greatly the value of the Spanish histories. The people undoubtedly resided in these houses, which were adapted to such a use only, and were also in the nature of fortresses, thus proving the insecurity in which they lived. Some portion of the tribe may have resided in inferior and common habitations in the vicinity of these pueblos, and under their protection; but the great houses of stone were built for residences and not for temples, and were the homes of the body of the people. There were many of these pueblos, nearly all of them composed of one or two large structures, sprinkled over the face of the country in eligible situations after the manner of Village Indian life. The

---

[1] History of America, iv, 162, 163, 165.   [1] Ib., iv, 162.

same adaptation to communism in living in large households is found impressed upon all the houses now in ruins in these areas.   They are joint-tenement houses of the American type, and very similar to those still found in New Mexico and on the San Juan.   At the epoch of the Spanish conquest, they were occupied pueblos, and were deserted by the Indians to escape the rapacity of Spanish military adventurers by whom they were oppressed and abused beyond Indian endurance.   Instances are mentioned by Herrera where large numbers destroyed themselves to escape the exactions of Spanish masters, whom they were unable to resist.[1]   The numerous pueblos in ruins scattered through the forests of Yucatan and southward are so many monuments of Spanish misrule, oppression, and rapacity.

The most extensive group of ruins in Yucatan is that at Uxmal.   Its several structures are known as the "Governor's House"; the "House of the Nuns," which consists of four disconnected buildings, facing the four sides of a court; the "House of the Pigeons," consisting of two quadrangles; the "House of the Turtles"; the "House of the Old Woman"; and the "House of the Dwarf"; with some trace of smaller buildings of inconsiderable size, and one or two pyrimidal elevations unoccupied by structures. Of these, the "Governor's House" may have been the *Tecpan*, or *Official House of the Tribe*, from the unusual size of the central rooms.   The "House of the Dwarf" was probably designed for the observance of religious rites. The remaining structures were evidently the residence portions of the pueblo.

Among the Aztecs, three kinds of houses were distinguished: 1. *Calli*, the ordinary dwelling house, of which the "House of the Nuns" is an example.   2. *Ticplantlacalli*, the "Stone House," which contained council halls, etc., of which the "Governor's House" is an example.   3. *Teocalli*, "House of God," such as the "House of the Dwarf."   The *estufas* in New Mexican pueblos took the place of the last two in Mexico and Yucatan.

Ground plans of the principal structures will be given for comparison with those in New Mexico.   The pyramidal elevations on which they stand are situated quite near each other, and form one Indian pueblo.   The houses are constructed of stone laid in courses, and dressed to a uniform surface,

---

[1] History of America, iii, 346.

with the upper half of the exterior walls decorated with grotesque ornaments cut on the faces of the stone. Foster states that "these structures
are composed of a soft coralline limestone of comparatively recent geological formation, probably of the Tertiary period."[1]

The so-called idols at Copan are the largest stones worked by the
Central Americans. They are about eleven feet high by three feet wide
and three feet deep, each face being covered with sculptures and hieroglyphics.
In a field near the ruins, and near each other, are nine of these elaborately
ornamented statues. By the side of each is a so-called altar, about six feet
square and four feet high, made of separate stone. These Idols and Altars
have been supposed to have some relation to their religious system, with
human sacrifices in the background. From their situation and character it
may be conjectured that we have here the Copan cemetery, and that these
idols are the grave-posts, and these altars are the graves of Copan chiefs.
The type of both may still be seen in Nebraska in the grave-posts and
grave-mounds by their side, of Iowas and Otoes, and formerly in all parts
of the United States east of the Mississippi. If Mr. Stephens had opened
one of these altars he would, if this conjecture is well taken, have found
within or under it an Indian grave, and perhaps a skeleton, with the personal articles usually entombed beside the dead. It was customary among
the Northern Indians for the chosen friend of the decedent, with whom he
formed this peculiar tie, to erect his grave-post, representing the chief exploits
of the departed upon one side, with ideographs and his own upon the opposite side. "The stone," Mr. Stephens observes, "of which all these altars
and statues are made, is a soft grit-stone."[2]

Norman had previously described the material used as a "fine concrete
limestone."[3] Elsewhere, with respect to the nature of the tools for cutting
this stone, he remarks that "flint was undoubtedly used."[4] Stephens makes
a similar statement. The exact size of the stones used is not given, but
they were not large. Norman remarks of Chichen Itza that "the stones
are cut in *parallelopipeds* of about twelve inches in length and six in breadth,
the interstices filled up with the same materials of which the terraces are

---

[1] Prehistoric Races of the United States, p. 398. [2] Central America, Chiapas, and Yucatan, 1–153.
[3] Rambles in Yucatan, p. 126. [4] Ib., p. 184.

composed."[1]   He also speaks of "large blocks of hewn stone used in the doorways."[2]   A soft coralline limestone could be easily worked with flint implements when first taken from the quarry, and would harden after exposure to the air.   The size and nature of the stones used is some evidence of limited advancement in solid stone architecture.[5]

These structures, as reproduced in engravings by Stephens and Catherwood, may well excite surprise and admiration for the taste, skill, and industry they display, and the degree of progress they reveal.   When rightly understood, they will enable us to estimate the extent of the progress actually made, which was truly remarkable for a people still in barbarism, and no further advanced than the Middle Status.

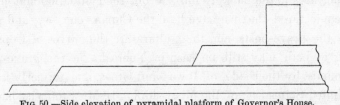

FIG. 50.—Side elevation of pyramidal platform of Governor's House.

We have seen that the style of architecture in New Mexico brought the Indians to the house-tops as the common place of living.   At first suggested for security, it became in time a settled habit of life.   The same want was met in Yucatan and Chiapas by a new expedient, namely, a pyramidal platform or elevation of earth, twenty, thirty, and forty feet high, upon the level summits of which their great houses were erected.   These platforms were made still higher for small buildings.   A natural elevation being, when practicable, selected, the top was leveled or raised by artificial means, the sides made rectangular and sloping, and faced on the four sides with a dry stone wall, the ascent being made by a flight of stone steps.   It was not uncommon to find two such platforms, and sometimes three, one above the other, as shown in the figure.   These platforms, called terraces, were the gathering and the lounging places of the inhabitants.

The edifices in the regions named are almost invariably but one story high, and but two rooms deep, the walls being carried up vertically to an

---

[1] Rambles in Yucatan, p. 127.   [2] Ib., p. 128.

equal height on the sides and ends, and terminating in a flat roof. The doorways opened upon the platform area or terrace when the building was single, and where it was carried around the four sides of an inclosed court they opened usually upon the court. As their elevation above the level of the surrounding area invested them with the character of fortresses, they were defended on the line or edge of the terrace-walls, or, rather, at the head of the flight of steps by means of which the summit-level was reached. Neither adobe brick, nor rubble masonry, nor timber roofs could withstand the tropical climate, with its pouring rains during a portion of the year. Stone walls and a vaulted ceiling were indispensable to a permanent structure. There were, doubtless, pueblos of timber-framed houses with thatched roofs here and there in Yucatan, Chiapas, and Honduras, as there were further south towards the Isthmus; but the prevailing material used was stone, as the number of small pueblos in ruins still attest. Upon these elevated platforms they enjoyed the same security as the Village Indians of New Mexico upon their roof-tops and within the walls of their houses. They were also raised above the flight of the mosquitoes and flies, the scourge of this hot region. Considering the surrounding conditions, single-storied houses upon raised platforms was a natural suggestion, harmonizing with a style of architecture, the communal character of which was predetermined by their social condition. For the details of this architecture reference must be made to published works, which are easily accessible, its general features and the principles from which they sprang being the only subjects within the scope of this inquiry.

The front elevation of the Governor's House at Uxmal, shown in the engraving, and which was taken from Stephens' work, will answer as a sample of the whole. It stands upon the upper of three platforms, of which the lowest is five hundred and seventy-five feet long, fifteen feet broad to the base of the middle platform, and three feet high. The second is five hundred and forty-five feet long, two hundred and fifty feet broad to the base of the upper platform, and twenty feet high. The third is three hundred and sixty feet long, thirty feet broad in front of the edifice, and nineteen feet high. The upper one is formed upon the back half of the middle platform, of which last Mr. Stephens observes that "this great terrace was not entirely artificial. The substratum was a natural rock, and showed that advantage had been taken of a natural elevation as far as it went, and by this means some portion of the immense labor of constructing the terrace had been saved."[1] The three terraces with their sloping walls are shown in the engraving, the house standing upon an elevation forty-two feet above the surrounding area. The ascent from terrace to terrace was made by flights of stone steps, which are not distinctly shown. When newly constructed and inhabited, this structure, from its commanding situation, its great size, and conspicuous terraces, must have presented a striking appearance. It is doubtful whether any of the Aryan tribes, when in the Middle Status of barbarism, have produced houses superior to those in Yucatan.

The house is symmetrical in structure, three hundred and twenty-two feet long, thirty-nine feet deep, and about twenty-five feet high. It has eleven doorways, besides two small openings in front, and contains twenty-two apartments, two of which are each sixty feet long. The rear wall is solid, and in the central part is nine feet thick. A parallel wall through the center divides the interior into two rows of apartments, of which those in front are eleven feet six inches deep and twenty-three feet high to the top of the arch, and those back of them are thirteen feet deep and twenty-two feet high. Both inside and out the walls are of dressed stone laid in courses. No drawings of the rooms in the Governor's House are furnished in Mr. Stephens' work. The back rooms are dark, excepting the light received through the front doorway.

"The House of the Nuns," says Mr. Stephens, "is quadrangular, with a court yard in the center. It stands on the highest of three terraces. The lowest is three feet high and twenty feet wide; the second, twelve feet high and forty-five feet wide; and the third, four feet high and five feet wide, extending the whole length of the front of the building. The front [building] is two hundred and seventy-nine feet long, and above the cornice, from one end to the other, is ornamented with sculpture. In the centre is a gateway ten feet eight inches wide, spanned by the triangular arch, and leading to the court yard. On each side of this gateway are four doorways

---

[1] Incidents of Travel in Yucatan, i, 128.

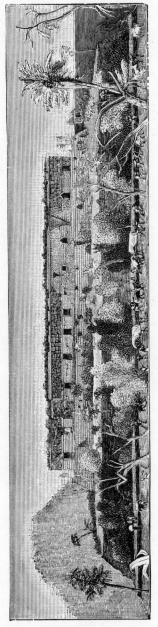

FIG. 51.—Governor's House at Uxmal.

FIG. 52.—Ground plan of Governor's House at Uxmal.

with wooden lintels, opening to apartments averaging twenty-four feet long, ten feet wide, seventeen feet high to the top of the arch, but having no connection with each other. The building that forms the right or eastern side of the quadrangle measures one hundred and fifty-eight feet long; that on the left is one hundred and seventy-three feet long, and the range opposite, or at the end of the quadrangle, measures two hundred and sixty-four

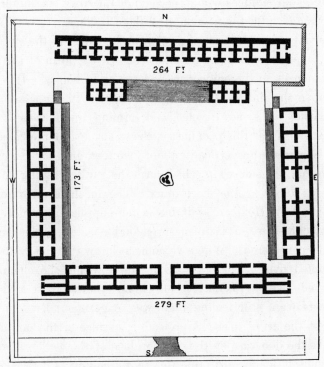

Fig. 53.—Ground-plan of the House of the Nuns.

feet. These three ranges have no doorways outside, but the exterior of each is a dead wall, and above the cornice all are ornamented with the same rich and elaborate sculptures."[1]

Altogether, these four structures contain seventy-six apartments, which vary in size from twenty to thirty feet long, and from ten to twelve feet wide. There are twenty single apartments, and twenty-five pairs of apart-

[1] Incidents of travel in Yucatan, i, 299.

ments, half of which, as in the Governor's House, are dark, except as they are lighted from the doorways connecting with the rooms in front. In the fifth structure, not described, there are six pairs of similar apartments. In the building on the right there are six rooms connecting with each other, one of which, the front room, is shown in Fig. 54. This number of connecting rooms is so unusual in Yucatan architecture as to attract attention. Each of the four edifices would accommodate from six hundred to one thousand persons, after the fashion of Village Indians.

In this view of the interior of a room in the House of the Nuns, Fig. 54, which was taken from Stephens' work, is shown the form of the triangular ceiling common in all the edifices in Yucatan and Chiapas. It is a triangular arch above the line of the exterior cornice, without a keystone, and with the faces of the stones beveled, and forming a perfect vault over each apartment. But it has this peculiarity, that a space a foot or more wide in the center is carried up vertically about two feet, and covered with a cap of stone, so that the side walls which form the vaulted ceiling do not come together so as to rest against each other. The mechanical principle is the same as in the New Mexican arch, but is here applied in a more extended and more difficult scale. It is the most remakable feature in this architecture, mechanically considered. When we come to know that this vaulted ceiling was constructed over a core of solid masonry within the chamber, afterwards removed—which was the fact—it will be seen that these Indian masons and architects were still feeling their way experimentally to a scientific knowledge of the art of arts. A projecting cornice or median entablature is seen above the doorway on the exterior face of the wall, which balances somewhat the interior inward projection of the ceiling as it rises, and, since the wall is carried up flush with the cornice, the down-weight of the superincumbent mass sustained the masonry. The room shown is thirty-three feet long, thirteen wide, and twenty-three feet high to the cap-stone, and the room communicating with it is of the same width, and nine feet long. The apartments back of these are of corresponding size.[1] There were originally lintels of hard sapote wood over the doorways, upon the decay of which a portion of the masonry has fallen. Those over the doorways through

---

[1] Incidents of Travel, etc., i, 308.

Fig. 54.—Section of room in House of the Nuns.

the partition walls are found in place. The proof of the comparatively modern date of these structures is conclusive from these facts alone.

It will be observed that there are six single apartments in the building on the right of the "House of Nuns" which have no connection with the remaining rooms of the building, and that the others are in pairs, a back room connecting with the one in front, and neither with any others. It seems to show very plainly, in the plan of the house itself, that it was designed to be occupied by distinct groups composed of related families, each group a large household by itself. If the communal principle in living existed in fact among them, its expression in the interior arrangement of the house, and in this form, might have been expected. This striking and significant feature runs through all the structures, in these areas, of which ground-plans have been obtained.

The triangular ceiling, in effect, is an attempt to extend the lintel in sections across the vault of a chamber in the place of joists, and, so far as the writer is aware, the only attempt ever made by any barbarous people to form a ceiling of stone over ordinary residence rooms. In a wall and ceiling formed in this manner, and carried up several feet above the apex of the triangular arch, there would be no lateral thrust outward of the masonry.

It should be stated that there are neither fire-place, chimneys, nor windows in any of these houses; neither have any been found, so far as the writer is aware, in any ancient structure in Yucatan or Central America. Fires were not needed for warmth; but since they were for cooking, it shows very plainly that no cooking was done within these houses. A presumption at once arises that their inmates prepared their food in the open court, or on the middle terrace, by household groups, making a common stock of their provisions, and dividing from the earthen cauldron, like the Iroquois. The communistic character of these houses is shown by their great size, and by the separation of the rooms, generally in pairs, having no connection with the remainder of the house. Each pair of rooms would accommodate several married pairs with their children; and so would each single apartment, according to the mode of life of the Village Indians. Moreover, communism in living appears to have been a law of man's condition both in the Lower and in the Middle Status of barbarism. Among the Iroquois, one regular meal each day was all their mode of life permitted; hunger being allayed by hominy kept constantly prepared, or such other food as their domestic resources allowed. It is not probable that the Aborigines of Yucatan were able to superadd either a regular breakfast or a supper. These belong to the more highly developed house-keeping of the mono-gamian family in civilization.

Another custom, usual in the Lower Status of barbarism, seems to have been continued in the Middle Status; namely, of the men eating first and by themselves, and the women and children afterwards. Without a knowl-edge of tables or of chairs, the dinner was of necessity a solitary affair between the person and his earthen bowl or platter. The time, however, for the dinner was the same to all the men, and afterwards to the women and children. Herrera, in his summary of the habits of the people of Yucatan, drops the remark incidentally, that at their festivals the women "did eat apart from the men."[1] This is precisely what would have been expected had nothing been said on the subject.

There are some proofs bearing directly upon the question of the ancient practice of communism in these Uxmal houses. They are found in the present usages of the Maya Indians of Yucatan, the descendants of the builders of these houses, which they may reasonably be supposed to have derived from their ancestors. At Nohcacab, a short distance east of the ruins of Uxmal, there was a settlement of Maya Indians, whose commun-ism in living was accidentally discovered by Mr. Stephens, when among them to employ laborers. He remarks as follows: "Their community con-sists of a hundred labradores or working men; their lands are held in common, and the products are shared by all. Their food is prepared at one hut, and every family sends for its portion; which explains a singular spectacle we had seen on our arrival [in 1841], a procession of women and children, each carrying an earthen bowl containing a quantity of smoking hot broth, all coming down the same road, and dispersing among different huts * * * From our ignorance of the language, and the number of other and more pressing matters claiming our attention, we could not learn

---

[1] History of America, iv, 175.

all the details of their internal economy, but it seemed to approximate that improved state of association which is sometimes heard of among us; and as this has existed for an unknown length of time, and can no longer be considered experimental, Owen and Fourier might perhaps take lessons from them with advantage.   *   *   *   I never before regretted so much my ignorance of the Maya language."[1]   A hundred working men indicate a total of five hundred persons who were then depending for their daily food upon a single fire, and a single cooking-house, the provisions being supplied from common stores, and divided from the kettle.   It is not unlikely a truthful picture of the mode of life in the House of the Nuns, and in the Governor's House at the period of European discovery.   Each group practising communism, for convenience and for economy, may have included all the inmates of a single house, or its occupants may have subdivided into lesser groups; but the presumption is in favor of the larger.   Evidence has elsewhere been adduced of the existence of the organization into gentes among the Mayas, with descent in the male line, from which it may be

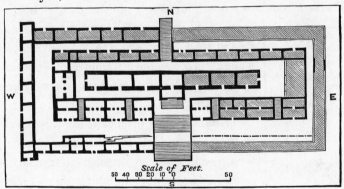

FIG. 55.—Ground Plan of Zayi.

inferred that the occupation of these houses was on the basis of gentile kinship among the families in each, the fathers and their children belonging to the same gens, and the wives and mothers to other gentes.   All the facts seem to indicate that communism in living was practiced among the Village Indians in general upon a scale then unknown in other parts of the world, because they alone represented the culture and mode of life of the Middle

[1] Incidents of Travel, etc., ii, 14.

Status of barbarism.   The dinner of Montezuma, before considered, is an illustration.

Near Uxmal are the interesting ruins of Zayi, which present a new feature in Yucatan house architecture.   Upon a low eminence are three independent structures, the second within and above the first or lowest, and the third within and above the second, presenting the appearance, in the distance, of a single quadrangular edifice in three receding stories.   But each stands on a separate terrace, and is built against the one within, which rises above it, except the inner one, a single edifice occupying the summit. The outer quadrangle stands on the lowest terrace.   The measurements of the several buildings are indicated on the plan.   Together they contain eighty-seven apartments, assuming the parts in ruins to have corresponded with the parts preserved.   The rooms, as usual, are either single or in pairs. An external staircase upon the front and rear sides interrupts the buildings on these sides from the lower terrace to the upper.   The dots in the apertures indicate columns, which are found in this and several other structures. In case of attack, the outer quadrangle was not defensible; but its inhabitants could retire to the second terrace above, and defend their fortress at the head of the staircases, which were the only avenues of approach except by scaling the outer quadrangle, a very improbable undertaking.

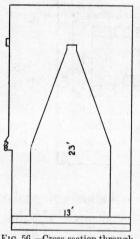

Attention has been called to this pueblo, which would accommodate two thousand or more persons, for a special reason.   It seems to furnish conclusive proof of the manner in which these great edifices were erected in order to construct the peculiar triangular stone ceiling, which is the striking characteristic of this architecture.

FIG. 56.—Cross-section through one apartment.

To understand the problem, the annexed cross-section of a single room will afford some aid by showing the relations of the walls to the chamber and its ceiling.   The chamber, with its vaulted ceiling, was constructed over a solid core of masonry, laid simultaneously with the walls, which was removed after the latter had seasoned and settled. It tends to show that with small stones of the size used, about a foot long and six inches thick, the triangular ceiling as it projected toward the center in rising, required the interior support of a core to insure the possibility of construction by their methods. Once put together over such a core and carried up several feet above the top of the arch, the down weight of the superincumbent mass would articulate and hold the masonry together. It shows further that the essential feature of the arch is wanting in this contrivance.

The proof of this assertion is found in the actual presence of the unre-moved core in one of these edifices in all of its apartments. Mr. Stephens found every room of the back building on the second terrace filled with masonry from bottom to top, left precisely as it was when the building was finished. He remarks that "the north half of the second range has a curious and unaccountable feature. It is called the *Casa Cerrada*, or 'closed house,' having ten doorways, all of which are blocked up on the inside with stone and mortar. * * * In front of several were piles of stones which they [his workmen] had worked out from the doorways, and under the lintels were holes through which we were able to crawl inside; and here we found ourselves in apartments finished with walls and ceilings like all the others, but filled up, except so far as they had been emptied by the Indians, with solid masses of mortar and stone. There were ten of these apartments in all, two hundred and twenty feet long and ten feet deep, which thus being filled up made the whole building a solid mass; and the strangest feature was that the filling up of the apartments must have been simultaneous with the erection of the buildings; for, as the filling in rose above the tops of the doorways, the men who performed it never could have entered to their work through the doors. It must have been done as the walls were built, and the ceiling must have closed over a solid mass."[1]

It does not seem to have occurred to Mr. Stephens that the masonry within each room was a core, without which a vaulted chamber in this form could not have been constructed with their knowledge of the art of build-ing. It shows the rudeness of their mechanical resources as well as the real condition of the art among them, but at the same time increases our

---

[1] Incidents of Travel, etc., ii, 22.

appreciation of their originality, ingenuity, and industry. They were working their way upward experimentally in architecture, as all other peoples have done, having richly earned the right to point with pride to these structures as extraordinary memorials of the progress they had made.

An important conclusion follows, namely, that this "closed house" was the last, in the order of time, erected in this pueblo, and had not been emptied of its core and brought into use when the Spanish irruption forced the people to abandon this pueblo. It would fix the period of its construction at or after A. D. 1520, thus settling the question of its modern date and removing one of the delusions concerning the antiquity of the ruins in Yucatan and Central America. This structure is as much decayed as any other in Yucatan. There are many other structures even better preserved than this.

A brief reference to Palenque will conclude this notice, but without dealing with the facts as fully as they deserve. There are four or five pyramidal elevations at this pueblo quite similar in plan and general situation with those at Uxmal. One is much the largest, and the structures upon it are called the "Palace." It has generally been regarded as the paragon of American Indian architecture. As a palace implies a potentate for its occupation, a character who never existed and could not exist under their institutions, it has been a means of self-deception with respect to the condition of the Aborigines which ought to be permanently discarded. Several distinct buildings are here grouped upon one elevated terrace, and are more or less connected. Altogether they are two hundred and twenty-eight feet long, front and rear, and one hundred and eighty feet deep, occupying not only the four sides of a quadrangle, but the greater part of what originally was, in all probability, an open court. The use of the interior court for additional structures shows a decadence of architecture and of ethnic life in the people, because it implies an unwillingness to raise a new pyramidal site to gain accommodations for an increased number of people. Thus to appropriate the original court so essential for light and air as well as room, and which is such a striking feature in the general plan of the architecture of the Village Indians, was a departure from the principles of this architecture. Nearly all the edifices in Yucatan and Central America agree in one particular, namely, in being constructed with three parallel walls with partition walls at intervals, giving two rows of apartments under one roof, usually, if not invariably, flat. Where several are grouped together on the same platform, as at Palenque, they are severally under independent roofs, and the spaces between, called courts, are simply open lanes or passageways between the structures. An inspection of the ground plan of the Palenque ruins in the folio volume of Dupaix, or in the work of Mr. Stephens, will be apt to mislead unless this feature of the architecture is kept in mind There are in reality seven or eight distinct edifices crowded together upon the summit level of the platform. Mr. Stephens speaks of it as one structure. " The building," he remarks, "was constructed of stone, and the whole front was covered with stucco and painted. * * * The doorways have no doors, nor are there the remains of any. * * * The tops of the doorways were all broken. They had evidently been square, and over every one were large niches in the wall on each side, in which the lintels had been laid. These lintels had all fallen, and the stones above formed broken natural arches."[1] The interior walls in two rooms shown by engravings were plastered over. Architecturally, Palenque is inferior to the House of the Nuns; but it is more ornamental. It also has one peculiar feature not generally found in the Yucatan structures, namely, a corridor about nine feet wide, supposed to have run around the greater part of the exterior on the four sides. The exterior walls of these corridors rest on a series of piers, and the central or next parallel wall is unbroken, except by one doorway on each of three sides and two in the fourth, thus forming a narrow promenade. One of the interior buildings consists of two such corridors, but wider, on opposite sides of a central longitudinal wall. All the rooms in the several edifices are large. In one of the open spaces is a tower about thirty feet square, rising three stories. The Palenque structures are quite remarkable, standing upon an artificial eminence about forty feet high, and large enough to accommodate three thousand people living in the fashion of Village Indians.

The plan of these houses, as well as of those in Yucatan, seems to show that they were designed to be occupied by groups of persons composed of

---

[1] Central America, &c., ii, 310-312.

a number of families, whose private boundaries were fixed by solid partition walls. They are exactly adapted to this mode of occupation, and this special adaptation, so plainly impressed upon all this architecture, leads irresistibly to the conclusion that they were occupied on the communal principle, and were, consequently, neither more nor less than joint-tenement houses, of a model which may be called, distinctively, that of the American aborigines. None of these edifices are as large as those on the Rio Chaco, nor does either of them possess equal accommodations with the Pueblo Bonito, which possessed six hundred and forty rooms.[1] But in this warm climate, and with the raised terraces used as gathering places, more persons could manage to live in equal spaces.

Each structure, or group of structures, thus elevated, was a fortress. They prove the insecurity in which the people lived; for the labor involved in constructing these platform elevations, in part, at least, artificial, would never have been undertaken without a powerful motive. One of the chief blessings of civilization is the security which a higher organization of society gives to the people, under the protection of which they are able as cultivators to occupy broad areas of land. In the Middle Status of barbarism they were compelled to live generally in villages, which were fortified in various ways; and each village, we must suppose, was an independent, self-governing community, except as several kindred in descent, and speaking the same dialect or dialects of the same language, confederated for mutual protection. An impression has been propagated that Palenque and other pueblos in these regions were surrounded by dense populations living in cheaply constructed tenements. Having assigned the structures found, and which undoubtedly were all that ever existed, to Indian kings or potentates, the question might well be asked, if such palaces were provided for the rulers of the land, what has become of the residences of the people? Mr. Stephens has given direct countenance to this preposterous suggestion.[2] In his valuable works he has shown a disposition to feed the flames of fancy with respect to these ruins. After describing the "palace," so called, at Palenque, and remarking that "the whole extent of ground covered by

---

[1] Lieutenant Simpson's Report, Senate Ex. Doc., 1st Sess. 31st Congress, 1850, p. 81.
[2] Central America, &c., ii, 235.

those [ruins] as yet known, as appears by the plan, is not larger than our Park or Battery" [in New York], he proceeds: "It is proper to add, however, that considering the space now occupied by the ruins as the site of palaces, temples, and public buildings, and supposing the houses of the inhabitants to have been, like those of the Egyptians and the present race of Indians, of frail and perishable materials as at Memphis and Thebes, to have disappeared altogether, the city may have covered an immense extent."[1] This is a clear case of *suggestio falsi* by Mr. Stephens, who is usually so careful and reliable and, even here, so guarded in his language. He had fallen into the mistake of regarding these remains as a city in ruins, instead of a small Indian pueblo in ruins. But he had furnished a general ground plan of all the ruins found of the Palenque pueblo, which made it plain that four or five structures upon pyramidal platforms at some distance from each other, with the whole space over which they were scattered about equal to the Battery, made a poor show for a city. The most credulous reader would readily perceive that it was a misnomer to call them the ruins of a city; wherefore the suggestions of Mr. Stephens, that "*considering* the space now occupied by the ruins as the site of palaces, temples, and public buildings, and *supposing* the houses of the inhabitants * * * of frail and perishable materials to have disappeared * * * the city *may have* covered an immense extent." That Mr. Stephens himself considered or supposed either to be true may have been the case, but it seems hardly supposable, and in either event he is responsible for the false coloring thus put upon those ruins, and the deceptive inferences drawn from them.

These structures are highly creditable to the intelligence of their builders, and can be made to reveal the manner of their use and the actual progress they had made in the arts of life; but they never can be rationally explained while such wild views are entertained concerning them. Until the actual character and signification of these ruins are made known, such opinions may be expected to prevail concerning them. They spring from the assumed existence of a state of society far enough advanced to develop potentates and privileged classes, with power to enforce labor from the people for personal objects. There is no evidence whatever in

---

[1] Incidents of Travel, Central America, Chiapas and Yucatan, ii, 355.

support of such an assumption. It is quite probable that small numbers belonging to every pueblo lived a portion of the year in the forests in temporary habitations, engaged in cultivation, or in hunting and fishing; but enough is known from the brief accounts of the early explorers to show us that the body of the inhabitants of Yucatan and Central America were gathered in pueblos or villages. Moreover, they were animated by the same spirit as the Cibolans in what related to personal independence. Rather than live in subjection to Spanish taskmasters, the very Indians who erected these houses with so much labor, as Coronado states of the Cibolans, " Set in order all their goods and substance, their women and children, and fled to the hills, leaving their towns, as it were, abandoned," [1] preferring a return to a lower stage of barbarism rather than a loss of personal freedom. In 1524 Cortez sent an officer "to reduce the people of Chiapas, who had revolted, which that commander effectually performed, for, when they could resist no longer, these desperate wretches cast themselves with their wives and children headlong from precipices, so that not above two thousand of them remained, whose offspring inhabit that province at this time." [2] The inhabitants of Palenque may have been included in this description.

The profiles of the Palenque Indians, copied by Stephens from representations in plaster in different parts of the several structures, show that they were flat-heads, like the Chinook Indians of the Columbia River; their foreheads having been flattened by artificial compression. Herrera, speaking generally of the inhabitants of Yucatan, remarks, " that they flattened their heads and foreheads.." [3] Whether it was a general practice does not appear, aside from the Palenque monuments, and the off-hand statement of Herrera.

Another important question still remains, namely, whether or not the Indians of Yucatan and Central America had reached the first stage of scientific architecture, the use of the post and lintel of stone as a principle of construction in stone masonry. The Egyptians used the post and lintel, whence their architecture has been characterized as the horizontal. The Greeks did not get beyond this, although they brought in the three orders of architecture. The round and the pointed arch, used as principles of construction, with all they gave to architecture, were beyond even the

---

[1] Herrera, History of America, iii, 346, cf. 348.   [2] Ib., iv, 169.   [3] Ib., iv, 169.

Greeks. Speaking of the Governor's House, Mr. Stephens remarks, that "the doors are all gone, and the wooden lintels over them have fallen."[1] In some of the inner apartments, the lintels were still in place over the doorways, and some were lying on the floor, sound and solid, which latter condition was no doubt owing to their being more sheltered than those over the outer doorway."[2] The same is true of the House of the Nuns, and of a number of other structures figured and described in Mr. Stephens' works. But lintels of stone are found in some houses. Thus, of one of the buildings at Kabah, he says: "The lintels over the doors are of stone."[3] In this case there was a stone column in the middle of the doorway, and the lintel was in two sections. Norman, speaking of the ruins at Chichen Itza, remarks that the "doorways are nearly a square of about seven feet, somewhat resembling the Egyptian; the sides of which are formed of large blocks of hewn stone. In some instances the lintels are of the same material."[4] They used sapote wood usually for lintels, a wood remarkable for its solidity and durability. It may safely be said that the lintel of wood was the rule in Yucatan, and not the exception. While they understood the use of the stone lintel, which alone was capable of affording a durable structure, its common and ordinary use was beyond their ability. The use of stone of the size required overmatched their ability in stone masonry, as a rule. It cannot, therefore, be said that the post and lintel of stone became a principle of construction in their architecture. As the Mayas, who constructed these edifices, were in the Middle Status of barbarism, it was not to have been expected that their architecture would reach the scientific stage.

American aboriginal history and ethnology have been perverted, and even caricatured in various ways, and, among others, by a false terminology, which of itself is able to vitiate the truth. When we have learned to substitute Indian confederacy for Indian kingdom; Teuchtli, or head war-chief, sachem, and chief, for king, prince, and lord; Indian villages in the place of "great cities"; communal houses for "palaces," and democratic for monarchic institutions; together with a number of similar substitutions of appropriate for deceptive and improper terms, the Indian of the

---

[1] Incidents of Travel in Yucatan, i, 175. [2] Ib., p. 178. [3] Ib., i, 398. [4] Rambles in Yucatan, p. 128.

past and present will be presented understandingly, and placed in his true position in the scale of human advancement. While the Aryan family has lost nearly all traces of its experiences anterior to the closing period of barbarism, the Indian family, in its different branches, offered for our investigation not only the state of savagery, but also that of both the opening and of the middle period of barbarism in full and ample development. The American aborigines had enjoyed a continuous and undisturbed progress upon a great continent, through two ethnical periods, and the latter part of a previous period, on a remarkable scale. If the opportunity had been wisely improved, a rational knowledge of the experience of our own ancestors, while in the same status, might have been gained through a study of these progressive conditions. Beside this, before a science of ethnology applied to the American aborigines can come into existence, the misconceptions, and erroneous interpretations which now encumber the original memorials must be removed. Unless this can in some way be effectually accomplished, this science can never be established among us.

Our ethnography was initiated for us by European investigators, and corrupted in its foundation from a misconception of the facts. The few Americans who have taken up the subject have generally followed in the same track, and intensified the original errors of interpretation until romance has swept the field. Whether it is possible to commence anew, and retrieve what has been lost, I cannot pretend to determine. It is worth the effort.

Finally, with respect to the condition and structures of the Village Indians of Yucatan and Central America, the following conclusions may be stated as reasonable from the facts presented:[1]

---

[1] Whether the Indian tribes of any part of North America had learned to quarry stone to use for building purposes, is still a question. In New Mexico there is no evidence that they quarried stone. They picked up and used such stones as were found in broken masses at the base of cliffs, or as were found on the surface and could be easily removed from their bed. In Central America, if anywhere they must have quarried stone, in the strict sense of this term, but as yet there is no decisive evidence of the fact. It will be necessary to find the quarries from which the stones were taken, with such evidence of their having been worked as these quarries may exhibit. The stones used in the edifices in Yucatan and Central America are represented as a "soft coralline limestone," and, in some cases, as in that of the Copan Idols, so called, of a "soft grit stone." It requires the application of more than ordinary intelligence and skill to quarry stone, even of this character. The native tribes had no metals except native copper gold and silver, and these were without the hardness requisite for a lever or chisel; and they had no explosives to use in blasting. Other agencies may have been used. We find the stone lintel for the doorway beyond their ability for ordinary use, and that for the want of it, they were unable to erect permanent structures in stone. The art of quarrying stone is gained by

First: That the Family among them was too weak an organization to face alone the struggle of life, and therefore sheltered itself in large households, composed probably of related families.

Second: That they were probably organized in gentes, and, as a consequence, were broken up into independent tribes, with confederacies here and there for mutual protection; and that their institutions were essentially democratic.

Third: That from the plan and interior arrangement of these houses the practice of communism in living in households may be inferred.

Fourth: That the people were Village Indians in the Middle Status of barbarism; living in a single joint-tenement house or in several such houses grouped together, and forming one pueblo.

Fifth: That hospitality and communism in living were laws of their condition, which found expression in the form of the houses, which were adapted to communism in living in large households.

Sixth: That all there ever was of Uxmal, Palenque, Copan, and other pueblos in these areas, building for building, and stone for stone, are there now in ruins.

Seventh: That nothing herein stated is inconsistent with the supposition that some of these structures were devoted to religious uses.

Finally: That a common principle runs through all this architecture, from the Columbia River and the Saint Lawrence, to the Isthmus of Panama, namely, that of adaptation to communism in living.

When we attempt to understand the "Palace at Palenque" or the Governor's House at Uxmal, as the residences of Indian potentates, they are wholly unintelligible; but as communal joint-tenement houses, embody-

mankind before civilization is gained, but it must commence in rude form before more effective means are discovered through experience. If any of the American Indian tribes had advanced to this knowledge, and possessed the skill and ability to quarry stone, it is important that the fact should be established, and that they should have credit for the progress in knowledge implied by this skill and ability. Dressed stone from the walls at Uxmal, Palenque, and elsewhere in Yucatan and Central America should be proved by applying the square to find whether a level surface and a true angle were formed upon them. It should also be ascertained whether the walls are truly vertical, and also whether they had learned to make a mortar of quicklime and sand. Before our adventurous writers use in connection with our native tribes and their works such terms as "*civilization, great cities, palaces*, and *temples*," and apply such imposing titles as "*king, prince*, and *lord*" to Indian chiefs, they should be prepared to show that some at least of their tribes had learned the use of wells and how to dig them, and how to quarry stone; to prepare a mortar of lime and sand; to form a right angle and a level face upon a stone, and lay up vertical walls. These necessary acquisitions precede the first beginnings of civilization.

ing the social, the defensive, and the communal principles, we can understand how they could have been created, and so elaborately and laboriously finished.   It is evident that they were the work of the people, constructed for their own enjoyment and protection.   Enforced labor never created them   On the contrary, it is the charm of all these edifices, roomy, and tasteful and remarkable as they are, that they were raised by the Indians for their own use, with willing hands, and occupied by them on terms of entire equality.   Liberty, equality, and fraternity are emphatically the three great principles of the gens, and this architecture responds to these sentiments.   And it is highly creditable to the Indian mind that while in the Middle Status of barbarism they had developed the capacity to plan, and the industry to rear, structures of such architectural design and imposing magnitude.

I have now submitted all I intended to present with respect to the house architecture of the American aborigines.   It covers but a small part of a great subject.   As a key to the interpretation of this architecture, two principles, the practice of hospitality and the practice of communism in living, have been employed.   They seem to afford a satisfactory explanation of its peculiar features in entire harmony with Indian institutions. Should the general reader be able to acquiesce in this interpretation, it will lead to a reconstruction of our aboriginal history, now so imperatively demanded.

INDEX

Abert, J. W., 144
Aborigines, American: classification of, 42–43, 225–26; origin of, 43–44. *See also* Northern Tribes; Village Indians
Acoma pueblo, 140–41. *See also* New Mexico, Village Indians of
Acosta, José de, 220, 256
Adair, James, 54–55, 68, 100, 103
Adobe, use of, 141, 159, 168, 203, 232–33, 261, 289
Africa, gentile organization in tribes of, 3
Aleüts: architecture, house, of, 71; communal life of, seen in households, 71; hospitality, law of, among, 53
Algonkins: architecture, house, of, 124–25; communal life of, 124–25; displacement of, by Iroquois, 25; food customs among, 124–25; hospitality, law of, among, 47–48. *See also* Nyacks; Pomeiock
Alto pueblo: architecture, house, in, 190, 193; size of, 190. *See also* Chaco River pueblos
Alvarado, Pedro de, 260
Amidas, Philip, 47
Ancient Monuments of the Mississippi Valley (Squier and Davis), 228–29, 243, 246
Ancient Society; or, Researches in the Lines of Human Progress from Savagery through Barbarism to Civilization (Morgan), 8, 21
Animas River ruins: architecture, house, in, 169, 200–203, 205–12; communal life in, seen in joint-tenement houses, 210; compared to Chaco River pueblos, 169, 210; population of, 214; site of, 198, 214; size of, 198–99, 210–12. *See also* San Juan River ruins
Apaches, 168
Apoxpalan, house architecture in, 260
Architecture, house: in Acoma pueblo, 140–41; of Aleüts, 71; of Algonkins, 124–25; in Alto pueblo, 190; in Animas River ruins, 169, 200–203, 205–12; in Apoxpalan, 260; of Arickarees, 138; in Arroyo pueblo, 186; of Assiniboines, 119; of Aztecs, 141, 179, 258, 262–63; of Blackfeet, 119; in Bonito pueblo, 185–86; of California tribes, 105–13; in Cempoala, 204, 260–61; in Chaco

River pueblos, 169–70, 196–97; in Chettro Kettle pueblo, 179–80, 185; in Chiapas ruins, 205, 282, 284, 294; in Chichén Itzá, 202, 287–88, 307; of Chinooks, 115–16; in Cíbola, 137; of Clahclellahs, 115; of Clatsops, 115–16; of Columbia Valley tribes, 114–17; of Creeks, 68; of Crees, 119; of Crows, 119; of Dakotas, 118–19; in High Bank pueblo, 233–34, 237–38, 241–43, 245; in Hungo Pavie pueblo, 170, 176, 179, 186, 210; of Iowas, 119; of Iroquois, 64–65, 68, 105, 125–29, 142; in Iztapalapa, 259–60; in Jemez pueblo, 141; in Kabah, 307; of Kŭtchĭn (Louchoux), 113; of Lolsels, 106; of McElmo Cañon cliff houses, 217–18; of Makahs, 117; of Mancos River cliff houses, 143, 168, 221; of Mandans, 72, 133–38, 241; of Maricopas, 138–39; of Mayas, 75–76; of Minnetarees, 133, 138, 241, 245; in Mi-shong'-i-ni'-vi pueblo, 153–55; of Mohaves, 138–39; in Montezuma Valley ruins, 168, 215, 218; of Ncerchokioo, 114–15; of New Mexican Village Indians, 74–75, 141–42, 144–67; of Nez Percés, 114–15; of Northern Tribes, 104–39; of Nyacks, 124–25; of Ojibwas, 117–18, 120; of Onondagas, 129–30, 133; of Otoes, 119; in Palenque, 105, 142, 204, 302–6; of Pawnees, 119; in Peñasca Blanca pueblo, 189–90; of Pimas, 138; in Pintado pueblo, 170, 173–75; in Pomeiock, 119–20, 123; of Powhatans, 67–68, 123–24; in Santo Domingo pueblo, 144; of Sauks, 73; in Secotan, 120, 123; of Senecas, 65, 125–27, 130; of Se-nels, 110; of Sokulks, 70; in Taos pueblo, 141, 156, 159–61, 164, 208–13; of Tatus, 110; in Tenochtitlán, 255–56, 258–59, 262–66; in Tututlepec, 260; in Una Vida pueblo, 176; in Ute Mountain ruins, 216–17; of Utes, 119; in Uxmal, 75, 105, 120, 185–86, 202–4, 233, 284–94, 297–300, 303, 307, 309; of Village Indians, 105–6, 212–13; in Wege'-gi pueblo, 175–76; in Wolpi pueblo, 153; of Yo-kai'-as, 110; of Yokuts, 109; of Yucatán, Chiapas, and Central American Village Indi-